50% OFF TABE 11 & 12 Prep Course!

Dear Customer,

We consider it an honor and a privilege that you chose our TABE 11 & 12 Study Guide. As a way of showing our appreciation and to help us better serve you, we have partnered with Mometrix Test Preparation to offer you **50% off their online TABE 11 & 12 Prep Course.** Many TABE courses are needlessly expensive and don't deliver enough value. With their course, you get access to the best TABE 11 & 12 prep material, and **you only pay half price.**

Mometrix has structured their online course to perfectly complement your printed study guide. The TABE 11 & 12 Test Prep Course contains **in-depth lessons** that cover all the most important topics, over **600 practice questions** to ensure you feel prepared, more than **500 flashcards** for studying on the go, and over **250 instructional videos.**

Online TABE 11 & 12 Prep Course

Topics Covered:

- Reading
  - Main Ideas & Author's Purpose
  - Reading Informational Texts
  - Persuasive & Argumentative Writing

- Language
  - Word Meaning and Context Clues
  - Sentence Structure
  - The Writing Process

- Mathematics
  - Proportions and Ratios
  - Inequalities
  - Quadratics

And More!

Course Features:

- TABE 11 & 12 Study Guide
  - Get access to content from the best reviewed study guide available.

- Track Your Progress
  - Their customized course allows you to check off content you have studied or feel confident with.

- 5 Full-Length Practice Tests
  - With 600+ practice questions and lesson reviews, you can test yourself again and again to build confidence.

- TABE 11 & 12 Flashcards
  - Their course includes a flashcard mode consisting of over 500 content cards to help you study.

To receive this discount, visit them at www.mometrix.com/university/tabe-11-12 or simply scan this QR code with your smartphone. At the checkout page, enter the discount code: **TPBTABE50**

If you have any questions or concerns, please contact Mometrix at support@mometrix.com.

Sincerely,

SCAN HERE

 in partnership with

FREE Test Taking Tips Video/DVD Offer

To better serve you, we created videos covering test taking tips that we want to give you for FREE. **These videos cover world-class tips that will help you succeed on your test.**

We just ask that you send us feedback about this product. Please let us know what you thought about it—whether good, bad, or indifferent.

To get your **FREE videos**, you can use the QR code below or email freevideos@studyguideteam.com with "Free Videos" in the subject line and the following information in the body of the email:

   a. The title of your product
   b. Your product rating on a scale of 1-5, with 5 being the highest
   c. Your feedback about the product

If you have any questions or concerns, please don't hesitate to contact us at info@studyguideteam.com.

Thank you!

TABE Test Study Guide 2024-2025
3 Practice Exams and Prep Book for TABE 11/12 Levels A and D
[6th Edition]

Lydia Morrison

Written and edited by TPB Publishing.

Interested in buying more than 10 copies of our product? Contact us about bulk discounts:
bulkorders@studyguideteam.com

ISBN 13: 9781637759042

Table of Contents

Welcome

Dear Reader,

Welcome to your new Test Prep Books study guide! We are pleased that you chose us to help you prepare for your exam. There are many study options to choose from, and we appreciate you choosing us. Studying can be a daunting task, but we have designed a smart, effective study guide to help prepare you for what lies ahead.

Whether you're a parent helping your child learn and grow, a high school student working hard to get into your dream college, or a nursing student studying for a complex exam, we want to help give you the tools you need to succeed. We hope this study guide gives you the skills and the confidence to thrive, and we can't thank you enough for allowing us to be part of your journey.

In an effort to continue to improve our products, we welcome feedback from our customers. We look forward to hearing from you. Suggestions, success stories, and criticisms can all be communicated by emailing us at info@studyguideteam.com.

Sincerely,
Test Prep Books Team

FREE Videos/DVD OFFER

Doing well on your exam requires both knowing the test content and understanding how to use that knowledge to do well on the test. We offer completely FREE test taking tip videos. **These videos cover world-class tips that you can use to succeed on your test.**

To get your **FREE videos**, you can use the QR code below or email freevideos@studyguideteam.com with "Free Videos" in the subject line and the following information in the body of the email:

> a. The title of your product
> b. Your product rating on a scale of 1-5, with 5 being the highest
> c. Your feedback about the product

If you have any questions or concerns, please don't hesitate to contact us at info@studyguideteam.com.

1

Quick Overview

As you draw closer to taking your exam, effective preparation becomes more and more important. Thankfully, you have this study guide to help you get ready. Use this guide to help keep your studying on track and refer to it often.

This study guide contains several key sections that will help you be successful on your exam. The guide contains tips for what you should do the night before and the day of the test. Also included are test-taking tips. Knowing the right information is not always enough. Many well-prepared test takers struggle with exams. These tips will help equip you to accurately read, assess, and answer test questions.

A large part of the guide is devoted to showing you what content to expect on the exam and to helping you better understand that content. In this guide are practice test questions so that you can see how well you have grasped the content. Then, answer explanations are provided so that you can understand why you missed certain questions.

Don't try to cram the night before you take your exam. This is not a wise strategy for a few reasons. First, your retention of the information will be low. Your time would be better used by reviewing information you already know rather than trying to learn a lot of new information. Second, you will likely become stressed as you try to gain a large amount of knowledge in a short amount of time. Third, you will be depriving yourself of sleep. So be sure to go to bed at a reasonable time the night before. Being well-rested helps you focus and remain calm.

Be sure to eat a substantial breakfast the morning of the exam. If you are taking the exam in the afternoon, be sure to have a good lunch as well. Being hungry is distracting and can make it difficult to focus. You have hopefully spent lots of time preparing for the exam. Don't let an empty stomach get in the way of success!

When travelling to the testing center, leave earlier than needed. That way, you have a buffer in case you experience any delays. This will help you remain calm and will keep you from missing your appointment time at the testing center.

Be sure to pace yourself during the exam. Don't try to rush through the exam. There is no need to risk performing poorly on the exam just so you can leave the testing center early. Allow yourself to use all of the allotted time if needed.

Remain positive while taking the exam even if you feel like you are performing poorly. Thinking about the content you should have mastered will not help you perform better on the exam.

Once the exam is complete, take some time to relax. Even if you feel that you need to take the exam again, you will be well served by some down time before you begin studying again. It's often easier to convince yourself to study if you know that it will come with a reward!

Test-Taking Strategies

1. Predicting the Answer

When you feel confident in your preparation for a multiple-choice test, try predicting the answer before reading the answer choices. This is especially useful on questions that test objective factual knowledge. By predicting the answer before reading the available choices, you eliminate the possibility that you will be distracted or led astray by an incorrect answer choice. You will feel more confident in your selection if you read the question, predict the answer, and then find your prediction among the answer choices. After using this strategy, be sure to still read all of the answer choices carefully and completely. If you feel unprepared, you should not attempt to predict the answers. This would be a waste of time and an opportunity for your mind to wander in the wrong direction.

2. Reading the Whole Question

Too often, test takers scan a multiple-choice question, recognize a few familiar words, and immediately jump to the answer choices. Test authors are aware of this common impatience, and they will sometimes prey upon it. For instance, a test author might subtly turn the question into a negative, or he or she might redirect the focus of the question right at the end. The only way to avoid falling into these traps is to read the entirety of the question carefully before reading the answer choices.

3. Looking for Wrong Answers

Long and complicated multiple-choice questions can be intimidating. One way to simplify a difficult multiple-choice question is to eliminate all of the answer choices that are clearly wrong. In most sets of answers, there will be at least one selection that can be dismissed right away. If the test is administered on paper, the test taker could draw a line through it to indicate that it may be ignored; otherwise, the test taker will have to perform this operation mentally or on scratch paper. In either case, once the obviously incorrect answers have been eliminated, the remaining choices may be considered. Sometimes identifying the clearly wrong answers will give the test taker some information about the correct answer. For instance, if one of the remaining answer choices is a direct opposite of one of the eliminated answer choices, it may well be the correct answer. The opposite of obviously wrong is obviously right! Of course, this is not always the case. Some answers are obviously incorrect simply because they are irrelevant to the question being asked. Still, identifying and eliminating some incorrect answer choices is a good way to simplify a multiple-choice question.

4. Don't Overanalyze

Anxious test takers often overanalyze questions. When you are nervous, your brain will often run wild, causing you to make associations and discover clues that don't actually exist. If you feel that this may be a problem for you, do whatever you can to slow down during the test. Try taking a deep breath or counting to ten. As you read and consider the question, restrict yourself to the particular words used by the author. Avoid thought tangents about what the author *really* meant, or what he or she was *trying* to say. The only things that matter on a multiple-choice test are the words that are actually in the question. You must avoid reading too much into a multiple-choice question, or supposing that the writer meant something other than what he or she wrote.

3

5. No Need for Panic

It is wise to learn as many strategies as possible before taking a multiple-choice test, but it is likely that you will come across a few questions for which you simply don't know the answer. In this situation, avoid panicking. Because most multiple-choice tests include dozens of questions, the relative value of a single wrong answer is small. As much as possible, you should compartmentalize each question on a multiple-choice test. In other words, you should not allow your feelings about one question to affect your success on the others. When you find a question that you either don't understand or don't know how to answer, just take a deep breath and do your best. Read the entire question slowly and carefully. Try rephrasing the question a couple of different ways. Then, read all of the answer choices carefully. After eliminating obviously wrong answers, make a selection and move on to the next question.

6. Confusing Answer Choices

When working on a difficult multiple-choice question, there may be a tendency to focus on the answer choices that are the easiest to understand. Many people, whether consciously or not, gravitate to the answer choices that require the least concentration, knowledge, and memory. This is a mistake. When you come across an answer choice that is confusing, you should give it extra attention. A question might be confusing because you do not know the subject matter to which it refers. If this is the case, don't

eliminate the answer before you have affirmatively settled on another. When you come across an answer choice of this type, set it aside as you look at the remaining choices. If you can confidently assert that one of the other choices is correct, you can leave the confusing answer aside. Otherwise, you will need to take a moment to try to better understand the confusing answer choice. Rephrasing is one way to tease out the sense of a confusing answer choice.

7. Your First Instinct

Many people struggle with multiple-choice tests because they overthink the questions. If you have studied sufficiently for the test, you should be prepared to trust your first instinct once you have carefully and completely read the question and all of the answer choices. There is a great deal of research suggesting that the mind can come to the correct conclusion very quickly once it has obtained all of the relevant information. At times, it may seem to you as if your intuition is working faster even than your reasoning mind. This may in fact be true. The knowledge you obtain while studying may be retrieved from your subconscious before you have a chance to work out the associations that support it. Verify your instinct by working out the reasons that it should be trusted.

8. Key Words

Many test takers struggle with multiple-choice questions because they have poor reading comprehension skills. Quickly reading and understanding a multiple-choice question requires a mixture of skill and experience. To help with this, try jotting down a few key words and phrases on a piece of scrap paper. Doing this concentrates the process of reading and forces the mind to weigh the relative importance of the question's parts. In selecting words and phrases to write down, the test taker thinks

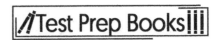

about the question more deeply and carefully. This is especially true for multiple-choice questions that are preceded by a long prompt.

9. Subtle Negatives

One of the oldest tricks in the multiple-choice test writer's book is to subtly reverse the meaning of a question with a word like *not* or *except*. If you are not paying attention to each word in the question, you can easily be led astray by this trick. For instance, a common question format is, "Which of the following is…?" Obviously, if the question instead is, "Which of the following is not…?," then the answer will be quite different. Even worse, the test makers are aware of the potential for this mistake and will include one answer choice that would be correct if the question were not negated or reversed. A test taker who misses the reversal will find what he or she believes to be a correct answer and will be so confident that he or she will fail to reread the question and discover the original error. The only way to avoid this is to practice a wide variety of multiple-choice questions and to pay close attention to each and every word.

10. Reading Every Answer Choice

It may seem obvious, but you should always read every one of the answer choices! Too many test takers fall into the habit of scanning the question and assuming that they understand the question because they recognize a few key words. From there, they pick the first answer choice that answers the question they believe they have read. Test takers who read all of the answer choices might discover that one of the latter answer choices is actually *more* correct. Moreover, reading all of the answer choices can remind you of facts related to the question that can help you arrive at the correct answer. Sometimes, a misstatement or incorrect detail in one of the latter answer choices will trigger your memory of the subject and will enable you to find the right answer. Failing to read all of the answer choices is like not reading all of the items on a restaurant menu: you might miss out on the perfect choice.

11. Spot the Hedges

One of the keys to success on multiple-choice tests is paying close attention to every word. This is never truer than with words like *almost*, *most*, *some*, and *sometimes*. These words are called "hedges" because they indicate that a statement is not totally true or not true in every place and time. An absolute statement will contain no hedges, but in many subjects, the answers are not always straightforward or absolute. There are always exceptions to the rules in these subjects. For this reason, you should favor those multiple-choice questions that contain hedging language. The presence of qualifying words indicates that the author is taking special care with his or her words, which is certainly important when composing the right answer. After all, there are many ways to be wrong, but there is only one way to be right! For this reason, it is wise to avoid answers that are absolute when taking a multiple-choice test. An absolute answer is one that says things are either all one way or all another. They often include words like *every*, *always*, *best*, and *never*. If you are taking a multiple-choice test in a subject that doesn't lend itself to absolute answers, be on your guard if you see any of these words.

12. Long Answers

In many subject areas, the answers are not simple. As already mentioned, the right answer often requires hedges. Another common feature of the answers to a complex or subjective question are qualifying clauses, which are groups of words that subtly modify the meaning of the sentence. If the question or answer choice describes a rule to which there are exceptions or the subject matter is complicated, ambiguous, or confusing, the correct answer will require many words in order to be expressed clearly and accurately. In essence, you should not be deterred by answer choices that seem excessively long. Oftentimes, the author of the text will not be able to write the correct answer without offering some qualifications and modifications. Your job is to read the answer choices thoroughly and completely and to select the one that most accurately and precisely answers the question.

13. Restating to Understand

Sometimes, a question on a multiple-choice test is difficult not because of what it asks but because of how it is written. If this is the case, restate the question or answer choice in different words. This process serves a couple of important purposes. First, it forces you to concentrate on the core of the question. In order to rephrase the question accurately, you have to understand it well. Rephrasing the question will concentrate your mind on the key words and ideas. Second, it will present the information to your mind in a fresh way. This process may trigger your memory and render some useful scrap of information picked up while studying.

14. True Statements

Sometimes an answer choice will be true in itself, but it does not answer the question. This is one of the main reasons why it is essential to read the question carefully and completely before proceeding to the answer choices. Too often, test takers skip ahead to the answer choices and look for true statements. Having found one of these, they are content to select it without reference to the question above. The savvy test taker will always read the entire question before turning to the answer choices. Then, having settled on a correct answer choice, he or she will refer to the original question and ensure that the selected answer is relevant. The mistake of choosing a correct-but-irrelevant answer choice is especially common on questions related to specific pieces of objective knowledge.

15. No Patterns

One of the more dangerous ideas that circulates about multiple-choice tests is that the correct answers tend to fall into patterns. These erroneous ideas range from a belief that B and C are the most common right answers, to the idea that an unprepared test-taker should answer "A-B-A-C-A-D-A-B-A." It cannot be emphasized enough that pattern-seeking of this type is exactly the WRONG way to approach a multiple-choice test. To begin with, it is highly unlikely that the test maker will plot the correct answers according to some predetermined pattern. The questions are scrambled and delivered in a random order. Furthermore, even if the test maker was following a pattern in the assignation of correct answers, there is no reason why the test taker would know which pattern he or she was using. Any attempt to discern a pattern in the answer choices is a waste of time and a distraction from the real work of taking the test. A test taker would be much better served by extra preparation before the test than by reliance on a pattern in the answers.

6

Bonus Content

We host multiple bonus items online, including all ## practice tests in digital format. Scan the QR code or go to this link to access this content:

testprepbooks.com/bonus/tabe

The first time you access the tests, you will need to register as a "new user" and verify your email address.

If you have any issues, please email support@testprepbooks.com.

Introduction to the TABE 11 & 12

Function of the Test

The Tests of Adult Basic Education (TABEs) are a series of tests offered by Data Recognition Corporation as assessment and diagnostic tests for use in the field of adult education. The tests are administered by a wide variety of adult education programs including GED programs, community colleges, adult literacy programs, and correctional institution literacy programs, among others. Most students who take the test do so at the request of the adult education program they are involved with or planning to enter, so that the program can determine each student's capabilities and what sort of curriculum would be most appropriate.

The TABE tests are used by adult education programs across the United States, and often administered by the programs in question to assist with placement and diagnostics within their own program. The typical test taker is an adult with a basic level of education.

This guide is for the TABE 11&12 test. More information about this can be found in the table on the next page.

Test Administration

Generally, test administration is handled by the organization conducting the assessment. Accordingly, the location, date, time, and administrative logistics are determined on a case-by-case basis by those organizations. Likewise, each organization is free to retest students, if and when they see fit.

Test takers with documented disabilities are generally able to receive reasonable accommodations during the TABE testing process. Among other accommodations, a large-print edition, a Braille edition, and an audio edition of the TABE tests are available. Accommodations are arranged through the entity administering the test.

Test Format

TABE tests are offered in a variety of formats, depending on the needs and circumstances of the administering entity. They can be given in a pencil-and-paper format, online via the internet, or on a local computer. Depending on the format used, there are also a variety of test scoring options, including hand scoring, local scanning, and online scoring.

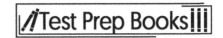

A summary of the content and purpose of some of the most prominent TABE tests follows:

Test	Summary	Purpose
TABE 9&10	Battery of subject tests including Reading, Math, and Language	Broad-based adult basic skills assessment
TABE 11&12	Updated battery of subject tests that align with the new College- and Career-Readiness Standards. It includes Literacy, Reading, Language, and Math	Broad-based adult basic skills assessment
TABE Advanced-Level Tests	Battery of subject tests including Science, Social Studies, Algebra/Geometry, and Writing	Supplemental tests to diagnose readiness for high school equivalency exams
TABE Complete Language Assessment System- English	Examination of English language skills including reading, writing, listening, and speaking	Assessing the language skills of adult English-speakers
TABE Online	Online version of the TABE 9 & 10 test	Quick evaluation of readiness for education or employment

Scoring

Scoring methodology varies among the different tests offered within the TABE series, but typically, the test taker receives a raw score based on the number of correct answers provided, with no penalty for incorrect answers. The raw score is translated to a scaled score, which represents a certain level of aptitude in adult education. The scaled scores can also be translated to a grade level correlation, which indicates an approximate grade level for the test taker in a given subject so that the student is placed in the appropriate curriculum for their needs.

Recent/Future Developments

Changes have gradually been taking place, including shifting test takers toward computer-based exams and adjusting the test content to meet national college readiness standards. These changes are likely to continue in the future.

Study Prep Plan for the TABE 11 & 12 Test

1 **Schedule** - Use one of our study schedules below or come up with one of your own.

2 **Relax** - Test anxiety can hurt even the best students. There are many ways to reduce stress. Find the one that works best for you.

3 **Execute** - Once you have a good plan in place, be sure to stick to it.

One Week Study Schedule		
Day 1	Reading	
Day 2	Language	
Day 3	Math	
Day 4	Functions	
Day 5	Practice Test #1	
Day 6	Practice Test #2	
Day 7	Take Your Exam!	

Two Week Study Schedule			
Day 1	Reading	Day 8	Statistics and Probability
Day 2	Analyze a Particular Point of View...	Day 9	Functions
Day 3	Language	Day 10	Use Properties of Exponents to Interpret...
Day 4	Vocabulary Acquisition and Use	Day 11	Practice Test #1
Day 5	Write Informative/ Explanatory Texts to...	Day 12	Practice Test #2
Day 6	Math	Day 13	Practice Test #3
Day 7	Expressions and Equations	Day 14	Take Your Exam!

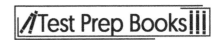

One Month Study Schedule

Day 1	Reading	Day 11	Math	Day 21	Use Properties of Exponents to Interpret...
Day 2	Determine a Theme or Central Idea of a Text	Day 12	Use Congruence and Similarity Criteria...	Day 22	Write a Function that Describes a Relationship...
Day 3	Craft and Structure	Day 13	Use Volume Formulas to Solve Problems	Day 23	Recognize Situations in Which a Quantity...
Day 4	Analyze a Particular Point of View...	Day 14	Expressions and Equations	Day 24	Practice Test #1
Day 5	Integration of Knowledge and Ideas	Day 15	Linear Inequalities in One Variable	Day 25	Answer Explanations #1
Day 6	Language	Day 16	Statistics and Probability	Day 26	Practice Test #2
Day 7	Knowledge of Language	Day 17	Interpret Differences in Shape, Center...	Day 27	Answer Explanations #2
Day 8	Vocabulary Acquisition and Use	Day 18	Interpret the Slope and the Intercept of a...	Day 28	Practice Test #3
Day 9	Text Types and Purposes	Day 19	Functions	Day 29	Answer Explanations #3
Day 10	Write Informative/ Explanatory Texts...	Day 20	For a Function that Models a Relationship...	Day 30	Take Your Exam!

Build your own prep plan by visiting:
testprepbooks.com/prep

As you study for your test, we'd like to take the opportunity to remind you that you are capable of great things! With the right tools and dedication, you truly can do anything you set your mind to. The fact that you are holding this book right now shows how committed you are. In case no one has told you lately, you've got this! Our intention behind including this coloring page is to give you the chance to take some time to engage your creative side when you need a little brain-break from studying. As a company, we want to encourage people like you to achieve their dreams by providing good quality study materials for the tests and certifications that improve careers and change lives. As individuals, many of us have taken such tests in our careers, and we know how challenging this process can be. While we can't come alongside you and cheer you on personally, we can offer you the space to recall your purpose, reconnect with your passion, and refresh your brain through an artistic practice. We wish you every success, and happy studying!

Math Reference Sheet

Symbol	Phrase
+	added to, increased by, sum of, more than
-	decreased by, difference between, less than, take away
×	multiplied by, 3 (4, 5 . . .) times as large, product of
÷	divided by, quotient of, half (third, etc.) of
=	is, the same as, results in, as much as
x, t, n, etc.	a variable which is an unknown value or quantity
<	is under, is below, smaller than, beneath
>	is above, is over, bigger than, exceeds
≤	no more than, at most, maximum; less than or equal to
≥	no less than, at least, minimum; greater than or equal to
√	square root of, exponent divided by 2

Geometry	Description
$P = 2l + 2w$	for perimeter of a rectangle
$P = 4 \times s$	for perimeter of a square
$P = a + b + c$	for perimeter of a triangle
$A = \frac{1}{2} \times b \times h = \frac{bh}{2}$	for area of a triangle
$A = b \times h$	for area of a parallelogram
$A = \frac{1}{2} \times h(b_1 + b_2)$	for area of a trapezoid
$A = \frac{1}{2} \times a \times P$	for area of a regular polygon
$C = 2 \times \pi \times r$	for circumference (perimeter) of a circle
$A = \pi \times r^2$	for area of a circle
$c^2 = a^2 + b^2; c = \sqrt{a^2 + b^2}$	for finding the hypotenuse of a right triangle
$SA = 2xy + 2yz + 2xz$	for finding surface area
$V = \frac{1}{3}xyh$	for finding volume of a rectangular pyramid
$V = \frac{4}{3}\pi r^3; \frac{1}{3}\pi r^2 h; \pi r^2 h$	for volume of a sphere; a cone; and a cylinder

Radical Expressions	Description
$\sqrt[n]{a} = a^{\frac{1}{n}}; \sqrt[n]{a^m} = (\sqrt[n]{a})^m = a^{\frac{m}{n}}$	a is the radicand, n is the index, m is the exponent
$\sqrt{x^2} = (x^2)^{\frac{1}{2}} = x$	to convert square root to exponent
$a^m \times a^n = a^{m+n}$	multiplying radicands with exponents
$(a^m)^n = a^{m \times n}$	multiplying exponents
$(a \times b)^m = a^m \times b^m$	parentheses with exponents

Property	Addition	Multiplication
Commutative	$a + b = b + a$	$a \times b = b \times a$
Associative	$(a + b) + c = a + (b + c)$	$(a \times b) \times c = a \times (b \times c)$
Identity	$a + 0 = a; 0 + a = a$	$a \times 1 = a; 1 \times a = a$
Inverse	$a + (-a) = 0$	$a \times \frac{1}{a} = 1; a \neq 0$
Distributive		$a(b + c) = ab + ac$

Data	Description
Mean	equal to the total of the values of a data set, divided by the number of elements in the data set
Median	middle value in an odd number of ordered values of a data set, or the mean of the two middle values in an even number of ordered values in a data set
Mode	the value that appears most often
Range	the difference between the highest and the lowest values in the set

Graphing	Description
(x, y)	ordered pair, plot points in a graph
$y = mx + b$	slope-intercept form; m represents the slope of the line and b represents the y-intercept
$f(x)$	read as f of x, which means it is a function of x
(x_2, y_2) and (x_2, y_2)	two ordered pairs used to determine the slope of a line
$m = \frac{y_2 - y_1}{x_2 - x_1}$	to find the slope of the line, m, for ordered pairs
$Ax + By = C$	standard form of an equation, also for solving a system of equations through the elimination method
$M = \left(\frac{x_1 + x_2}{2}, \frac{y_1 + y_2}{2}\right)$	for finding the midpoint of an ordered pair
$y = ax^2 + bx + c$	quadratic function for a parabola
$y = a(x - h)^2 + k$	quadratic function for a parabola with vertex
$y = ab^x; y = a \times b^x$	function for exponential curve
$y = ax^2 + bx + c$	standard form of a quadratic function
$x = \frac{-b}{2a}$	for finding axis of symmetry in a parabola; given quadratic formula in standard form
$f = \sqrt{\frac{\Sigma(x - \bar{x})^2}{n - 1}}$	function for standard deviation of the sample; where $\bar{x}$ = sample mean and n = sample size

Proportions and Percentage	Description
$\frac{gallons}{cost} = \frac{gallons}{cost} : \frac{7\ gallons}{\$14.70} = \frac{x}{\$20}$	written as equal ratios with a variable representing the missing quantity
$\frac{y_1}{x_1} = \frac{y_2}{x_2}$	for direct proportions
$(y_1)(x_1) = (y_2)(x_2)$	for indirect proportions
$\frac{change}{original\ value} \times 100 = percent\ change$	for finding percentage change in value
$\frac{new\ quantity - old\ quantity}{old\ quantity} \times 100$	for calculating the increase or decrease in percentage

Reading

Key Ideas and Details

Citing Strong and Thorough Textual Evidence

Supporting Details

Supporting details help readers better develop and understand the main idea. Supporting details answer questions like *who, what, where, when, why,* and *how*. Different types of supporting details include examples, facts and statistics, anecdotes, and sensory details.

Persuasive and informative texts often use supporting details. In persuasive texts, authors attempt to make readers agree with their point of view, and supporting details are often used as "selling points." If authors make a statement, they should support the statement with evidence in order to adequately persuade readers. Informative texts use supporting details such as examples and facts to inform readers. Let's take a look at the following "Cheetahs" passage to find examples of supporting details.

Cheetahs

> Cheetahs are one of the fastest mammals on land, reaching up to 70 miles an hour over short distances. Even though cheetahs can run as fast as 70 miles an hour, they usually only have to run half that speed to catch up with their choice of prey. Cheetahs cannot maintain a fast pace over long periods of time because they will overheat their bodies. After a chase, cheetahs need to rest for approximately 30 minutes prior to eating or returning to any other activity.

In the example above, supporting details include:

- Cheetahs reach up to 70 miles per hour over short distances.
- They usually only have to run half that speed to catch up with their prey.
- Cheetahs will overheat their bodies if they exert a high speed over longer distances.
- Cheetahs need to rest for 30 minutes after a chase.

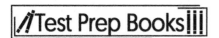

Look at the diagram below (applying the cheetah example) to help determine the hierarchy of topic, main idea, and supporting details.

Inferences in a Text

Readers should be able to make **inferences**. Making an inference requires you to read between the lines and look for what is implied rather than what is explicitly stated. That is, using information that is known from the text, the reader is able to make a logical assumption about information that is not explicitly stated but is probably true. Read the following passage:

"Hey, do you wanna meet my new puppy?" Jonathan asked.

"Oh, I'm sorry but please don't—" Jacinta began to protest, but before she could finish, Jonathan had already opened the passenger side door of his car and a perfect white ball of fur came bouncing towards Jacinta.

"Isn't he the cutest?" beamed Jonathan.

"Yes—achoo!—he's pretty—aaaachooo!!—adora—aaa—aaaachoo!" Jacinta managed to say in between sneezes. "But if you don't mind, I—I—achoo!—need to go inside."

Which of the following can be inferred from Jacinta's reaction to the puppy?
   a. She hates animals
   b. She is allergic to dogs
   c. She prefers cats to dogs
   d. She is angry at Jonathan

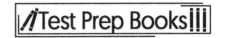

An inference requires the reader to consider the information presented and then form their own idea about what is probably true. Based on the details in the passage, what is the best answer to the question? Important details to pay attention to include the tone of Jacinta's dialogue, which is overall polite and apologetic, as well as her reaction itself, which is a long string of sneezes. Answer choices (a) and (d) both express strong emotions ("hates" and "angry") that are not evident in Jacinta's speech or actions. Answer choice (c) mentions cats, but there is nothing in the passage to indicate Jacinta's feelings about cats. Answer choice (b), "she is allergic to dogs," is the most logical choice. Based on the fact she began sneezing as soon as a fluffy dog approached her, it makes sense to guess that Jacinta might be allergic to dogs. Using the clues in the passage, it is reasonable to guess that this is true even though Jacinta never directly states, "Sorry, I'm allergic to dogs!"

Making inferences is crucial for readers of literature because literary texts often avoid presenting complete and direct information to readers about characters' thoughts or feelings, or they present this information in an unclear way, leaving it up to the reader to interpret clues given in the text. In order to make inferences while reading, readers should ask themselves:

- What details are being presented in the text?
- Is there any important information that seems to be missing?
- Based on the information that the author *does* include, what else is probably true?
- Is this inference reasonable based on what is already known?

Citing Specific Textual Evidence to Support Analysis of Primary and Secondary Sources

Primary and Secondary Sources

Primary sources are best defined as records or items that serve as historical evidence. To be considered primary, the source documents or objects must have been created during the time period in which they reference. Examples include diaries, newspaper articles, speeches, government documents, photographs, and historical artifacts. In today's digital age, primary sources, which were once in print, often are embedded in secondary sources. Secondary sources, such as websites, history books, databases, or reviews, contain analysis or commentary on primary sources. **Secondary sources** borrow information from primary sources through the process of quoting, summarizing, or paraphrasing.

Analyzing and Citing a Text

When analyzing a text, readers first want to understand what type of text they are dealing with. For example, is the text a primary or secondary source? Is it meant to entertain or persuade? Who is the intended audience of the text? Once you answer these basic questions, it is critical to read the passage until the passage is completely understood. Once the passage is read, briefly summarize the text. Summarizing, or "translating," a text in one's own words, will help you to better comprehend the meaning and intent of the passage. Once you begin analyzing the passage in your own writing, the audience will expect you to draw upon the original passage for text evidence. This kind of evidence supports authorial credibility.

One way to draw from the passage read is to cite direct quotations from the text; this will show readers that you are intimate with the passage and that you are able to show them the original source from whence your information came. Including a paraphrase of the passage you draw from is also substantial, as long as you cite the author's last name with the page number. Depending on what style you are using (APA, MLA, or Chicago), references can be added at the end of your analysis to show exactly where the

17

source is from. References will tell you if the information is found in a magazine article, journal, or website, who the author is, and when the text was published.

Citing Specific Textual Evidence to Support Analysis of Science and Technical Texts

Backing up analysis as a science and technical text writer is a must if the end goal is to have a credible standing with an audience. Primary sources of science and technical writing draw upon observation and experiments to inform the reader; before science writing is published in a reputable journal, it must be peer reviewed. Therefore, a credible citation of a science or technical source in order to support your own analysis of the text is key in convincing your audience that the material you have is valid.

Keep in mind that the material you cite in science and technical writing must be precise. Precision writing in a science or technical field is imperative. Analysis of science writing does not need your opinion or a vague generalization on what the text says; it needs *precise* details from the text, detailing specific information regarding how the experiment or process works. Let's say you are writing in a science field and you want to explain to your audience how light travels. If you say "light travels fast," this is a vague generalization of complex material that should be treated thoroughly. The following is a more precise explanation of how light travels, and it draws upon a credible source from Stanford University:

> The first person to measure how light travels was astronomer Ole Roemer in 1675. He noticed that light rays from Jupiter were later than expected, and thus figured that light actually *travelled*, like we do, instead of being this immediate energy source. Today, the best understanding that we have of light is that it is "a disturbance in the electromagnetic fields of charged bodies" (Dr. Sten Odenwald, 1997). In a sense, light is energy that comes from a charge and projects outward into space, and it travels at 186,282 miles per second.

A few things to notice in the above explanation is a summary of information as well as a direct quotation. Writers should use direct quotations when something is said that they cannot say better themselves, or when there is no other way to say a truth or phrase. Notice how, after the direct quotation, there is the author's name followed by the year written in parentheses. After you write your own analysis of a text in science or technical writing, it is important to ask the following questions: Have I explained the process in detail? Have I drawn upon the original source as an accurate reflection of the information? Always cite as many specifics from the original source as you can, while making sure to attribute the information to the proper source.

Determine a Theme or Central Idea of a Text

Main Idea or Primary Purpose

The **main idea** is what the writer wants to say about that topic. A writer may make the point that global warming is a growing problem that must be addressed in order to save the planet. Therefore, the topic is global warming, and the main idea is that it's *a serious problem needing to be addressed*. The topic can be expressed in a word or two, but the main idea should be a complete thought.

In order to illustrate the main idea, a writer will use supporting details—the details that provide evidence or examples to help make a point. Supporting details are typically found in nonfiction texts that seek to inform or persuade the reader.

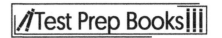

For example, in the example of global warming, where the author's main idea is to show the seriousness of this growing problem and the need for change, the use of supporting details would be critical in effectively making that point. Supporting details used here might include statistics on an increase in global temperatures and studies showing the impact of global warming on the planet. The author could also include projections regarding future climate change in order to illustrate potential lasting effects of global warming.

Some questions may also ask you what the best title is for the passage. Going back to the **topic**, for these questions, it's important give a narrower answer that still encompasses the main idea of the passage. Asking for the appropriate title for passages is rare, but it's best to be prepared for anything.

Summarizing

At the end of a text or passage, it is important to summarize what the readers read. **Summarizing** is a strategy in which readers determine what is important throughout the text or passage, shorten those ideas, and rewrite or retell it in their own words. A summary should identify the main idea of the text or passage. Important details or supportive evidence should also be accurately reported in the summary. If writers provide irrelevant details in the summary, it may cloud the greater meaning of the summary in the text. When summarizing, writers should not include their opinions, quotes, or what they thought the author should have said. A clear summary provides clarity of the text or passage to the readers. Let's review the checklist of items writers should include in their summary.

Summary Checklist

- Title of the story
- Who is or are the main character(s)?
- What did the character(s) want?
- What was the problem?
- How did the character(s) solve the problem?
- How did the story end? What was the resolution?

Determine the central ideas or conclusions of a text

How Authors Develop Theme

Authors employ a variety of techniques to present a **theme**. They may compare or contrast characters, events, places, ideas, or historical or invented settings to speak thematically. They may use analogies, metaphors, similes, allusions, or other literary devices to convey the theme. An author's use of diction, syntax, and tone can also help convey the theme. Authors will often develop themes through the development of characters, use of the setting, repetition of ideas, use of symbols, and through contrasting value systems. Authors of both fiction and nonfiction genres will use a variety of these techniques to develop one or more themes.

Regardless of the literary genre, there are commonalities in how authors, playwrights, and poets develop themes or central ideas.

Authors often do research, the results of which contribute to theme. In prose fiction and drama, this research may include real historical information about the setting the author has chosen or include elements that make fictional characters, settings, and plots seem realistic to the reader. In nonfiction, research is critical since information contained within this literature must be accurate.

In fiction, authors present a narrative conflict that will contribute to the overall theme. This conflict may involve the storyline itself and some trouble within characters that needs resolution. In nonfiction, this conflict may be an explanation or commentary on factual people and events.

Authors will sometimes use character motivation to convey theme, such as in the example from *Hamlet* regarding revenge. In fiction, the characters an author creates will think, speak, and act in ways that effectively convey the theme to readers. In nonfiction, the characters are factual, as in a biography, but authors pay particular attention to presenting those motivations to make them clear to readers.

Authors also use literary devices as a means of conveying theme. For example, the use of moon symbolism in Mary Shelley's *Frankenstein* is significant as its phases can be compared to the phases that the Creature undergoes as he struggles with his identity.

The selected point of view can also contribute to a work's theme. The use of first-person point of view in a fiction or non-fiction work engages the reader's response differently than third person point of view. The central idea or theme from a first-person narrative may differ from a third-person limited text.

In literary nonfiction, authors usually identify the purpose of their writing, which differs from fiction, where the general purpose is to entertain. The purpose of nonfiction is usually to inform, persuade, or entertain the audience. The stated purpose of a non-fiction text will drive how the central message or theme, if applicable, is presented.

Authors identify an audience for their writing, which is critical in shaping the theme of the work. For example, the audience for J.K. Rowling's *Harry Potter* series would be different than the audience for a biography of George Washington. The audience an author chooses to address is closely tied to the purpose of the work. The choice of an audience also drives the choice of language and level of diction an author uses. Ultimately, the intended audience determines the level to which that subject matter is presented and the complexity of the theme.

Paraphrasing

Another strategy readers can use to help them fully comprehend a text or passage is **paraphrasing**. Paraphrasing is when readers take the author's words and put them into their own words. When readers and writers paraphrase, they should avoid copying the text—that is plagiarism. It is also important to include as many details as possible when restating the facts. Not only will this help readers and writers recall information, but by putting the information into their own words, they demonstrate whether or not they fully comprehend the text or passage. Look at the example below showing an original text and how to paraphrase it.

> *Original Text*: Fenway Park is home to the beloved Boston Red Sox. The stadium opened on April 20, 1912. The stadium currently seats over 37,000 fans, many of whom travel from all over the country to experience the iconic team and nostalgia of Fenway Park.

> *Paraphrased*: On April 20, 1912, Fenway Park opened. Home to the Boston Red Sox, the stadium now seats over 37,000 fans. Many spectators travel to watch the Red Sox and experience the spirit of Fenway Park.

Paraphrasing, summarizing, and quoting can often cross paths with one another. Review the chart below showing the similarities and differences between the three strategies.

Paraphrasing	Summarizing	Quoting
Uses own words	Puts main ideas into own words	Uses words that are identical to text
References original source	References original source	Requires quotation marks
Uses own sentences	Shows important ideas of source	Uses author's own words and ideas

Analyzing a Complex Set of Ideas or Sequence of Events

Logical Sequence

Even if the writer includes plenty of information to support their point, the writing is only coherent when the information is in a logical order. **Logical sequencing** is really just common sense, but it's also an important writing technique. First, the writer should introduce the main idea, whether for a paragraph, a section, or the entire piece. Second, they should present evidence to support the main idea by using transitional language. This shows the reader how the information relates to the main idea and the sentences around it. The writer should then take time to interpret the information, making sure necessary connections are obvious to the reader. Finally, the writer can summarize the information in a closing section.

Though most writing follows the above pattern, it isn't a set rule. Sometimes writers change the order for effect. For example, the writer can begin with a surprising piece of supporting information to grab the reader's attention, and then transition to the main idea. Thus, if a passage doesn't follow the logical order, don't immediately assume it's wrong. However, most writing usually settles into a logical sequence after a nontraditional beginning.

As a reader, you are expected to pursue the author's logic regardless of the confusing transitions or complex content. For example, postmodern literary theory is all about deconstruction of texts. Deconstructing texts is picking apart a text in order to understand it better, or to understand it through an alternate lens or perspective. Some theorists who write about deconstruction, such as Jacques Derrida, do not follow traditional logic as a rule, because their intent is to interrupt traditional logic and to disturb the "supposed" order of processes and systems.

This makes his writing extremely hard to understand. As readers, it is our job to go through the text, even a literary deconstructionist text, line by line, in order to understand it. Sometimes what helps with analyzing a complex text is to write your own observations when transitions occur from one subject to the next, and to mark them in the text. Or, after each paragraph or section, write a brief summary in your own words about what you just read. Drawing diagrams also helps, if the author is trying to explain a phenomenon or process that is not easily understood. Use all your faculties to follow the author and uncover the truth of what they are trying to relay to their audience.

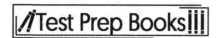

Analyzing in Detail a Series of Events Described in a Text

<u>Causality</u>

Causality is simply cause and effect; Event A causes Effect B to come into existence. Determining the strength of the relationship between the cause and effect will make evaluating the argument much easier. The more the events are directly related, the greater the causality.

Be wary of language that implies that there is direct causation when none actually exists. This trick usually involves **correlation**, which is a separate concept. **Correlating events** simply occur at the same time. One event does not cause or affect the other. Here's an example:

> Jeffrey Johnston is having the best year of his career. He hit twice as many home runs as last year and increased his batting average by one hundred points. He clearly must have wanted to earn more money in the offseason.

The author is unreasonably identifying an athlete's desire to enhance his value as the cause of his career year. It's illogical to say that some intangible increase in motivation is the reason why a player doubled his productivity. There could be any number of reasons why Jeffrey Johnston is playing much better. Maybe he was a young player who was still developing? Maybe a new coach fixed his batting swing? Maybe he is finally healthy for the first time in his career? There are a number of explanations as to why he improved. There is not enough evidence to suggest that desiring more money caused the spike in production. An addition of more information to the argument is:

> Jeffrey Johnston is having the best year of his career. He hit twice as many home runs as last year and increased his batting average by one hundred points. He clearly must have wanted to earn more money in the offseason. After all, he spent the whole offseason talking about how he increased his training regimen to put himself in a better position to earn more money as a free agent.

This argument adds more justification for attributing the desire for more money to the player's successful career year. This argument states that Jeffrey Johnston publicly discussed working harder to get a bigger contract. However, a strong causation is still not established. Some other causal agent could have been a much bigger reason for the bump in productivity. Another addition to the argument is:

> Jeffrey Johnston is having the best year of his career. He hit twice as many home runs as last year and increased his batting average by one hundred points. He clearly must have wanted to earn more money in the offseason. After all, he spent the whole offseason talking about how he increased his training regimen to put himself in a better position to earn more money as a free agent. Not to mention, he tattooed dollar signs on his forearms and painted his bat green.

The author has now included Jeffrey's tattoo and custom bat as evidence of his complete focus on money. This is the strongest causation since it has the most evidence directly related to the conclusion. According to the argument, Jeffrey knew he was a free agent before the season, he made public comments about working hard for better compensation, and he illustrated his mindset on his forearm and baseball bat. It seems likely that a desire for more money caused Jeffrey's career year.

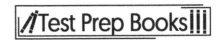

Following a Complex Multistep Procedure When Carrying Out Experiments

Interpreting Observed Data or Information

An important skill for scientific comprehension is the ability to interpret observed data and information. Scientific studies and research articles can be challenging to understand, but by familiarizing oneself with the format, language, and presentation of such information, fluency regarding the research process, results, and significance of such results can be improved. Most scientific research articles published in a journal follow the same basic format and contain the following sections:

- Abstract: A brief summary in paragraph form of each of the individual sections that are detailed below.
- Introduction or background: this section introduces the research question, states why the question is important, lays the groundwork for what is already known and what remains unknown, and states the hypothesis. Typically, this section includes a miniature literature review of previously published studies and details the results and or gaps in the research that these studies failed to achieve.
- Methods: this section details the experimental process that was conducted including information about how subjects were recruited, their demographic information, steps that were followed in the methodology, and what statistical analyses were performed on the data.
- Results: this section includes a narrative description of the results that were found as well as tables and graphs of the findings.
- Conclusion: this section interprets the results to put meaning to the numbers. Essentially, it answers the question, so what? It also discusses strengths, weaknesses, and shortcomings of the performed experiment as well as needed areas of future research.

Applying Scientific Principles

The scientific method provides the framework for studying and learning about the world in a scientific fashion. The scientific method has been around since at least the 17th century and is a codified way to answer natural science questions. Due to objectivity, the scientific method is impartial and its results are highly repeatable; these are its greatest advantages. There is no consensus as to the number of steps involved in executing the scientific method, but the following six steps are needed to fulfill the criteria for correct usage of the scientific method:

- Ask a question: Most scientific investigations begin with a question about a specific problem.
- Make observations: Observations will help pinpoint research objectives on the quest to answer the question.
- Create or propose a hypothesis: The hypothesis represents a possible solution to the problem. It is a simple statement predicting the outcome of an experiment designed to investigate the research question.
- Formulate an experiment: The experiment tests the proposed hypothesis.
- Test the hypothesis: The outcome of the experiment to test the hypothesis is the most crucial step in the scientific method.
- Accept or reject the hypothesis: Using results from the experiment, a scientist can conclude to accept or reject the hypothesis.

Several key nuances of the scientific method include:

- The hypothesis must be verifiable and falsifiable. Falsifiable refers to the possibility of a negative solution to the hypothesis. The hypothesis should also have relevance, compatibility, testability, simplicity, and predictive power.
- Investigation must utilize both deductive and inductive reasoning. Deductive reasoning employs a logical process to arrive at a conclusion using premises considered true, while inductive reasoning employs an opposite approach. Inductive reasoning allows scientists to propose hypotheses in the scientific method, while deductive reasoning allows scientists to apply hypotheses to particular situations.
- An experiment should incorporate an independent, or changing, variable and a dependent, or non-changing, variable. It should also utilize both a control group and an experimental group. The experimental group will ultimately be compared against the control group.

A **scientific explanation** has three crucial components—a claim, evidence, and logical reasoning. A claim makes an assertion or conclusion focusing on the original question or problem. The evidence provides backing for the claim and is usually in the form of scientific data. The scientific data must be appropriate and sufficient. The scientific reasoning connects the claim and evidence and explains why the evidence supports the claim.

Scientific explanations must fit certain criteria and be supported by logic and evidence. The following represent scientific explanation criteria. The proposed explanation:

- Must be logically consistent
- Must abide by the rules of evidence
- Must report procedures and methods
- Must be open to questions and possible modification
- Must be based on historical and current scientific knowledge

The scientific method encourages the growth and communication of new information and procedures among scientists. Explanations of how the natural changes and works based on fiction, personal convictions, religious morals, mystical influences, superstitions, or authorities are not scientific; therefore, these explanations are irrelevant to the scientific community.

Scientific explanations have two fundamental characteristics. First, they should explain all scientific data and observations gleaned from experiments. Second, they should allow for predictions that can be verified with future experiments.

Craft and Structure

Determining the Meaning of Words and Phrases in a Literary Text

Meaning of Words in Context
There will be many occasions in one's reading career in which an unknown word or a word with multiple meanings will pop up. There are ways of determining what these words or phrases mean that do not require the use of the dictionary, which is especially helpful during a test where one may not be available. Even outside of the exam, knowing how to derive an understanding of a word via context clues will be a critical skill in the real world. The context is the circumstances in which a story or a

24

passage is happening and can usually be found in the series of words directly before or directly after the word or phrase in question. The clues are the words that hint towards the meaning of the unknown word or phrase.

There may be questions that ask about the meaning of a particular word or phrase within a passage. There are a couple ways to approach these kinds of questions:

1. Define the word or phrase in a way that is easy to comprehend (using context clues).
2. Try out each answer choice in place of the word.

To demonstrate, here's an example from *Alice in Wonderland*:

> Alice was beginning to get very tired of sitting by her sister on the bank, and of having nothing to do: once or twice she <u>peeped</u> into the book her sister was reading, but it had no pictures or conversations in it, "and what is the use of a book," thought Alice, "without pictures or conversations?"

Q: As it is used in the selection, the word <u>peeped</u> means:

Using the first technique, before looking at the answers, define the word peeped using context clues and then find the matching answer. Then, analyze the entire passage in order to determine the meaning, not just the surrounding words.

To begin, imagine a blank where the word should be and put a synonym or definition there: "once or twice she _____ into the book her sister was reading." The context clue here is the book. It may be tempting to put read where the blank is, but notice the preposition word into. One does not read into a book, one simply reads a book, and since reading a book requires that it is seen with a pair of eyes, then look would make the most sense to put into the blank: "once or twice she <u>looked</u> into the book her sister was reading."

Once an easy-to-understand word or synonym has been supplanted, readers should check to make sure it makes sense with the rest of the passage. What happened after she looked into the book? She thought to herself how a book without pictures or conversations is useless. This situation in its entirety makes sense.

Now check the answer choices for a match:
a. To make a high-pitched cry
b. To smack
c. To look curiously
d. To pout

Since the word was already defined, Choice *C* is the best option.

Using the second technique, replace the figurative blank with each of the answer choices and determine which one is the most appropriate. Remember to look further into the passage to clarify that they work, because they could still make sense out of context.
a. Once or twice, she <u>made a high pitched cry</u> into the book her sister was reading
b. Once or twice she <u>smacked</u> into the book her sister was reading
c. Once or twice she <u>looked curiously</u> into the book her sister was reading
d. Once or twice she <u>pouted</u> into the book her sister was reading

25

For Choice *A*, it does not make much sense in any context for a person to cry into a book, unless maybe something terrible has happened in the story. Given that afterward Alice thinks to herself how useless a book without pictures is, this option does not make sense within context.

For Choice *B*, smacking a book someone is reading may make sense if the rest of the passage indicates a reason for doing so. If Alice was angry or her sister had shoved it in her face, then maybe smacking the book would make sense within context. However, since whatever she does with the book causes her to think, "what is the use of a book without pictures or conversations?" then answer Choice *B* is not an appropriate answer. Answer Choice *C* fits well within context, given her subsequent thoughts on the matter. Answer Choice *D* does not make sense in context or grammatically, as people do not pout into things.

This is a simple example to illustrate the techniques outlined above. There may, however, be a question in which all of the definitions are correct and also make sense out of context, in which the appropriate context clues will really need to be honed in on in order to determine the correct answer. For example, here is another passage from *Alice in Wonderland*:

> ... but when the Rabbit actually took a watch out of its waistcoat pocket, and looked at it, and then hurried on, Alice <u>started</u> to her feet, for it flashed across her mind that she had never before seen a rabbit with either a waistcoat-pocket or a watch to take out of it, and burning with curiosity, she ran across the field after it, and was just in time to see it pop down a large rabbit-hole under the hedge.

Q: As it is used in the passage, the word started means _____.
  a. to turn on
  b. to begin
  c. to move quickly
  d. to be surprised

All of these words qualify as a definition of start, but using context clues, the correct answer can be identified using one of the two techniques above. It's easy to see that one does not turn on, begin, or be surprised to one's feet. The selection also states that she "ran across the field after it," indicating that she was in a hurry. Therefore, to move quickly would make the most sense in this context.

The same strategies can be applied to vocabulary that may be completely unfamiliar. In this case, focus on the words before or after the unknown word in order to determine its definition. Take this sentence, for example:

> Sam was such a <u>miser</u> that he forced Andrew to pay him twelve cents for the candy, even though he had a large inheritance and he knew his friend was poor.

Unlike with assertion questions, for vocabulary questions, it may be necessary to apply some critical thinking skills when something isn't explicitly stated within the passage. Think about the implications of the passage, or what the text is trying to say. With this example, it is important to realize that it is considered unusually stingy for a person to demand so little money from someone instead of just letting their friend have the candy, especially if this person is already wealthy. Hence, a <u>miser</u> is a greedy or stingy individual.

Questions about complex vocabulary may not be explicitly asked, but this is a useful skill to know. If there is an unfamiliar word while reading a passage and its definition goes unknown, it is possible to

Determining the Meaning of Words and Phrases in an Informational Text

The previous section looks at meaning of word choice in literary text. In addition to literary text, you are also expected to know how to find out the meaning of word choice in informational text. Remember that in any kind of writing, it is important to look at the context surrounding the word in question. Informational texts include the following:

- Science articles
- History books
- Magazines
- Autobiographies
- Instruction Manuals
- Newspaper
- Court Opinion

Let's look at an example of how to look at the meaning of words in technical documents and how they affect tone. The following passage explains what lethal force is and can be found in a journal on crime reports:

> Lethal force, or deadly force, is defined as the physical means to cause death or serious harm to another individual. The law holds that lethal force is only acceptable when you or another person are in immediate and unavoidable danger of death or severe bodily harm. For example, a person could be beating someone in such a way that the victim is suffering severe trauma that could result in death or serious harm. This would be an instance where lethal force would be acceptable and possibly the only way to save the victim from irrevocable damage.

Now let's look at this passage from a travel agency:

> Vacationers looking for a perfect experience should opt out of Disney parks and try a trip on Disney Cruise Lines. While a park offers rides, characters, and show experiences, it also includes long lines, often very hot weather, and enormous crowds. A Disney cruise, on the other hand, is a relaxing, luxurious vacation that includes many of the same experiences as the parks, minus the crowds and lines. The cruise has top-notch food, maid service, water slides, multiple pools, Broadway-quality shows, and daily character experiences for kids. There are also many activities, such as bingo, trivia contests, and dance parties that can entertain guests of all ages. The cruise even stops at Disney's private island for a beach barbecue with characters, water slides, and water sports. Those looking for the Disney experience without the hassle should book a Disney cruise.

What is the tone of each passage and how does the author's word choice affect that tone? Let's look at the first passage and the word choice they use. They "define" lethal force in the first sentence and refer to people as "individuals." Right off we know that we are dealing with formal language, and this creates a serious tone. We also know that the first passage does not wish to undermine the seriousness of their subject by words like "unavoidable danger of death" and "severe bodily harm." In contrast, let's look at the passage from the travel agency. Some of the more memorable words they use are "relaxing,"

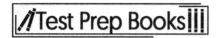
"luxurious," and "perfect experience"—these words choices are fun and fancy, which creates a lighthearted, desirable tone.

Both of these are technical texts which are meant to inform the reader. The difference is in their word choice affecting their tone. The authors here paid close attention to who their audience was. The audience of the first passage is possibly a police officer or a judge reading about the definition of lethal force for a case or a court trial. The audience for the second passage is probably a family looking to have fun and go on vacation. Both passages identified their audience and constructed the tone accordingly.

Determining the Meaning of Symbols

Determining unknown symbols or terms in a scientific or technical textbook is much easier today than one would expect. Textbooks almost always have a chart to depict what various symbols mean throughout their pages. Textbooks also have key terms bolded or italicized to help readers find the unknown word either at the bottom of a page in a footnote or in the back of a textbook inside a glossary. Electronic textbooks will even have links to click that will take you to a definition source or for extra resources to find if the textbook information does not suffice.

For example, let's say you are asked to do a research project on earthquakes. In order to do a comprehensive project explaining what earthquakes are and what they do, you would have to learn the symbols used to measure the earthquakes and the tools used to locate them. We would learn that earthquakes are measured by the symbol MS, meaning the standard surface-wave formula. The MS number goes from a 6.0 to an 8.9. The text depicting the term "MS" would probably be in parentheses after the words or in a footnote to explain what it stands for and how it measures the earthquake. The term "standard surface-wave" might be in italics or bold to highlight the importance of the word.

Whatever source you are looking into for information, if it is credible, such as a textbook, scientific journal, or a book written by a meteorologist with a PhD, it should have the information you are looking for within the text, as well as additional resources to navigate to, such as a hyperlink or an appendix, in order to guide readers to the best information possible. Don't ignore the information in the margins or in the footnotes—this will be your best key to unlock the information you are struggling to comprehend. Also, don't just glance over words or symbols you don't know. Chances are, they will be listed somewhere on that page with more information. If all else fails and there is no additional resources or information available for a symbol or key word, you can always use a search engine, such as google, to look up a definition or key word. Once you find a credible source online to read, you will be able to find the information you are looking for.

Analyzing an Author's Ideas or Claims

In non-fiction writing, authors employ argumentative techniques to present their opinion to readers in the most convincing way. Persuasive writing usually includes at least one type of appeal: an appeal to logic (logos), emotion (pathos), or credibility and trustworthiness (ethos). When a writer appeals to logic, they are asking readers to agree with them based on research, evidence, and an established line of reasoning. An author's argument might also appeal to readers' emotions, perhaps by including personal stories and anecdotes (a short narrative of a specific event). A final type of appeal, appeal to authority, asks the reader to agree with the author's argument on the basis of their expertise or credentials. Consider three different approaches to arguing the same opinion:

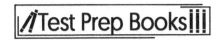

Logic (Logos)

This is an example of an appeal to logic:

> Our school should abolish its current ban on campus cell phone use. The ban was adopted last year as an attempt to reduce class disruptions and help students focus more on their lessons. However, since the rule was enacted, there has been no change in the number of disciplinary problems in class. Therefore, the rule is ineffective and should be done away with.

The author uses evidence to disprove the logic of the school's rule (the rule was supposed to reduce discipline problems, but the number of problems has not been reduced; therefore, the rule is not working) and call for its repeal.

Emotion (Pathos)

An author's argument might also appeal to readers' emotions, perhaps by including personal stories and anecdotes. The next example presents an appeal to emotion. By sharing the personal anecdote of one student and speaking about emotional topics like family relationships, the author invokes the reader's empathy in asking them to reconsider the school rule.

> Our school should abolish its current ban on campus cell phone use. If students aren't able to use their phones during the school day, many of them feel isolated from their loved ones. For example, last semester, one student's grandmother had a heart attack in the morning. However, because he couldn't use his cell phone, the student didn't know about his grandmother's accident until the end of the day—when she had already passed away, and it was too late to say goodbye. By preventing students from contacting their friends and family, our school is placing undue stress and anxiety on students.

Credibility (Ethos)

Finally, an appeal to authority includes a statement from a relevant expert. In this case, the author uses a doctor in the field of education to support the argument. All three examples begin from the same opinion—the school's phone ban needs to change—but rely on different argumentative styles to persuade the reader.

> Our school should abolish its current ban on campus cell phone use. According to Dr. Bartholomew Everett, a leading educational expert, "Research studies show that cell phone usage has no real impact on student attentiveness. Rather, phones provide a valuable technological resource for learning. Schools need to learn how to integrate this new technology into their curriculum." Rather than banning phones altogether, our school should follow the advice of experts and allow students to use phones as part of their learning.

Analyzing and Evaluating the Effectiveness of Structure

Evaluating the Effectiveness of a Piece of Writing

An effective and engaging piece of writing will cause the reader to forget about the author entirely. Readers will become so engrossed in the subject, argument, or story at hand that they will almost identify with it, readily adopting beliefs proposed by the author or accepting all elements of the story as believable. On the contrary, poorly written works will cause the reader to be hyperaware of the author, doubting the writer's knowledge of a subject or questioning the validity of a narrative. Persuasive or expository works that are poorly researched will have this effect, as well as poorly planned stories with

29

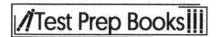

significant plot holes. An author must consider the task, purpose, and audience to sculpt a piece of writing effectively.

When evaluating the effectiveness of a piece, the most important thing to consider is how well the purpose is conveyed to the audience through the mode, use of rhetoric, and writing style.

The purpose must pass through these three aspects for effective delivery to the audience. If any elements are not properly considered, the reader will be overly aware of the author, and the message will be lost. The following is a checklist for evaluating the effectiveness of a piece:

- Does the writer choose the appropriate writing mode—argumentative, narrative, descriptive, informative—for their purpose?
- Does the writing mode employed contain characteristics inherent to that mode?
- Does the writer consider the personalities/interests/demographics of the intended audience when choosing rhetorical appeals?
- Does the writer use appropriate vocabulary, sentence structure, voice, and tone for the audience demographic?
- Does the author properly establish himself/herself as having authority on the subject, if applicable?
- Does the piece make sense?

Another thing to consider is the medium in which the piece was written. If the medium is a blog, diary, or personal letter, the author may adopt a more casual stance towards the audience. If the piece of writing is a story in a book, a business letter or report, or a published article in a journal or if the task is to gain money or support or to get published, the author may adopt a more formal stance. Ultimately, the writer will want to be very careful in how he or she addresses the reader.

Finally, the effectiveness of a piece can be evaluated by asking how well the purpose was achieved. For example, if students are assigned to read a persuasive essay, instructors can ask whether the author influences students' opinions. Students may be assigned two differing persuasive texts with opposing perspectives and be asked which writer was more convincing. Students can then evaluate what factors contributed to this—for example, whether one author uses more credible supporting facts, appeals more effectively to readers' emotions, presents more believable personal anecdotes, or offers stronger counterargument refutation. Students can then use these evaluations to strengthen their own writing skills.

Analyzing a Particular Point of View or Cultural Experience

Developing a knowledge of diverse texts other than those in western literature is an important part of learning about other cultures and their point of view. Since literature reflects the time period, consciousness, and perspectives of a culture, reading diverse texts in alternate time periods is a

30

fundamental way to experience cultures other than our own. We might not only learn compassion but a well-rounded view of life and experiences around the world. The following list depicts world literature classics from other cultures, although the list is not comprehensive:

- *Don Quixote* by Miguel de Cervantes
- *Things Fall Apart* by Chinua Achebe
- *Pride and Prejudice* by Jane Austen
- *Wuthering Heights* by Emily Bronte
- *Heart of Darkness* by Joseph Conrad
- *The Stranger* by Albert Camus
- *The Divine Comedy* by Dante Alighieri
- *Canterbury Tales* by Geoffrey Chaucer
- *Great Expectations* by Charles Dickens
- *Madame Bovary* by Gustave Flaubert
- *One Hundred Years of Solitude* by Gabriel Garcia Marquez
- *The Iliad* and *The Odyssey* by Homer
- *The Trial* by Franz Kafka
- *The Sound of the Mountain* by Yasunari Kawabata
- *Diary of a Madman and Other Stories* by Lun Xun
- *The Tale of Genji* by Murasaki Shikibu
- *Lolita* by Vladimir Nabokov
- *The Book of Disquiet* by Fernando Pessoa
- *War and Peace* by Leo Tolstoy
- *Mrs. Dalloway* by Virginia Woolf
- *Nectar in a Sieve* by Kamala Markandaya
- *Obasan* by Joy Kogawa
- *The House of the Spirits* by Isabel Allende

Let's look at an example of a world literature classic and its surrounding context. The following is a passage from the narrative poem, The *Divine Comedy*, written by Dante Alighieri, an Italian poet in the late Middle ages.

> Benign Apollo! this last labour aid,
> And make me such a vessel of thy worth,
> As thy own laurel claims of me belov'd.
> Thus far hath one of steep Parnassus' brows
> Suffic'd me; henceforth there is need of both
> For my remaining enterprise Do thou
> Enter into my bosom, and there breathe
> So, as when Marsyas by thy hand was dragg'd
> Forth from his limbs unsheath'd. O power divine!
> If thou to me of shine impart so much,
> That of that happy realm the shadow'd form
> Trac'd in my thoughts I may set forth to view,
> Thou shalt behold me of thy favour'd tree
> Come to the foot, and crown myself with leaves;
> For to that honour thou, and my high theme

Will fit me. If but seldom, might Sire!
To grace his triumph gathers thence a wreath
Caesar or bard (more shame for human wills
Deprav'd!) joy to the Delphic god must spring
From the Pierian foliage, when one breast
Is with such thirst inspir'd. From a small spark
Great flame hath risen; after me perchance
Others with better voice may pray, and gain
From the Cirrhaean city answer kind.

This text was written in the Middle Ages, as you can probably tell from the language using "thy" and "thou." Remember that most texts in world literature from other countries that you read in English are probably translated into English. This poem was originally written in Italian. The original poem in Italian has a different rhyme scheme and metrical line than the one above. The above is iambic pentameter, which is a popular line for a poet to write in in English because it fits nicely with the way we stress our words.

In the original Italian, the poem is written in terza rima, which is a rhyme scheme that fits well with the Italian language because many of the word-endings in Italian are easier to rhyme than in English. In the poem above, the poet is calling on Apollo for inspiration, who is the god of poetry. This rhetorical device of calling out to an abstract thing is called an apostrophe and is used by many poets throughout the centuries, though this device is less common now. In epic poems or medieval narrative poems, it was very popular for the author to dedicate a passage to the gods before embarking on the journey, or narrative. Knowing characteristics and context of world literature can help us to understand cultures better in the past and why they did certain things.

Analyzing Double Meanings

Satire

Satire is a genre of literature that is humorous on the surface but deals with social commentary on a deeper level. Satire uses irony and sarcasm to deal with its subject and usually seeks to shame or shed light on a society that is corrupt or acting on irrational principles. The most famous example of satire is Jonathan Swift's "A Modest Proposal," an essay that sheds light on England's treatment of the Irish at the time. The essay proposes that poor Irish parents sell their children as food to the wealthy to help with economic circumstances, thus addressing harsh attitudes toward the poor. Satire is a genre that shows widely accepted behavior in a new perspective and works at changing social consciousness.

Some modern examples of satire are late night TV shows, such as *The Late Show* with Stephen Colbert or *Saturday Night Live*, horror movies, or political cartoons. Many modern satire mediums deal with political figures and discourse and the policies that affect the public. Horror movies often deal with self-parody, such as *Scream*, which is a horror movie that makes fun of other horror movies in American culture. Although it is sometimes harsh, satire can be an intelligent way for a society to laugh at itself even under grim circumstances.

Sarcasm

Depending on the tone of voice or the words used, sarcasm can be expressed in many different ways. **Sarcasm** is defined as a bitter or ambiguous declaration that intends to cut or taunt. Most of the ways we use sarcasm is saying something and not really meaning it. In a way, sarcasm is a contradiction that is

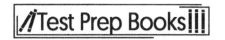

understood by both the speaker and the listener to convey the opposite meaning. For example, let's say Bobby is struggling to learn how to play the trumpet. His sister, Gloria, walks in and tells him: "What a great trumpet player you've become!" This is a sort of verbal irony known as sarcasm. Gloria is speaking a contradiction, but Bobby and Gloria both know the truth behind what she's saying: that Bobby is not a good trumpet player. Sarcasm can also be accompanied by nonverbal language, such as a smirk or a head tilt. Remember that sarcasm is not always clear to the listener; sometimes sarcasm can be expressed by the speaker but lost on the listener.

Irony

Irony is a device that authors use when pitting two contrasting items or ideas against each other in order to create an effect. It's frequently used when an author wants to employ humor or convey a sarcastic tone. Additionally, it's often used in fictional works to build tension between characters, or between a particular character and the reader. An author may use **verbal irony** (sarcasm), **situational irony** (where actions or events have the opposite effect than what's expected), and **dramatic irony** (where the reader knows something a character does not). Examples of irony include:

- Dramatic Irony: An author describing the presence of a hidden killer in a murder mystery, unbeknownst to the characters but known to the reader.
- Situational Irony: An author relating the tale of a fire captain who loses her home in a five-alarm conflagration.
- Verbal Irony: This is where an author or character says one thing but means another. For example, telling a police officer "Thanks a lot" after receiving a ticket.

Understatement

Making an understatement means making a statement that gives the illusion of something being smaller than it actually is. Understatement is used, in some instances, as a humorous rhetorical device. Let's say that there are two friends. One of the friends, Kate, meets the other friend's, Jasmine's, boyfriend. Jasmine's boyfriend, in Kate's opinion, is attractive, funny, and intelligent. After Kate meets her friend's boyfriend, Kate says to Jasmine, "You could do worse." Kate and Jasmine both know from Kate's tone that this means Kate is being ironic—Jasmine could do much, much worse, because her boyfriend is considered a "good catch." The understatement was a rhetorical device used by Kate to let Jasmine know she approves.

Determine an Author's Point of View or Purpose in a Text

Identifying the Author's Purpose

Every story has a **narrator**, or someone who tells the story. This is sometimes also referred to as the story's **point of view**. Don't make the mistake of assuming that the narrator and the author are the same person—on the contrary, they may have completely different opinions and personalities. There are also several types of narrators commonly found in fiction, and each type serves a different purpose.

The first type of narrator is a **first-person narrator** who tells the story from an "I" perspective. A first-person narrator is almost always a character in the story. They might be a main protagonist (like Jane Eyre in the novel of the same name) or a side character (such as Nelly in *Wuthering Heights*). Also, first-person narrator has an immediate response to the events of the story. However, keep in mind that they are reporting the story through their own perspective, so this narrator may not be totally objective or reliable. Pay attention to language that shows the narrator's tone and consider how the events of the story might be interpreted differently by another character.

Another type of narrator is a **second-person narrator** who tells the story from a "you" perspective. Readers probably won't encounter this type of narrator often, although it's becoming slightly more common in modern literature. A second-person narrator forces the reader to insert themselves into the story and consider how they would respond to the action themselves.

Much more common is a **third-person narrator**. This type of narrator is further divided into two subtypes: **third-person limited** and **third-person omniscient**. In both cases, the story is told from an outside perspective ("he," "she," and "they," rather than "I," "me," or "you"). In this way, a third-person narrator is more distanced and objective than a first-person narrator. A third-person limited narrator tends to follow one main character in the story, reporting only that character's thoughts and only events that directly involve that character (think of the Harry Potter books, which are told by a third-person narrator but primarily limited to Harry's thoughts and experiences). A third-person omniscient narrator isn't limited to one character, but instead reports freely on the thoughts, actions, and events of all characters and situations in the story (omniscient means "all knowing"). Third-person omniscient is generally the most flexible and objective type of narrator. Readers can find this narrator in the novels of writers like Charles Dickens and Alexandre Dumas, whose stories are spread across dozens of different characters and locations.

By identifying the type of narrator, readers can assess a narrator's objectivity as well as how the narrator's perspective is limited to a single character's experience. When a narrator is unbiased, readers can take their account of events at face value; when a narrator is less objective, readers have to consider how the narrator's personal perspective influences the reader's understanding.

In addition to the point of view, another important factor to consider is the writer's **purpose**. This answers the question, "Why did the author write this?" Three of the most common purposes are to persuade, to inform, or to entertain. Of course, it's possible for these purposes to overlap.

Generally, literary texts are written to *entertain*. That is, the reader is simply supposed to enjoy the story! The romantic, dramatic, and adventurous elements are all designed to get readers involved with the fates of the characters. When the primary purpose of a text is to entertain, the focus is on the plot elements, the characters' thoughts and emotions, and descriptions of places, events, and characters. Examples of texts that entertain include novels, plays, poetry, and memoirs. Within the more general purpose of entertaining, literary texts might include passages to convey emotion or to describe a character's thoughts or feelings.

Another common writing purpose is to *inform*. Informative writing intends to teach the reader about a particular topic. Generally, this type of writing is objective and unbiased. Informative writing may also be descriptive. However, instead of describing thoughts and emotions, informative writing tends to describe concrete facts. After reading an informative text, the reader should be more knowledgeable about the text's subject. Examples of informative writing include textbooks, research articles, and texts about academic topics like science and history. Sometimes, informative writing is also described as writing that intends to teach or give information about a subject.

The third common writing purpose is to *persuade*. Unlike the objective writing found in informative texts, persuasive texts are more subjective. Rather than being neutral, the author expresses an opinion about the subject and tries to convince readers to agree. As with informative texts, persuasive texts often include facts and statistics—however, these are used to support the writer's perspective. Examples of persuasive writing include newspaper editorials and texts about controversial topics like politics or social issues. Sometimes, persuasive writing is also described as writing that intends to convince, argue, or express an opinion about a subject.

In order to determine the purpose of a text, readers can keep the following questions in mind:

- What type of details are included (facts, emotions, imagery, etc.)?
- Facts and statistics tend to indicate informative or persuasive writing, while emotions or imagery point to writing that entertains.
- Is the author neutral or opinionated?
- An opinionated or biased author is probably writing to persuade, while a neutral author writes to inform.
- Is this passage teaching information?
- If readers gained a lot of new knowledge about a subject after reading a text, the primary purpose was probably to inform.

Comparing the Point of View of Multiple Authors

At some point in your life you will be asked to compare two different things. Comparing two different texts can be difficult because it is tedious—you are being asked to read each text, formulate an analysis of each, and then compare the differences between the two texts. There are many instances where you might run into this in everyday life. Let's say you are being asked to compare two separate proposals for your workplace and you have to give a report on the characteristics of each. Some details you will look at are rhetorical devices used, effectiveness of the language, organization, style, and content, among others. Although the subject of the text is important, you will inevitably look at how each author connects to their audience and how *well* they do so.

The following two passages are written about seat belts. For the sake of discussion afterwards, let's pretend that they are written for an oral presentation for a college class. After you read each of them carefully, we will analyze the impact of each:

Passage A

Seat belts save more lives than any other automobile safety feature. Many studies show that airbags save lives as well; however, not all cars have airbags. For instance, some older cars don't. Furthermore, air bags aren't entirely reliable. For example, studies show that in 15% of accidents, airbags don't deploy as designed; but, on the other hand, seat belt malfunctions are extremely rare. The number of highway fatalities has plummeted since laws requiring seat belt usage were enacted.

Passage B

You are probably wondering about seat belts. A lot of studies show that seat belts help with car accidents. My friend got in a car accident one time and the seat belt saved him, although it left bruises on his chest. It took weeks for the bruises to go away. His name is Chris. But yes it did save his life. You should wear a seat belt every single time you get in a car because some cars do not have airbags or sometimes the airbags do not work and you never know when that will happen.

35

Let's talk about the overall difference between them. Which one is more convincing? Which one is better suited to fit its audience? After reading each, Passage A fits a college audience better than Passage B. It "flows" better and doesn't feel so awkward. But why?

First, let's look at point of view. Passage A sticks with a consistent perspective of a neutral third-person account. There are no "you's" or I's." Passage B, on the other hand, inserts second-person "you" in its passage and intermixes it with a neutral third person. When choosing a point of view, it's important to be consistent with one or the other. To personalize a text, sometimes "you" or "I" is used to create a familiarity with the readers. However, in a passage as short as this that's trying to convince its audience of something, third person is the best option.

Next, let's look at the evidence used in each of these passages. Passage A uses concrete evidence with data-driven statistics. We see that in "15% of accidents, airbags don't deploy as designed" in Passage A, but in Passage B, we receive information like this: "A lot of studies show that seat belts help with car accidents." The phrase "a lot" is vague, but more importantly, what do they mean by "seat belts help with car accidents"? *How* do they help with car accidents? The author of Passage B, maybe unintholds important information from its audience. Clear evidence is very important to the credibility of the author. While Passage A has straightforward claims ("Seat belts save more lives than any other automobile safety feature"), Passage B uses vague language to hedge around the information they are providing.

Finally, the difference in organization between the two passages is important. Passage A begins with a straightforward claim, offers a counterclaim, and then proceeds to provide evidence against the counterclaim, thus proving the claim by the end of the passage. The organization of Passage B is a little more confusing. The author does not begin with a claim, but begins with an assumption that the audience "is wondering about seatbelts." Then the author provides a personal testimony, which is fine, but proceeds to get off track with the name of his friend and how long it took for his bruises to go away, which is not part of the author's claim that "seat belts help with car accidents." The author concludes the claim but gets off track in the body of the passage. Thus, Passage A is better organized than Passage B.

Integration of Knowledge and Ideas

Delineating and Evaluating the Argument and Specific Claims in a Text

In order to evaluate the claims made in a text, it's important to look at the evidence offered to support those claims. Knowing whether an argument is faulty or valid will put you in a better starting point. Claims that are supported will usually have concrete evidence to back it up, like our seatbelt example in the previous section. Claims that are not supported will have generalizations, like "everyone who wears a seatbelt is safe." The word "everyone" is an absolute, and avoiding absolutes like "always" or "all" or "everyone" is important for the validity of a claim. Let's look at the flaws authors can make while presenting arguments:

Red Herring

A **red herring** is a logical fallacy in which irrelevant information is introduced to alter the argument's trajectory. Red herrings are the irrelevant information used to fallaciously and slyly divert the argument into an unrelated topic. This fallacy is common in thriller movies or television shows in which the audience is led to believe that a character is the villain or mastermind, while the true villain remains a

36

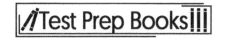

secret. In terms of the Logical Reasoning section, red herrings will attempt to distract the reader with irrelevant information in either the question or answer choice. A red herring is sometimes referred to as a **straw man**, since this fallacy attacks a different argument than the one presented. Consider the following example of a red herring:

> The government must immediately issue tax cuts to strengthen the economy. A strong middle class is the backbone of a fully functional economy, and tax cuts will increase the discretionary spending necessary to support the middle class. After all, it's extremely important for our society to be open-minded and to limit racial discord.

On its face, the argument looks fine. The conclusion is obvious—the government needs to pass tax cuts to strengthen the economy. This is based on the premise that the cuts will increase discretionary spending, which will strengthen the middle class, and the economy will be stronger. However, the last sentence is a red herring. The argument does not address how a society should be open-minded and avoid racism; it holds no connection with the main thrust of the argument. In this scenario, look out for answer choices that address the red herring rather than the essential argument.

Extreme Language
The test makers commonly write appealing answer choices, but take the language to such an unjustified extreme that it is rendered incorrect. The extreme language usually will take the argument too far.

An example of an argument appealing to the extreme is:

> Weight lifting breaks down muscles and rebuilds them. If one just kept exercising and never stopped, their body would deteriorate and eventually fall apart.

This argument is clearly illogical. The author correctly describes what weight lifting does to the body, but then takes the argument to an unjustified extreme. If someone continually lifted weights, their body would not deteriorate and fall apart due to the weights breaking down muscle. The weightlifter may eventually die from a heart attack or dehydration, but it would not be because of how weight lifting rebuilds muscle.

Appeals to Authority Fallacy
Arguing from authority occurs when an author uses an expert to justify their argument. Whether the appeal is fallacious depends on the status, authority, or expertise of the cited authority. If the authority cannot reasonably be relied upon, then the author is committing a logical fallacy.

Always keep in mind that **appealing to authority** can be valid or invalid argumentation. It all depends on the authority's credibility. How is the credibility of a cited authority evaluated? Indicators are listed below:

- Whatever expertise is stated in the field. The required qualifications will depend on the field, such as a PhD in chemistry or two decades experience as the top bricklayer.
- Whether the claim being asserted by the qualified authority is actually within their field of expertise.
- Whether the majority of other similarly qualified experts agree, or if there is open disagreement on the subject.
- Whether the author is biased in some manner.

- Whether the claimed field of expertise is legitimate. For example, be cautious of claimed expertise in psychic abilities or horoscope readings.
- Whether the authority is identified. The author will sometimes preface the argument with phrases like, *experts say*, *a book stated*, *a documentary reported*, and *they say*. The unidentified authority is almost always a sign of fallacious argumentation.

Always ask yourself these questions when an argument cites an authority. They will help you determine if the authority is reliable and relevant to the argument at hand. If the authority can be trusted, this may lend weight to one of the answer choices. If, however, the authority is in question, this can divert you to a better option. Here's an example of a flawed argument from authority:

> Bill Gates is the preeminent mathematical and computer genius of his era. Bill Gates believes in our government making huge economic investments in the research of renewable energy. The government should obviously follow this advice.

The argument relates Bill Gates' genius in math and computers. The author is hoping the inference is that math and computer genius translates to expertise in government fiscal and energy policy. The argument offers no support as to why the expertise would apply to this seemingly unrelated field. This is flawed reasoning. Although Bill Gates is an authority on computers, it does not mean that the government should follow his thoughts in an unrelated field.

Hasty Generalizations

A hasty generalization involves an argument relying on insufficient statistical data or inaccurately generalizing. One common generalization occurs when a group of individuals under observation have some quality or attribute that is asserted to be universal or true for a much larger number of people than actually documented. Here's an example of a hasty generalization:

> A man smokes a lot of cigarettes, but so did his grandfather. The grandfather smoked nearly two packs per day since his World War II service until he died at ninety years of age. Continuing to smoke cigarettes will clearly not impact the grandson's long-term health.

This argument is a hasty generalization because it assumes that one person's addiction and lack of consequences will naturally be reflected in a different individual. There is no reasonable justification for such extrapolation. It is common knowledge that any smoking is detrimental to one's health. The fact that the man's grandfather smoked two packs per day and lived a long life has no logical connection with the grandson engaging in similar behavior. The hasty generalization doesn't take into account other reasons behind the grandfather's longevity. Nor does the author offer evidence that might support the idea that the man would share a similar lifetime if he smokes. It might be different if the author stated that the man's family shares some genetic trait rendering them immune to the effects of tar and chemicals on the lungs. If this were in the argument, we would assume it as truth and find the generalization to be valid rather than hasty. Of course, this is not the case in our example.

COMMON LOGICAL FALLACIES		
Fallacy	**Summary**	**Example**
Red Herring	A red herring is a logical fallacy in which irrelevant information is introduced to alter the argument's trajectory and divert the argument into an unrelated topic.	The government must immediately issue tax cuts to strengthen the economy. A strong middle class is the backbone of a fully functional economy, and tax cuts will increase the discretionary spending necessary to support the middle class. After all, it's extremely important for our society to be open-minded and limit racial discord.
Extreme Language	Extreme arguments will take the language to such an unjustified extreme, or push it so far, that the extremeness will render the argument incorrect.	Weight lifting breaks down muscles and rebuilds them. If one just kept exercising and never stopped, their body would deteriorate and eventually fall apart.
Irrelevancy	Although usually persuasive, irrelevant information is unconnected to the argument's logic or context.	Argument only discusses the balance of speed and accuracy and does not mention history. Answer Choice: Historically, news organizations always waited to verify information and sources, and the change is due to the advent of the Internet.
Similar Language	Answer choices deceptively bear similar language, like the exact same words or phrases, as the argument.	Argument: This leads to some analysts jumping the gun and predicting outcomes inaccurately. Answer Choice: Jumping the gun is the worst mistake any analyst could make.
Parallel Reasoning	Parallel reasoning will make otherwise illogical answer choices seem more credible by mimicking the argument's structure.	Argument only involves news analysts prioritizing speed and accuracy. Answer Choice: The worst sports analysts prioritize speed over accuracy when announcing trades and other roster moves.
Appeal to Authority	Arguing from authority occurs when an author uses an expert to justify his argument, which is illogical if the supposed authority lacks the required status or expertise.	Bill Gates is the pre-imminent mathematical and computer genius of his era. Bill Gates believes in our government making huge economic investments in the research of renewable energy. The government should obviously follow this advice.
Hasty Generalizations	A hasty generalization involves an argument relying on insufficient statistical data or inaccurately generalizing.	I smoke a lot of cigarettes but so did my grandpa. He smoked nearly two packs per day from his World War II service until he died at ninety years of age. Continuing to smoke cigarettes will clearly not impact my long-term health.
Confusing Correlation with Causation	Arguments confuse correlation with causation by saying that one event caused another just because they occurred at the same time.	Jacob adopted a puppy last week. I saw him on Monday and he's lost fifty pounds since last summer. He looks really good. Adopting a puppy must be the secret to weight loss.

Confusing Correlation with Causation

Correlation means that two events occur at the same time; however, **causation** indicates that one event caused a separate event. It is a common logical fallacy for correlation to be confused with causation. Arguments confuse correlation with causation by stating that one event caused another just because they occurred at the same time.

When evaluating whether an argument's reasoning is confusing the terms causation and correlation, always identify the actual cause of the event. Is there another more likely or reasonable event that could have been the true cause? If there is no causation, then there is a logical error. Also, be mindful of the events' timing and relationship to each other. If the author is drawing undue attention to the fact that the events occurred close in time, then check for this fallacy. However, remain aware that it is always possible for events occurring at the same time to be the cause.

Below is an example of an argument confusing correlation with causation:

> Jacob adopted a puppy two months ago. I saw him on Monday, and he's lost fifty pounds since summer. He looks really good. Adopting a puppy must be the secret to his weight loss.

In this argument, the author is saying that he saw Jacob with a new puppy, and Jacob looked good; therefore, adopting the puppy caused Jacob to look better. This is clearly illogical. Jacob could have been on a serious juice cleanse. He could have started running or lifting weights. Although the events (adopting the puppy and losing weight) occurred at the same time, it does not necessarily mean that one caused the other.

This is often a judgment decision. The argument must justify the assumption of causation in some meaningful way. For example, in the sample argument it would not be fallacious if the author stated that Jacob adopted the puppy a while ago, and they often run together. This would not be a logical flaw since starting to exercise with a new dog could reasonably cause the weight loss and improved looks.

Practice Quiz

Questions 1–5 are based upon the following passage:

> Four score and seven years ago our fathers brought forth on this continent, a new nation, conceived in Liberty, and dedicated to the proposition that all men are created equal.
>
> Now we are engaged in a great civil war, testing whether that nation, or any nation so conceived and so dedicated, can long endure. We are met on a great battle-field of that war. We have come to dedicate a portion of that field, as a final resting place for those who here gave their lives that that nation might live. It is altogether fitting and proper that we should do this.
>
> But, in a larger sense, we can not dedicate—we can not consecrate—we can not hallow—this ground. The brave men, living and dead, who struggled here, have consecrated it, far above our poor power to add or detract. The world will little note, nor long remember what we say here, but it can never forget what they did here. It is for us the living, rather, to be dedicated here to the unfinished work which they who fought here have thus far so nobly advanced. It is rather for us to be here dedicated to the great task remaining before us—that from these honored dead we take increased devotion to that cause for which they gave the last full measure of devotion—that we here highly resolve that these dead shall not have died in vain—that this nation, under God, shall have a new birth of freedom—and that government of the people, by the people, for the people, shall not perish from the earth.

From Abraham Lincoln's address delivered at the dedication of the cemetery at Gettysburg, November 19, 1863.

1. The best description for the phrase "Four score and seven years ago" is:
    a. A unit of measurement
    b. A period of time
    c. A literary movement
    d. A statement of political reform

2. What is the setting of this text?
    a. A battleship off of the coast of France
    b. A desert plain on the Sahara Desert
    c. A battlefield in a North American town
    d. The residence of Abraham Lincoln

3. Which war is Abraham Lincoln referring to in the following passage?

    Now we are engaged in a great civil war, testing whether that nation, or any nation so conceived and so dedicated, can long endure.

    a. World War I
    b. The War of Spanish Succession
    c. World War II
    d. The American Civil War

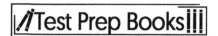

4. What message is the speaker trying to convey through this address?
   a. The audience should perpetuate the ideals of freedom that the soldiers died fighting for.
   b. The audience should honor the dead by establishing an annual memorial service.
   c. The audience should form a militia that would overturn the current political structure.
   d. The audience should forget the lives that were lost and discredit the soldiers.

5. What is the effect of Lincoln's statement in the following passage?

But, in a larger sense, we can not dedicate—we can not consecrate—we can not hallow—this ground. The brave men, living and dead, who struggled here, have consecrated it, far above our poor power to add or detract.

   a. His comparison emphasizes the great sacrifice of the soldiers who fought in the war.
   b. His comparison serves as a reminder of the inadequacies of his audience.
   c. His comparison serves as a catalyst for guilt and shame among audience members.
   d. His comparison suggests that the dedication ceremony was inappropriate.

See answers on the next page.

Answer Explanations

1. B: "Four score and seven years ago" is 87 because the word "score" means 20.

2. C: The setting of this text is a battlefield in Gettysburg, Pennsylvania. Choices *A, B*, and *D* are incorrect because the text specifies that they "met on a great battlefield of that war."

3. D: Though the U.S. was involved in World War I and II, Choices *A* and *C* are incorrect because they occurred long after the Gettysburg address. Choice *B* is incorrect, as the War of Spanish Succession involved Spain, Italy, Germany, and the Netherlands, and not the United States.

4. A: The speech calls on the audience to consider the soldiers who died on the battlefield and to perpetuate the ideals of freedom so that their deaths would not be in vain. Choice *B* is incorrect because, although they are there to "dedicate a portion of that field," there is no mention in the text of an annual memorial service. Choice *C* is incorrect because there is no aggressive language in the text, only reverence for the dead. Choice *D* is incorrect because forgetting the lives that were lost is the opposite of what Lincoln is suggesting.

5. A: Choice *A* is correct because Lincoln's intention was to memorialize the soldiers who had fallen as a result of war as well as celebrate those who had put their lives in danger for the sake of their country. Choices *B, C*, and *D* are incorrect because Lincoln's speech was supposed to foster a sense of pride among the members of the audience while connecting them to the soldiers' experiences, not to alienate or discourage them.

Language

Conventions of Standard English

Standard English Capitalization, Punctuation, and Spelling

Capitalization

Here's a non-exhaustive list of things that should be capitalized:

- The first word of every sentence
- The first word of every line of poetry
- The first letter of proper nouns (World War II)
- Holidays (Valentine's Day)
- The days of the week and months of the year (Tuesday, March)
- The first word, last word, and all major words in the titles of books, movies, songs, and other creative works (In the novel, *To Kill a Mockingbird*, note that *a* is lowercase since it's not a major word, but *to* is capitalized since it's the first word of the title.)
- Titles when preceding a proper noun (President Roberto Gonzales, Aunt Judy)

When simply using a word such as president or secretary, though, the word is not capitalized.

> Officers of the new business must include a *president* and *treasurer*.

Seasons—spring, fall, etc.—are not capitalized.

North, *south*, *east*, and *west* are capitalized when referring to regions but are not when being used for directions. In general, if it's preceded by *the* it should be capitalized.

> I'm from the South.
> I drove south.

Punctuation

Ellipses

An **ellipsis (...)** is used to show that there is more to the quoted text than is necessary for the current discussion. Writers use them in place of words, lines, phrases, list content, or paragraphs that might just as easily have been omitted from a passage of writing. This can be done to save space or to focus only on the specifically relevant material.

> Exercise is good for some unexpected reasons. Watkins writes, "Exercise has many benefits such as ... reducing cancer risk."

In the example above, the ellipsis takes the place of the other benefits of exercise that are more expected.

The ellipsis may also be used to show a pause in sentence flow.

> "I'm wondering ... how this could happen," Dylan said in a soft voice.

44

Commas

A **comma (,)** is the punctuation mark that signifies a pause—breath—between parts of a sentence. It denotes a break of flow. As with so many aspects of writing structure, authors will benefit by memorizing all of the different ways in which commas can be used so as not to abuse them.

In a complex sentence—one that contains a subordinate (dependent) clause or clauses—the use of a comma is dictated by where the subordinate clause is located. If the subordinate clause is located before the main clause, a comma is needed between the two clauses.

> I will not pay for the steak, *because I don't have that much money.*

Generally, if the subordinate clause is placed after the main clause, no punctuation is needed.

> I did well on my exam because I studied two hours the night before.

Notice how the last clause is dependent, because it requires the earlier independent clauses to make sense.

Use a comma on both sides of an interrupting phrase.

> I will pay for the ice cream, *chocolate and vanilla*, and then will eat it all myself.

The words forming the phrase in italics are nonessential (extra) information. To determine if a phrase is nonessential, try reading the sentence without the phrase and see if it's still coherent.

A comma is not necessary in this next sentence because no interruption—nonessential or extra information—has occurred. Read sentences aloud when uncertain.

> I will pay for his chocolate and vanilla ice cream and then will eat it all myself.

If the nonessential phrase comes at the beginning of a sentence, a comma should only go at the end of the phrase. If the phrase comes at the end of a sentence, a comma should only go at the beginning of the phrase.

Other types of interruptions include the following:

- interjections: Oh no, I am not going.
- abbreviations: Barry Potter, M.D., specializes in heart disorders.
- direct addresses: Yes, Claudia, I am tired and going to bed.
- parenthetical phrases: His wife, lovely as she was, was not helpful.
- transitional phrases: Also, it is not possible.

The second comma in the following sentence is called an Oxford comma.

> I will pay for ice cream, syrup, and pop.

It is a comma used after the second-to-last item in a series of three or more items. It comes before the word *or* or *and*. Not everyone uses the Oxford comma; it is optional, but many believe it is needed. The comma functions as a tool to reduce confusion in writing. So, if omitting the Oxford comma would cause confusion, then it's best to include it.

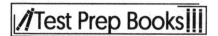

Commas are used in math to mark the place of thousands in numerals, breaking them up so they are easier to read. Other uses for commas are in dates (*March 19, 2016*), letter greetings (*Dear Sally,*), and in between cities and states (*Louisville, KY*).

Semicolons

The **semicolon (;)** might be described as a heavy-handed comma. Take a look at these two examples:

> I will pay for the ice cream, but I will not pay for the steak.
> I will pay for the ice cream; I will not pay for the steak.

What's the difference? The first example has a comma and a conjunction separating the two independent clauses. The second example does not have a conjunction, but there are two independent clauses in the sentence. So something more than a comma is required. In this case, a semicolon is used.

Two independent clauses can only be joined in a sentence by either a comma and conjunction or a semicolon. If one of those tools is not used, the sentence will be a run-on. Remember that while the clauses are independent, they need to be closely related in order to be contained in one sentence.

Another use for the semicolon is to separate items in a list when the items themselves require commas.

> The family lived in Phoenix, Arizona; Oklahoma City, Oklahoma; and Raleigh, North Carolina.

Colons

Colons have many miscellaneous functions. Colons can be used to precede further information or a list. In these cases, a colon should only follow an independent clause.

> Humans take in sensory information through five basic senses: sight, hearing, smell, touch, and taste.

> The meal includes the following components:

- Caesar salad
- spaghetti
- garlic bread
- cake

Colons can also be used to introduce an appositive.

> The family got what they needed: a reliable vehicle.

While a comma is more common, a colon can also precede a formal quotation.

> He said to the crowd: "Let's begin!"

The colon is used after the greeting in a formal letter.

> Dear Sir:
> To Whom It May Concern:

In the writing of time, the colon separates the minutes from the hour (*4:45 p.m.*). The colon can also be used to indicate a ratio between two numbers (*50:1*).

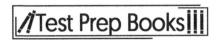

Hyphens

The **hyphen** (-) is a small dash mark that can be used to join words to show that they are linked.

Hyphens can connect two words that work together as a single adjective (a compound adjective).

    honey-covered biscuits

Some words always require hyphens even if not serving as an adjective.

    merry-go-round

Hyphens always go after certain prefixes like *anti-* & *all-*.

Hyphens should also be used when the absence of the hyphen would cause a strange vowel combination (*semi-engineer*) or confusion. For example, *re-collect* should be used to describe something being gathered twice rather than being written as *recollect*, which means to remember.

Parentheses and Dashes

Parentheses are half-round brackets that look like this: ( ). They set off a word, phrase, or sentence that is an afterthought, explanation, or side note relevant to the surrounding text but not essential. A pair of commas is often used to set off this sort of information, but parentheses are generally used for information that would not fit well within a sentence or that the writer deems not important enough to be structurally part of the sentence.

    The picture of the heart (see above) shows the major parts you should memorize.
    Mount Everest is one of three mountains in the world that are over 28,000 feet high (K2 and Kanchenjunga are the other two).

See how the sentences above are complete without the parenthetical statements? In the first example, *see above* would not have fit well within the flow of the sentence. The second parenthetical statement could have been a separate sentence, but the writer deemed the information not pertinent to the topic.

The **em-dash (—)** is a mark longer than a hyphen used as a punctuation mark in sentences and to set apart a relevant thought. Even after plucking out the line separated by the dash marks, the sentence will be intact and make sense.

    Looking out the airplane window at the landmarks—Lake Clarke, Thompson Community College, and the bridge—she couldn't help but feel excited to be home.

The dashes use is similar to that of parentheses or a pair of commas. So, what's the difference? Many believe that using dashes makes the clause within them stand out while using parentheses is subtler. It's advised to not use dashes when commas could be used instead.

Quotation Marks

Quotation marks (" ") are used in a number of ways. Here are some instances where quotation marks should be used: to indicate a quote that was taken from somewhere else, either from a verbal or written source...

- To indicate a quote that was taken from somewhere else, either from a verbal or written source
- Dialogue for characters in narratives. When characters speak, the first word should always be capitalized, and the punctuation goes inside the quotes. For example:
  Janie said, "The tree fell on my car during the hurricane."

- Around titles of songs, short stories, essays, and chapters in books
- To emphasize a certain word
- To refer to a word as the word itself

Apostrophes

This punctuation mark, the **apostrophe (')**, is a versatile little mark. It has a few different functions:

- Quotes: Apostrophes are used when a second quote is needed within a quote.
  In my letter to my friend, I wrote, "The girl had to get a new purse, and guess what Mary did? She said, 'I'd like to go with you to the store.' I knew Mary would buy it for her."
- Contractions: Another use for an apostrophe in the quote above is a contraction. *I'd* is used for *I would.*
- Possession: An apostrophe followed by the letter *s* shows possession (*Mary's* purse). If the possessive word is plural, the apostrophe generally just follows the word.
  The trees' leaves are all over the ground.

Spelling

Spelling might or might not be important to some, or maybe it just doesn't come naturally, but those who are willing to discover some new ideas and consider their benefits can learn to spell better and improve their writing. Misspellings reduce a writer's credibility and can create misunderstandings. Spell checkers built into word processors are not a substitute for accuracy. They are neither foolproof nor without error. In addition, a writer's misspelling of one word may also be a word. For example, a writer intending to spell *herd* might accidentally type *s* instead of *d* and unintentionally spell *hers*. Since *her*s is a word, it would not be marked as a misspelling by a spell checker. In short, use spell check, but don't rely on it.

Guidelines for Spelling

Saying and listening to a word serves as the beginning of knowing how to spell it. Keep these subsequent guidelines in mind, remembering there are often exceptions because the English language is replete with them.

Guideline #1: Syllables must have at least one vowel. In fact, every syllable in every English word has a vowel.

- d*o*g
- h*a*yst*a*ck
- *a*nsw*e*r*i*ng
- *a*bst*e*nt*iou*s
- s*i*mpl*e*

Guideline #2: The long and short of it. When the vowel has a short vowel sound as in *mad* or *bed,* only the single vowel is needed. If the word has a long vowel sound, add another vowel, either alongside it or separated by a consonant: bed/*bead*; mad/*made.* When the second vowel is separated by two consonants— *madder*—it does not affect the first vowel's sound.

Guideline #3: Suffixes. Refer to the examples listed above.

Guideline #4: Which comes first; the *i* or the *e*? Remember the saying, "*I* before *e* except after *c* or when sounding as *a* as in *neighbor* or *weigh*." Keep in mind that these are only guidelines and that there are always exceptions to every rule.

Guideline #5: Vowels in the right order. Another helpful rhyme is, "When two vowels go walking, the first one does the talking." When two vowels are in a row, the first one sometimes has a long vowel sound and the other is silent. An example is *team*. This rule is true for about half of the occurrences of two vowels next to each other.

If you have difficulty spelling words, determine a strategy to help. Work on spelling by playing word games like Scrabble or Words with Friends. Consider using phonics, which is sounding words out by slowly and surely stating each syllable. Try repeating and memorizing spellings as well as picturing words in your head. Try making up silly memory aids. See what works best.

Homophones

Homophones are two or more words that have no particular relationship to one another except their identical pronunciations. Homophones make spelling English words fun and challenging like these:

Common Homophones		
affect, effect	cell, sell	it's, its
allot, a lot	do, due, dew	knew, new
barbecue, barbeque	dual, duel	mantle, mantel
bite, byte	eminent, imminent	principal, principle
brake, break	flew, flu, flue	their, there, they're
capital, capitol	gauge, gage	to, too, two
cash, cache	holy, wholly	yoke, yolk

Irregular Plurals

Irregular plurals are words that aren't made plural the usual way.

- Most nouns are made plural by adding –s (book*s*, television*s*, skyscraper*s*).
- Most nouns ending in *ch, sh, s, x,* or *z* are made plural by adding –es (church*es,* marsh*es*).
- Most nouns ending in a vowel + *y* are made plural by adding –s (day*s,* toy*s*).
- Most nouns ending in a consonant + *y,* are made plural by the *-y* becoming *-ies* (baby becomes *babies*).
- Most nouns ending in an *o* are made plural by adding –s (piano*s,* photo*s*).
- Some nouns ending in an *o,* though, may be made plural by adding –es (example: potato*es,* volcano*es*), and, of note, there is no known rhyme or reason for this!
- Most nouns ending in an *f* or *fe* are made plural by the *-f* or *-fe* becoming *-ves*! (example: wolf becomes *wolves*).
- Some words function as both the singular and plural form of the word (fish, deer).
- Other exceptions include *man* becomes *men, mouse* becomes *mice, goose* becomes *geese,* and *foot* becomes *feet.*

Contractions

The basic rule for making **contractions** is one area of spelling that is pretty straightforward: combine the two words by inserting an apostrophe (') in the space where a letter is omitted. For example, to combine *you* and *are,* drop the *a* and put the apostrophe in its place: *you're.*

> he + is = he's
> you + all = y'all (informal but often misspelled)

Note that *it's,* when spelled with an apostrophe, is always the contraction for *it is.* The possessive form of the word is written without an apostrophe as *its.*

Correcting Misspelled Words

A good place to start looking at commonly misspelled words here is with the word *misspelled.* While it looks peculiar, look at it this way: *mis* (the prefix meaning *wrongly*) + *spelled* = *misspelled.*

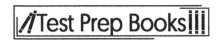
Let's look at some commonly misspelled words.

Commonly Misspelled Words					
accept	benign	existence	jewelry	parallel	separate
acceptable	bicycle	experience	judgment	pastime	sergeant
accidentally	brief	extraordinary	library	permissible	similar
accommodate	business	familiar	license	perseverance	supersede
accompany	calendar	February	maintenance	personnel	surprise
acknowledgement	campaign	fiery	maneuver	persuade	symmetry
acquaintance	candidate	finally	mathematics	possess	temperature
acquire	category	forehead	mattress	precede	tragedy
address	cemetery	foreign	millennium	prevalent	transferred
aesthetic	changeable	foremost	miniature	privilege	truly
aisle	committee	forfeit	mischievous	pronunciation	usage
altogether	conceive	glamorous	misspell	protein	valuable
amateur	congratulations	government	mortgage	publicly	vengeance
apparent	courtesy	grateful	necessary	questionnaire	villain
appropriate	deceive	handkerchief	neither	recede	Wednesday
arctic	desperate	harass	nickel	receive	weird
asphalt	discipline	hygiene	niece	recommend	
associate	disappoint	hypocrisy	ninety	referral	
attendance	dissatisfied	ignorance	noticeable	relevant	
auxiliary	eligible	incredible	obedience	restaurant	
available	embarrass	intelligence	occasion	rhetoric	
balloon	especially	intercede	occurrence	rhythm	
believe	exaggerate	interest	omitted	schedule	
beneficial	exceed	irresistible	operate	sentence	

Knowledge of Language

Standard English Grammar and Usage

Sentence Structure

Sentence Types

There are four ways in which we can structure sentences: simple, compound, complex, and compound-complex. Sentences can be composed of just one clause or many clauses joined together.

51

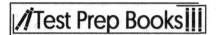

When a sentence is composed of just one clause (an independent clause), we call it a **simple sentence.** Simple sentences do not necessarily have to be short sentences. They just require one independent clause with a subject and a predicate. For example:

Thomas marched over to Andrew's house.

Jonah and Mary constructed a simplified version of the Eiffel Tower with Legos.

When a sentence has two or more independent clauses we call it a **compound sentence**. The clauses are connected by a comma and a coordinating conjunction—*and, but, or, nor, for*—or by a semicolon. Compound sentences do not have dependent clauses. For example:

We went to the fireworks stand, and we bought enough fireworks to last all night.

The children sat on the grass, and then we lit the fireworks one at a time.

When a sentence has just one independent clause and includes one or more dependent clauses, we call it a **complex sentence**:

Because she slept well and drank coffee, Sarah was quite productive at work.

Although Will had coffee, he made mistakes while using the photocopier.

When a sentence has two or more independent clauses and at least one dependent clause, we call it a **compound-complex sentence**:

It may come as a surprise, but I found the tickets, and you can go to the show.

Jade is the girl who dove from the high-dive, and she stunned the audience silent.

Sentence Fragments

Remember that a complete sentence must have both a subject and a verb. Complete sentences consist of at least one independent clause. Incomplete sentences are called sentence fragments. A sentence fragment is a common error in writing. **Sentence fragments** can be independent clauses that start with subordinating words, such as *but, as, so that,* or *because,* or they could simply be missing a subject or verb.

A fragment error can be corrected by adding the fragment to a nearby sentence or by adding or removing words to make it an independent clause. For example,

Dogs are my favorite animals. Because cats are too independent. (Incorrect; the word because creates a sentence fragment)

Dogs are my favorite animals because cats are too independent. (Correct; the fragment becomes a dependent clause.)

Dogs are my favorite animals. Cats are too independent. (Correct; the fragment becomes a simple sentence.)

52

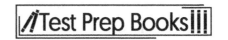

Run-on Sentences

Another common mistake in writing is the **run-on sentence**. A run-on is created when two or more independent clauses are joined without the use of a conjunction, a semicolon, a colon, or a dash. We don't want to use commas where periods belong. Here is an example of a run-on sentence:

> Making wedding cakes can take many hours I am very impatient, I want to see them completed right away.

There are a variety of ways to correct a run-on sentence. The method you choose will depend on the context of the sentence and how it fits with neighboring sentences:

> Making wedding cakes can take many hours. I am very impatient. I want to see them completed right away. (Use periods to create more than one sentence.)

> Making wedding cakes can take many hours; I am very impatient—I want to see them completed right away. (Correct the sentence using a semicolon, colon, or dash.)

> Making wedding cakes can take many hours and I am very impatient, so I want to see them completed right away. (Correct the sentence using coordinating conjunctions.)

> I am very impatient because I would rather see completed wedding cakes right away than wait for it to take many hours. (Correct the sentence by revising.)

Dangling and Misplaced Modifiers

A modifier is a word or phrase meant to describe or clarify another word in the sentence. When a sentence has a modifier but is missing the word it describes or clarifies, it's an error called a dangling modifier. We can fix the sentence by revising to include the word that is being modified. Consider the following examples with the modifier italicized:

> *Having walked five miles*, this bench will be the place to rest. (Incorrect; this version of the sentence implies that the bench walked the miles, not the person.)

> *Having walked five miles,* Matt will rest on this bench. (Correct; in this version, *having walked five miles* correctly modifies *Matt*, who did the walking.)

> *Since midnight,* my dreams have been pleasant and comforting. (Incorrect; in this version, the adverb clause *since midnight* cannot modify the noun *dreams*.)

> *Since midnight,* I have had pleasant and comforting dreams. (Correct; in this version, *since midnight* modifies the verb *have had*, telling us when the dreams occurred.)

Sometimes the modifier is not located close enough to the word it modifies for the sentence to be clearly understood. In this case, we call the error a misplaced modifier. Here is an example with the modifier italicized and the modified word in underlined.

> We gave the hot <u>cocoa</u> to the children *that was filled with marshmallows.* (Incorrect; this sentence implies that the children are what are filled with marshmallows.)

> We gave the hot <u>*cocoa that was filled with marshmallows*</u> to the children. (Correct; here, the cocoa is filled with marshmallows. The modifier is near the word it modifies.)

Parallelism and Subordination

Parallelism

To be grammatically correct we must use articles, prepositions, infinitives, and introductory words for dependent clauses consistently throughout a sentence. This is called **parallelism**. We use parallelism when we are matching parts of speech, phrases, or clauses with another part of the sentence. Being inconsistent creates confusion. Consider the following example.

Incorrect: Be ready for running and to ride a bike during the triathlon.

Correct: Be ready to run and to ride a bike during the triathlon.

Correct: Be ready for running and for riding a bike during the triathlon.

In the incorrect example, the gerund *running* does not match with the infinitive *to ride*. Either both should be infinitives or both should be gerunds.

Subordination

Sometimes we have unequal pieces of information in a sentence where one piece is more important than the other. We need to show that one piece of information is **subordinate** to the other. We can make the more important piece an independent clause and connect the other piece by making it a dependent clause. Consider this example:

Central thought: Kittens can always find their mother.

Subordinate: Kittens are blind at birth.

Complex Sentence: Despite being blind at birth, kittens can always find their mother.

The sentence "Kittens are blind at birth" is made subordinate to the sentence "Kittens can always find their mother" by placing the word "Despite" at the beginning and removing the subject, thus turning an independent clause ("kittens are blind at birth") into a subordinate phrase ("Despite being blind at birth").

Usage

Nouns

A noun is a person, place, thing ,or idea. All nouns fit into one of two types, common or proper.

A **common noun** is a word that identifies any of a class of people, places, or things. Examples include numbers, objects, animals, feelings, concepts, qualities, and actions. *A, an,* or *the* usually precedes the common noun. These parts of speech are called *articles*. Here are some examples of sentences using nouns preceded by articles.

A building is under construction.
The girl would like to move to *the* city.

A **proper noun** (also called a *proper name*) is used for the specific name of an individual person, place, or organization. The first letter in a proper noun is capitalized. "My name is *Mary*." "I work for *Walmart*."

Nouns sometimes serve as adjectives (which themselves describe nouns), such as "hockey player" and "state government."

54

An abstract noun is an idea, state, or quality. It is something that can't be touched, such as happiness, courage, evil, or humor.

A concrete noun is something that can be experienced through the senses (touch, taste, hear, smell, see). Examples of concrete nouns are birds, skateboard, pie, and car.

A collective noun refers to a collection of people, places, or things that act as one. Examples of collective nouns are as follows: team, class, jury, family, audience, and flock.

Pronouns

A word used in place of a noun is known as a **pronoun**. Pronouns are words like *I, mine, hers,* and *us.*

Pronouns can be split into different classifications (seen below) which make them easier to learn; however, it's not important to memorize the classifications.

- Personal pronouns: refers to people, places, things, etc.
- First person: we, I, our, mine
- Second person: you, yours
- Third person: he, them
- Possessive pronouns: demonstrate ownership (mine, his, hers, its, ours, theirs, yours)
- Interrogative pronouns: ask questions (what, which, who, whom, whose)
- Relative pronouns: include the five interrogative pronouns and others that are relative (whoever, whomever, that, when, where)
- Demonstrative pronouns: replace something specific (this, that, those, these)
- Reciprocal pronouns: indicate something was done or given in return (each other, one another)
- Indefinite pronouns: have a nonspecific status (anybody, whoever, someone, everybody, somebody)

Indefinite pronouns such as *anybody, whoever, someone, everybody,* and *somebody* command a singular verb form, but others such as *all, none,* and *some* could require a singular or plural verb form.

Antecedents

An **antecedent** is the noun to which a pronoun refers; it needs to be written or spoken before the pronoun is used. For many pronouns, antecedents are imperative for clarity. In particular, many of the personal, possessive, and demonstrative pronouns need antecedents. Otherwise, it would be unclear who or what someone is referring to when they use a pronoun like *he* or *this.*

Pronoun reference means that the pronoun should refer clearly to one, clear, unmistakable noun (the antecedent).

Pronoun-antecedent agreement refers to the need for the antecedent and the corresponding pronoun to agree in gender, person, and number. Here are some examples:

The *kidneys* (plural antecedent) are part of the urinary system. *They* (plural pronoun) serve several roles.

The kidneys are part of the *urinary system* (singular antecedent). *It* (singular pronoun) is also known as the renal system.

Pronoun Cases

The **subjective pronouns** —*I, you, he/she/it, we, they,* and *who*—are the subjects of the sentence.

> Example: *They* have a new house.

The **objective pronouns**—*me, you* (*singular*)*, him/her, us, them,* and *whom*—are used when something is being done for or given to someone; they are objects of the action.

> Example: The teacher has an apple for *us.*

The **possessive pronouns**—*mine, my, your, yours, his, hers, its, their, theirs, our,* and *ours*—are used to denote that something (or someone) belongs to someone (or something).

> Example: It's *their* chocolate cake.
> Even Better Example: It's *my* chocolate cake!

One of the greatest challenges and worst abuses of pronouns concerns *who* and *whom.* Just knowing the following rule can eliminate confusion. *Who* is a subjective-case pronoun used only as a subject or subject complement. *Whom* is only objective-case and, therefore, the object of the verb or preposition.

> *Who* is going to the concert?

> You are going to the concert with *whom*?

Hint: When using *who* or *whom,* think of whether someone would say *he* or *him.* If the answer is *he,* use *who.* If the answer is *him,* use *whom.* This trick is easy to remember because *he* and *who* both end in vowels, and *him* and *whom* both end in the letter *M.*

Verbs

The **verb** is the part of speech that describes an action, state of being, or occurrence.

A *verb* forms the main part of a predicate of a sentence. This means that the verb explains what the noun (which will be discussed shortly) is doing. A simple example is *time flies*. The verb *flies* explains what the action of the noun, *time,* is doing. This example is a *main* verb.

Helping (auxiliary) verbs are words like *have, do, be, can, may, should, must,* and *will.* "I *should* go to the store." Helping verbs assist main verbs in expressing tense, ability, possibility, permission, or obligation.

Particles are minor function words like *not, in, out, up,* or *down* that become part of the verb itself. "I might *not.*"

Participles are words formed from verbs that are often used to modify a noun, noun phrase, verb, or verb phrase.

> The *running* teenager collided with the cyclist.

Participles can also create compound verb forms.

> He is *speaking.*

Verbs have five basic forms: the *base* form, the *-s* form, the *-ing* form, the *past* form, and the **past participle** form.

56

The *past* forms are either *regular* (*love/loved; hate/hated*) or *irregular* because they don't end by adding the common past tense suffix "-ed" (*go/went; fall/fell; set/set*).

Verb Forms

Shifting verb forms entails *conjugation*, which is used to indicate *tense, voice,* or *mood*.

Verb tense is used to show when the action in the sentence took place. There are several different verb tenses, and it is important to know how and when to use them. Some verb tenses can be achieved by changing the form of the verb, while others require the use of helping verbs (e.g., *is, was,* or *has*).

- Present tense shows the action is happening currently or is ongoing:

    I walk to work every morning.

    She is stressed about the deadline.

- Past tense shows that the action happened in the past or that the state of being is in the past:

    I walked to work yesterday morning.

    She was stressed about the deadline.

- Future tense shows that the action will happen in the future or is a future state of being:

    I will walk to work tomorrow morning.

    She will be stressed about the deadline.

- Present perfect tense shows action that began in the past, but continues into the present:

    I have walked to work all week.

    She has been stressed about the deadline.

- Past perfect tense shows an action was finished before another took place:

    I had walked all week until I sprained my ankle.

    She had been stressed about the deadline until we talked about it.

- Future perfect tense shows an action that will be completed at some point in the future:

    By the time the bus arrives, I will have walked to work already.

Voice

Verbs can be in the active or passive voice. When the subject completes the action, the verb is in **active voice**. When the subject receives the action of the sentence, the verb is in *passive voice*.

Active: Jamie ate the ice cream.

Passive: The ice cream was eaten by Jamie.

In **active voice**, the subject (*Jamie*) is the "do-er" of the action (*ate*). In passive voice, the subject *ice cream* receives the action of being eaten.

While passive voice can add variety to writing, active voice is the generally preferred sentence structure.

Mood

Mood is used to show the speaker's feelings about the subject matter. In English, there is *indicative mood, imperative mood,* and *subjunctive mood.*

Indicative mood is used to state facts, ask questions, or state opinions:

> Bob will make the trip next week.

> When can Bob make the trip?

Imperative mood is used to state a command or make a request:

> Wait in the lobby.

> Please call me next week.

Subjunctive mood is used to express a wish, an opinion, or a hope that is contrary to fact:

> If I were in charge, none of this would have happened.

> Allison wished she could take the exam over again when she saw her score.

Adjectives

Adjectives are words used to modify nouns and pronouns. They can be used alone or in a series and are used to further define or describe the nouns they modify.

> Mark made us a delicious, four-course meal.

The words *delicious* and *four-course* are adjectives that describe the kind of meal Mark made.

Articles are also considered adjectives because they help to describe nouns. Articles can be general or specific. The three articles in English are: a, an, and the.

Indefinite articles *(a, an)* are used to refer to nonspecific nouns. The article *a* proceeds words beginning with consonant sounds, and the article *an* proceeds words beginning with vowel sounds.

> A car drove by our house.

> An alligator was loose at the zoo.

> He has always wanted a ukulele. (The first *u* makes a *y* sound.)

Note that *a* and *an* should only proceed nonspecific nouns that are also singular. If a nonspecific noun is plural, it does not need a preceding article.

> Alligators were loose at the zoo.

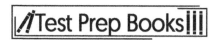

The **definite article** *(the)* is used to refer to specific nouns:

> The car pulled into our driveway.

Note that *the* should proceed all specific nouns regardless of whether they are singular or plural.

> The cars pulled into our driveway.

Comparative adjectives are used to compare nouns. When they are used in this way, they take on positive, comparative, or superlative form.

> The positive form is the normal form of the adjective:

>> Alicia is tall.

> The *comparative* form shows a comparison between two things:

>> Alicia is taller than Maria.

> *Superlative* form shows comparison between more than two things:

>> Alicia is the tallest girl in her class.

Usually, the comparative and superlative can be made by adding *–er* and *–est* to the positive form, but some verbs call for the helping verbs *more* or *most*. Other exceptions to the rule include adjectives like *bad*, which uses the comparative *worse* and the superlative *worst*.

An adjective phrase is not a bunch of adjectives strung together, but a group of words that describes a noun or pronoun and, thus, functions as an adjective. Very happy is an adjective phrase; so are way too hungry and passionate about traveling.

Adverbs
Adverbs have more functions than adjectives because they modify or qualify verbs, adjectives, or other adverbs as well as word groups that express a relation of place, time, circumstance, or cause. Therefore, adverbs answer any of the following questions: *How, when, where, why, in what way, how often, how much, in what condition,* and/or *to what degree. How good looking is he? He is <u>very</u> handsome.*

Here are some examples of adverbs for different situations:

- how: quickly
- when: daily
- where: there
- in what way: easily
- how often: often
- how much: much
- in what condition: badly
- what degree: hardly

As one can see, for some reason, many adverbs end in *-ly*.

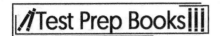

Adverbs do things like emphasize (*really, simply,* and *so*), amplify (*heartily, completely,* and *positively*), and tone down (*almost, somewhat,* and *mildly*).

Adverbs also come in phrases.

The dog ran as <u>though his life depended on it.</u>

Prepositions

Prepositions are connecting words and, while there are only about 150 of them, they are used more often than any other individual groups of words. They describe relationships between other words. They are placed before a noun or pronoun, forming a phrase that modifies another word in the sentence. *Prepositional phrases* begin with a preposition and end with a noun or pronoun, the *object of the preposition. A pristine lake is <u>near the store</u> and <u>behind the bank</u>.*

Some commonly used prepositions are *about, after, anti, around, as, at, behind, beside, by, for, from, in, into, of, off, on, to,* and *with.*

Complex prepositions, which also come before a noun or pronoun, consist of two or three words such as *according to, in regards to,* and *because of.*

Conjunctions

Conjunctions are vital words that connect words, phrases, thoughts, and ideas. Conjunctions show relationships between components. There are two types:

Coordinating conjunctions are the primary class of conjunctions placed between words, phrases, clauses, and sentences that are of equal grammatical rank; the coordinating conjunctions are *for, and, nor, but, or, yet,* and *so.* A useful memorization trick is to remember that the first letter of these conjunctions collectively spell the word *fanboys.*

I need to go shopping, *but* I must be careful to leave enough money in the bank.
She wore a black, red, *and* white shirt.

Subordinating-conjunctions are the secondary class of conjunctions. They connect two unequal parts, one *main* (or *independent*) and the other *subordinate* (or *dependent*). I must go to the store *even though* I do not have enough money in the bank.

Because I read the review, I do not want to go to the movie.

Notice that the presence of subordinating conjunctions makes clauses dependent. *I read the review* is an independent clause, but *because* makes the clause dependent. Thus, it needs an independent clause to complete the sentence.

Interjections

Interjections are words used to express emotion. Examples include *wow, ouch,* and *hooray.* Interjections are often separate from sentences; in those cases, the interjection is directly followed by an exclamation point. In other cases, the interjection is included in a sentence and followed by a comma. The punctuation plays a big role in the intensity of the emotion that the interjection is expressing. Using a comma or semicolon indicates less excitement than using an exclamation mark.

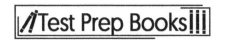

Subjects

Every sentence must include a subject and a verb. The **subject** of a sentence is who or what the sentence is about. It's often directly stated and can be determined by asking "Who?" or "What?" did the action:

Most sentences contain a direct subject, in which the subject is mentioned in the sentence.

> *Kelly mowed the lawn.*

> Who mowed the lawn? *Kelly*

> *The air-conditioner ran all night*

> What ran all night? *the air-conditioner*

The subject of imperative sentences is the implied *you*, because imperative subjects are commands:

> *Go home after the meeting.*

> Who should go home after the meeting? *you* (implied)

In **expletive sentences** that start with "there are" or "there is," the subject is found after the predicate. The subject cannot be "there," so it must be another word in the sentence:

> *There is a cup sitting on the coffee table.*

> What is sitting on the coffee table? *a cup*

Simple and Complete Subjects

A *complete subject* includes the simple subject and all the words modifying it, including articles and adjectives. A *simple subject* is the single noun without its modifiers.

> A warm, chocolate-chip cookie sat on the kitchen table.

> Complete subject: *a warm, chocolate-chip cookie*

> Simple subject: *cookie*

The words *a, warm, chocolate,* and *chip* all modify the simple subject *cookie.*

There might also be a *compound subject*, which would be two or more nouns without the modifiers.

> A little girl and her mother walked into the shop.

> Complete subject: *A little girl and her mother*

> Compound subject: *girl, mother*

In this case, *the girl and her mother* are both completing the action of walking into the shop, so this is a *compound subject*.

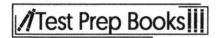

Predicates

In addition to the subject, a sentence must also have a **predicate**. The *predicate* contains a verb and tells something about the subject. In addition to the verb, a predicate can also contain a direct or indirect object, object of a preposition, and other phrases.

> The cats napped on the front porch.

In this sentence, cats is the subject because the sentence is about cats.

The **complete predicate** is everything else in the sentence: *napped on the front porch.* This phrase is the predicate because it tells us what the cats did.

This sentence can be broken down into a simple subject and predicate:

> Cats napped.

In this sentence, *cats* is the simple subject, and *napped* is the **simple predicate.**

Although the sentence is very short and doesn't offer much information, it's still considered a complete sentence because it contains a subject and predicate.

Like a compound subject, a sentence can also have a ***compound predicate***. This is when the subject is or does two or more things in the sentence.

> This easy chair reclines and swivels.

In this sentence, *this easy chair* is the complete subject. *Reclines and swivels* shows two actions of the chair, so this is the compound predicate.

Subject-Verb Agreement

The subject of a sentence and its verb must agree. The cornerstone rule of subject-verb agreement is that subject and verb must agree in number. Whether the subject is singular or plural, the verb must follow suit.

> Incorrect: The houses is new.
> Correct: The houses are new.
> Also Correct: The house is new.

In other words, a singular subject requires a singular verb; a plural subject requires a plural verb. The words or phrases that come between the subject and verb do not alter this rule.

> Incorrect: The houses built of brick is new.
> Correct: The houses built of brick are new.

> Incorrect: The houses with the sturdy porches is new.
> Correct: The houses with the sturdy porches are new.

The subject will always follow the verb when a sentence begins with *here* or *there.* Identify these with care.

> Incorrect: Here *is* the *houses* with sturdy porches.
> Correct: Here *are* the *houses* with sturdy porches.

The subject in the sentences above is not *here*, it is *houses*. Remember, *here* and *there* are never subjects. Be careful that contractions such as *here's* or *there're* do not cause confusion!

Two subjects joined by *and* require a plural verb form, except when the two combine to make one thing:

> Incorrect: Garrett and Jonathan is over there.
> Correct: Garrett and Jonathan are over there.

> Incorrect: Spaghetti and meatballs are a delicious meal!
> Correct: Spaghetti and meatballs is a delicious meal!

In the example above, *spaghetti and meatballs* is a compound noun. However, *Garrett and Jonathan* is not a compound noun.

Two singular subjects joined by *or, either/or,* or *neither/nor* call for a singular verb form.

> Incorrect: Butter or syrup are acceptable.
> Correct: Butter or syrup is acceptable.

Plural subjects joined by *or, either/or,* or *neither/nor* are, indeed, plural.

> The chairs or the boxes are being moved next.

If one subject is singular and the other is plural, the verb should agree with the closest noun.

> Correct: The chair or the boxes are being moved next.
> Correct: The chairs or the box is being moved next.

Some plurals of money, distance, and time call for a singular verb.

> Incorrect: Three dollars *are* enough to buy that.
> Correct: Three dollars *is* enough to buy that.

For words declaring degrees of quantity such as *many of, some of,* or *most of,* let the noun that follows *of* be the guide:

> Incorrect: Many of the books is in the shelf.
> Correct: Many of the books are in the shelf.

> Incorrect: Most of the pie *are* on the table.
> Correct: Most of the pie *is* on the table.

For indefinite pronouns like anybody or everybody, use singular verbs.

> Everybody *is* going to the store.

However, the pronouns *few, many, several, all, some,* and *both* have their own rules and use plural forms.

Some *are* ready.

Some nouns like *crowd* and *congress* are called *collective nouns* and they require a singular verb form.

Congress *is* in session.
The news *is* over.

Books and movie titles, though, including plural nouns such as *Great Expectations*, also require a singular verb. Remember that only the subject affects the verb. While writing tricky subject-verb arrangements, say them aloud. Listen to them. Once the rules have been learned, one's ear will become sensitive to them, making it easier to pick out what's right and what's wrong.

Direct Objects

The **direct object** is the part of the sentence that receives the action of the verb. It is a noun and can usually be found after the verb. To find the direct object, first find the verb, and then ask the question *who* or *what* after it.

The bear climbed the tree.

What did the bear climb? *the tree*

Indirect Objects

An **indirect object** receives the direct object. It is usually found between the verb and the direct object. A strategy for identifying the indirect object is to find the verb and ask the questions *to whom/for whom* or *to what/ for what*.

Jane made her daughter a cake.

For whom did Jane make the cake? *her daughter*

Cake is the direct object because it is what Jane made, and *daughter* is the indirect object because she receives the cake.

Complements

A **complement** completes the meaning of an expression. A complement can be a pronoun, noun, or adjective. A verb complement refers to the direct object or indirect object in the sentence. An object complement gives more information about the direct object:

The magician got the kids excited.

Kids is the direct object, and *excited* is the object complement.

A **subject complement** comes after a linking verb. It is typically an adjective or noun that gives more information about the subject:

The king was noble and spared the thief's life.

Noble describes the *king* and follows the linking verb *was*.

64

Predicate Nouns

A **predicate noun** renames the subject:

> John is a carpenter.

The subject is *John*, and the predicate noun is *carpenter*.

Predicate Adjectives

A **predicate adjective** describes the subject:

> Margaret is beautiful.

The subject is *Margaret*, and the predicate adjective is *beautiful*.

Homonyms

Homonyms are words that sound the same but are spelled differently, and they have different meanings. There are several common homonyms that give writers trouble.

There, They're, and Their

The word *there* can be used as an adverb, adjective, or pronoun:

> *There* are ten children on the swim team this summer.

> I put my book over *there*, but now I can't find it.

The word *they're* is a contraction of the words *they* and *are*:

> *They're* flying in from Texas on Tuesday.

The word *their* is a possessive pronoun:

> I store *their* winter clothes in the attic.

Its and It's

Its is a possessive pronoun:

> The cat licked *its* injured paw.

It's is the contraction for the words *it* and *is*:

> *It's* unbelievable how many people opted not to vote in the last election.

Your and You're

Your is a possessive pronoun:

> Can I borrow *your* lawnmower this weekend?

You're is a contraction for the words *you* and *are*:

> *You're* about to embark on a fantastic journey.

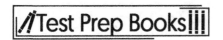
To, Too, and Two

To is an adverb or a preposition used to show direction, relationship, or purpose:

> We are going *to* New York.

> They are going *to* see a show.

Too is an adverb that means more than enough, also, and very:

> You have had *too* much candy.

> We are on vacation that week, *too*.

Two is the written-out form of the numeral 2:

> *Two* of the shirts didn't fit, so I will have to return them.

New and Knew

New is an adjective that means recent:

> There's a *new* customer on the phone.

Knew is the past tense of the verb *know*:

> I *knew* you'd have fun on this ride.

Affect and Effect

Affect and *effect* are complicated because they are used as both nouns and verbs, have similar meanings, and are pronounced the same.

	Affect	**Effect**
Noun Definition	emotional state	result
Noun Example	The patient's affect was flat.	The effects of smoking are well documented.
Verb Definition	to influence	to bring about
Verb Example	The pollen count affects my allergies.	The new candidate hopes to effect change.

Independent and Dependent Clauses

Independent clauses and **dependent clauses** are strings of words that contain both a subject and a verb. An independent clause *can* stand alone as complete thought, but a dependent clause *cannot*. A dependent clause relies on other words to be a complete sentence.

> Independent clause: The keys are on the counter.
> Dependent clause: If the keys are on the counter

Notice that both clauses have a subject (*keys*) and a verb (*are*). The independent clause expresses a complete thought, but the word *if* at the beginning of the dependent clause makes it *dependent* on other words to be a complete thought.

> Independent clause: If the keys are on the counter, please give them to me.

This example constitutes a complete sentence since it includes at least one verb and one subject and is a complete thought. In this case, the independent clause has two subjects (*keys* & an implied *you*) and two verbs (*are* & *give*).

> Independent clause: I went to the store.
> Dependent clause: Because we are out of milk,

> Complete Sentence: Because we are out of milk, I went to the store.
> Complete Sentence: I went to the store because we are out of milk.

Phrases

A **phrase** is a group of words that do not make a complete thought or a clause. They are parts of sentences or clauses. Phrases can be used as nouns, adjectives, or adverbs. A phrase does not contain both a subject and a verb.

Prepositional Phrases

A **prepositional phrase** shows the relationship between a word in the sentence and the object of the preposition. The object of the preposition is a noun that follows the preposition.

> The orange pillows are on the couch.

On is the preposition, and *couch* is the object of the preposition.

> She brought her friend with the nice car.

With is the preposition, and *car* is the object of the preposition. Here are some common prepositions:

about	as	at	after
by	for	from	in
of	on	to	with

Verbals and Verbal Phrases

Verbals are forms of verbs that act as other parts of speech. They can be used as nouns, adjectives, or adverbs. Though they are verb forms, they are not to be used as the verb in the sentence. A word group that is based on a verbal is considered a *verbal phrase*. There are three major types of verbals: *participles, gerunds,* and *infinitives*.

Participles are verbals that act as adjectives. The present participle ends in *–ing*, and the past participle ends in *–d, -ed, -n,* or *-t*.

Verb	Present Participle	Past Participle
walk	walking	walked
share	sharing	shared

Participial phrases are made up of the participle and modifiers, complements, or objects.

> Crying for most of an hour, the baby didn't seem to want to nap.

> Having already taken this course, the student was bored during class.

> *Crying for most of an hour* and *Having already taken this course* are the participial phrases.

Gerunds are verbals that are used as nouns and end in *–ing*. A gerund can be the subject or object of the sentence like a noun. Note that a present participle can also end in *–ing*, so it is important to distinguish between the two. The gerund is used as a noun, while the participle is used as an adjective.

> Swimming is my favorite sport.

> I wish I were sleeping.

A **gerund phrase** includes the gerund and any modifiers or complements, direct objects, indirect objects, or pronouns.

> Cleaning the house is my least favorite weekend activity.

Cleaning the house is the gerund phrase acting as the subject of the sentence.

> The most important goal this year is raising money for charity.

Raising money for charity is the gerund phrase acting as the direct object.

> The police accused the woman of stealing the car.

The *gerund* phrase *stealing the car* is the object of the preposition in this sentence.

An *infinitive* is a verbal made up of the word to and a verb. Infinitives can be used as nouns, adjectives, or adverbs.

> Examples: To eat, to jump, to swim, to lie, to call, to work

An **infinitive phrase** is made up of the infinitive plus any complements or modifiers. The infinitive phrase *to wait* is used as the subject in this sentence:

> To wait was not what I had in mind.

The infinitive phrase *to sing* is used as the subject complement in this sentence:

> Her dream is to sing.

The infinitive phrase *to grow* is used as an adverb in this sentence:

> Children must eat to grow.

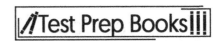

Appositive Phrases

An **appositive** is a noun or noun phrase that renames a noun that comes immediately before it in the sentence. An appositive can be a single word or several words. These phrases can be *essential* or *nonessential*. An essential appositive phrase is necessary to the meaning of the sentence and a nonessential appositive phrase is not. It is important to be able to distinguish these for purposes of comma use.

Essential: My sister Christina works at a school.

Naming which sister is essential to the meaning of the sentence, so no commas are needed.

Nonessential: My sister, who is a teacher, is coming over for dinner tonight.

Who is a teacher is not essential to the meaning of the sentence, so commas are required.

Absolute Phrases

An **absolute phrase** modifies a noun without using a conjunction. It is not the subject of the sentence and is not a complete thought on its own. Absolute phrases are set off from the independent clause with a comma.

Arms outstretched, she yelled at the sky.

All things considered, this has been a great day.

Vocabulary Acquisition and Use

Determining or Clarifying Meaning

Meaning of Words and Phrases

Another useful vocabulary skill is being able to understand meaning in context. A word's *context* refers to other words and information surrounding it, which can have a big impact on how readers interpret that word's meaning. Of course, many words have more than one definition. For example, consider the meaning of the word "engaged." The first definition that comes to mind might be "promised to be married," but consider the following sentences:

a. The two armies engaged in a conflict that lasted all night.

b. The three-hour lecture flew by because students were so engaged in the material.

c. The busy executive engaged a new assistant to help with his workload.

Were any of those sentences related to marriage? In fact, "engaged" has a variety of other meanings. In these sentences, respectively, it can mean: "battled," "interested or involved," and "appointed or employed." Readers may wonder how to decide which definition to apply. The appropriate meaning is prioritized based on context. For example, sentence *C* mentions "executive," "assistant," and "workload," so readers can assume that "engaged" has something to do with work—in which case, "appointed or employed" is the best definition for this context. Context clues can also be found in sentence *A*. Words like "armies" and "conflicts" show that this sentence is about a military situation, so in this context, "engaged" is closest in meaning to "battled." By using context clues—the surrounding words in the sentence—readers can easily select the most appropriate definition.

Context clues can also help readers when they don't know *any* meanings for a certain word. Test writers will deliberately ask about unfamiliar vocabulary to measure your ability to use context to make an educated guess about a word's meaning.

Which of the following is the closest in meaning to the word "loquacious" in the following sentence?

The *loquacious* professor was notorious for always taking too long to finish his lectures.
   a. knowledgeable
   b. enthusiastic
   c. approachable
   d. talkative

Even if the word "loquacious" seems completely new, it's possible to utilize context to make a good guess about the word's meaning. Grammatically, it's apparent that "loquacious" is an adjective that modifies the noun "professor"—so "loquacious" must be some kind of quality or characteristic. A clue in this sentence is "taking too long to finish his lectures." Readers should then consider qualities that might cause a professor's lectures to run long. Perhaps he's "disorganized," "slow," or "talkative"—all words that might still make sense in this sentence. Choice *D*, therefore, is a logical choice for this sentence— the professor talks too much, so his lectures run late. In fact, "loquacious" means "talkative or wordy."

One way to use context clues is to think of potential replacement words before considering the answer choices. You can also turn to the answer choices first and try to replace each of them in the sentence to see if the sentence is logical and retains the same meaning.

Another way to use context clues is to consider clues in the word itself. Most students are familiar with prefixes, suffixes, and root words—the building blocks of many English words. A little knowledge goes a long way when it comes to these components of English vocabulary, and these words can point readers in the right direction when they need help finding an appropriate definition.

Specific Word Choices on Meaning and Tone

Just as one word may have different meanings, the same meaning can be conveyed by different words or synonyms. However, there are very few synonyms that have *exactly* the same definition. Rather, there are slight nuances in usage and meaning. In this case, a writer's *diction*, or word choice, is important to the meaning meant to be conveyed.

Many words have a surface *denotation* and a deeper *connotation*. A word's *denotation* is the literal definition of a word that can be found in any dictionary (an easy way to remember this is that "denotation" and "dictionary definition" all begin with the letter "D"). For example, if someone looked up the word "snake" in the dictionary, they'd learn that a snake is a common reptile with scales, a long body, and no limbs.

A word's *connotation* refers to its emotional and cultural associations, beyond its literal definition. Some connotations are universal, some are common within a particular cultural group, and some are more personal. Let's go back to the word "snake." A reader probably already knows its denotation—a slithering animal—but readers should also take a moment to consider its possible connotations. For readers from a Judeo-Christian culture, they might associate a snake with the serpent from the Garden of Eden who tempts Adam and Eve into eating the forbidden fruit. In this case, a snake's connotations might include deceit, danger, and sneakiness.

Consider the following character description:

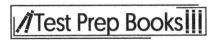

He slithered into the room like a snake.

Does this sound like a character who can be trusted? It's the connotation of the word "snake" that implies untrustworthiness. Connotative language, then, helps writers to communicate a deeper, more emotional meaning.

Read the following excerpt from "The Lamb," a poem by William Blake.

> Little lamb, who made thee?
> Dost thou know who made thee,
> Gave thee life, and bid thee feed
> By the stream and o'er the mead;
> Gave thee clothing of delight,
> Softest clothing, woolly, bright;
> Gave thee such a tender voice,
> Making all the vales rejoice?
> Little lamb, who made thee?
> Dost thou know who made thee?

Think about the connotations of a "lamb." Whereas a snake might make readers think of something dangerous and dishonest, a lamb tends to carry a different connotation: innocence and purity. Blake's poem contains other emotional language—"delight," "softest," "tender," "rejoice"—to support this impression.

Some words have similar denotations but very different connotations. "Weird" and "unique" can both describe something distinctive and unlike the norm. But they convey different emotions:

> You have such a weird fashion sense!

> You have such a unique fashion sense!

Which sentence is a compliment? Which sentence is an insult? "Weird" generally has more negative connotations, whereas "unique" is more positive. In this way, connotative language is a powerful way for writers to evoke emotion.

A writer's diction also informs their tone. *Tone* refers to the author's attitude toward their subject. A writer's tone might be critical, curious, respectful, dismissive, or any other possible attitude. The key to understanding tone is focusing not just on *what* is said, but on *how* it's said.

> a. Although the latest drug trial did not produce a successful vaccine, medical researchers are one step further on the path to eradicating this deadly virus.

> b. Doctors faced yet another disappointing setback in their losing battle against the killer virus; their most recent drug trial has proved as unsuccessful as the last.

Both sentences report the same information: the latest drug trial was a failure. However, each sentence presents this information in a different way, revealing the writer's tone. The first sentence has a more hopeful and confident tone, downplaying the doctors' failure ("although" it failed) and emphasizing their progress ("one step further"). The second sentence has a decidedly more pessimistic and defeatist

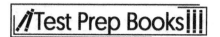

tone, using phrases like "disappointing setback" and "losing battle." The details a writer chooses to include can also help readers to identify their attitude towards their subject matter.

Identifying emotional or connotative language can be useful in determining the tone of a text. Readers can also consider questions such as, "Who is the speaker?" or "Who is their audience?" (Remember, particularly in fiction, that the speaker or narrator may not be the same person as the author.) For example, in an article about military conflict written by a notable anti-war activist, readers might expect their tone to be critical, harsh, or cynical. If they are presented with a poem written between newlyweds, readers might expect the tone to be loving, sensitive, or infatuated. If the tone seems wildly different from what's expected, consider if the writer is using *irony*. When a writer uses irony, they say one thing but imply the opposite meaning.

Acquiring and Using Words and Phrases Accurately

Vocabulary is the words a person uses on a daily basis. Having a good vocabulary is important. It's important in writing and also when you talk to people. Many of the questions on the test may have words that you don't know. Therefore, it's important to learn ways to find out a word's meaning.

It's hard to use vocabulary correctly. Imagine being thrust into a foreign country. If you didn't know right words to use to ask for the things you need, you could run into trouble! Asking for help from people who don't share the same vocabulary is hard. Language helps us understand each other. The more vocabulary words a person knows, the easier they can ask for things they need. This section of the study guide focuses on getting to know vocabulary through basic grammar.

Prefixes and Suffixes

In this section, we will look at the *meaning* of various prefixes and suffixes when added to a root word. A **prefix** is a combination of letters found at the beginning of a word. A **suffix** is a combination of letters found at the end. A *root word* is the word that comes after the prefix, before the suffix, or between them both. Sometimes a root word can stand on its own without either a prefix or a suffix.

More simply put:

Prefix + Root Word = Word

Root Word + Suffix = Word

Prefix + Root Word + Suffix = Word

Root Word = Word

Knowing the definitions of common prefixes and suffixes is helpful. It's helpful when you are trying to find out the meaning of a word you don't know. Also, knowing prefixes can help you find out the number of things, the negative of something, or the time and space of an object! Understanding suffixes can help when trying to find out the meaning of an adjective, noun, or verb.

The following charts look at some of the most common prefixes, what they mean, and how they're used to find out a word's meaning:

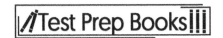

Number and Quantity Prefixes

Prefix	Definition	Example
bi-	two	bicycle, bilateral
mono-	one, single	monopoly, monotone
poly-	many	polygamy, polygon
semi-	half, partly	semiannual, semicircle
uni-	one	unicycle, universal

Here's an example of a number prefix:

The girl rode on a *bicycle* to school.

Look at the word *bicycle*. The root word (*cycle*)comes from the Greek and means *wheel*. The prefix *bi-* means *two*. The word *bicycle* means two wheels! When you look at any bicycles, they all have two wheels. If you had a unicycle, your bike would only have one wheel, because *uni-* means *one*.

Negative Prefixes

Prefix	Definition	Example
a-	without, lack of	amoral, atypical
in-	not, opposing	inability, inverted
non-	not	nonexistent, nonstop
un-	not, reverse	unable, unspoken

Here's an example of a negative prefix:

The girl was *insensitive* to the boy who broke his leg.

Look at the word *insensitive*. In the chart above, the prefix *in-* means *not* or *opposing*. Replace the prefix with *not*. Now place *not* in front of the word *sensitive*. Now we see that the girl was "not sensitive" to the boy who broke his leg. In simpler terms, she showed that she did not care. These are easy ways to use prefixes and suffixes in order to find out what a word means.

Time and Space Prefixes

Prefix	Definition	Example
a-	in, on, of, up, to	aloof, associate
ab-	from, away, off	abstract, absent
ad-	to, towards	adept, adjacent
ante-	before, previous	antebellum, antenna
anti-	against, opposing	anticipate, antisocial
cata-	down, away, thoroughly	catacomb, catalogue
circum-	around	circumstance, circumvent
com-	with, together, very	combine, compel
contra-	against, opposing	contraband, contrast
de-	from	decrease, descend

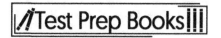

Prefix	Definition	Example
dia-	through, across, apart	diagram, dialect
dis-	away, off, down, not	disregard, disrespect
epi-	upon	epidemic, epiphany
ex-	out	example, exit
hypo-	under, beneath	hypoallergenic, hypothermia
inter-	among, between	intermediate, international
intra-	within	intrapersonal, intravenous
ob-	against, opposing	obtain, obscure
per-	through	permanent, persist
peri-	around	periodontal, periphery
post-	after, following	postdate, postoperative
pre-	before, previous	precede, premeditate
pro-	forward, in place of	program, propel
retro-	back, backward	retroactive, retrofit
sub-	under, beneath	submarine, substantial
super-	above, extra	superior, supersede
trans-	Across, beyond, or over	transform, transmit
ultra-	beyond, excessively	ultraclean, ultralight

Here's an example of a space prefix:

> The teacher's motivational speech helped *propel* her students toward greater academic achievement.

Look at the word *propel*. The prefix *pro-* means *forward*. *Forward* means something related to time and space. *Propel* means to drive or move in a forward direction. Therefore, knowing the prefix *pro-* helps interpret that the students are moving forward *toward greater academic achievement*.

Miscellaneous Prefixes

Prefix	Definition	Example
belli-	war, warlike	bellied, belligerent
bene-	well, good	benediction, beneficial
equi-	equal	equidistant, equinox
for-	away, off, from	forbidden, forsaken
fore-	previous	forecast, forebode
homo-	same, equal	homogeneous, homonym
hyper-	excessive, over	hyperextend, hyperactive
in-	in, into	insignificant, invasive
magn-	large	magnetic, magnificent
mal-	bad, poorly, not	maladapted, malnourished
mis-	bad, poorly, not	misplace, misguide
mor-	death	mortal, morgue
neo-	new	neoclassical, neonatal
omni-	all, everywhere	omnipotent, omnipresent
ortho-	right, straight	orthodontist, orthopedic
over-	above	overload, overstock,

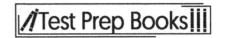

Prefix	Definition	Example
pan-	all, entire	panacea, pander
para-	beside, beyond	paradigm, parameter
phil-	love, like	philanthropy, philosophic
prim-	first, early	primal, primer
re-	backward, again	reload, regress
sym-	with, together	symmetry, symbolize
vis-	to see	visual, visibility

Here's another prefix example:

The computer was *primitive*; it still had a floppy disk drive!

The word *primitive* has the prefix *prim-*. The prefix *prim-*indicates being *first* or *early*. *Primitive* means the early stages of evolution. It also could mean the historical development of something. Therefore, the sentence is saying that the computer is an older model, because it no longer has a floppy disk drive.

The charts that follow review some of the most common suffixes. They also include examples of how the suffixes that are used to determine the meaning of a word. Remember, suffixes are added to the *end* of a root word:

Adjective Suffixes

Suffix	Definition	Example
-able (-ible)	capable of being	teachable, accessible
-esque	in the style of, like	humoresque, statuesque
-ful	filled with, marked by	helpful, deceitful
-ic	having, containing	manic, elastic
-ish	suggesting, like	malnourish, tarnish
-less	lacking, without	worthless, fearless
-ous	marked by, given to	generous, previous

Here's an example of an adjective suffix:

The live model looked so *statuesque* in the window display; she didn't even move!

Look at the word *statuesque*. The suffix *-esque* means *in the style of* or *like*. If something is *statuesque*, it's *like a statue*. In this sentence, the model looks like a statue.

Noun Suffixes

Suffix	Definition	Example
-acy	state, condition	literacy, legacy
-ance	act, condition, fact	distance, importance
-ard	one that does	leotard, billiard
-ation	action, state, result	legislation, condemnation
-dom	state, rank, condition	freedom, kingdom
-er (-or)	office, action	commuter, spectator
-ess	feminine	caress, princess
-hood	state, condition	childhood, livelihood

75

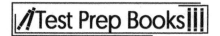

Suffix	Definition	Example
-ion	action, result, state	communion, position
-ism	act, manner, doctrine	capitalism, patriotism
-ist	worker, follower	stylist, activist
-ity (-ty)	state, quality, condition	community, dirty
-ment	result, action	empowerment, segment
-ness	quality, state	fitness, rudeness
-ship	position	censorship, leadership
-sion (-tion)	state, result	tension, transition
-th	act, state, quality	twentieth, wealth
-tude	quality, state, result	attitude, latitude

Look at the following example of a noun suffix:

The *spectator* cheered when his favorite soccer team scored a goal.

Look at the word *spectator*. The suffix *-or* means *action*. In this sentence, the *action* is to *spectate* (watch something). Therefore, a *spectator* is someone involved in watching something.

Verb Suffixes

Suffix	Definition	Example
-ate	having, showing	facilitate, integrate
-en	cause to be, become	frozen, written
-fy	make, cause to have	modify, rectify
-ize	cause to be, treat with	realize, sanitize

Here's an example of a verb suffix:

The preschool had to *sanitize* the toys every Tuesday and Thursday.

In the word *sanitize*, the suffix *-ize* means *cause to be* or *treat with*. By adding the suffix *-ize* to the root word *sanitary*, the meaning of the word becomes active: *cause to be sanitary*.

Text Types and Purposes

Writing Arguments to Support Claims

Understanding the Task, Purpose, and Audience
Identifying the Task, Purpose, and Intended Audience
An author's **writing style**—the way in which words, grammar, punctuation, and sentence fluidity are used—is the most influential element in a piece of writing, and it is dependent on the purpose and the audience for whom it is intended. Together, a writing style and mode of writing form the foundation of a written work, and a good writer will choose the most effective mode and style to convey a message to readers.

Writers should first determine what they are trying to say and then choose the most effective mode of writing to communicate that message. Different writing modes and *word choices* will affect the tone of a piece—that is, its underlying attitude, emotion, or character. The argumentative mode may utilize

76

words that are earnest, angry, passionate, or excited whereas an informative piece may have a sterile, germane, or enthusiastic tone. The tones found in narratives vary greatly, depending on the purpose of the writing. *Tone* will also be affected by the audience—teaching science to children or those who may be uninterested would be most effective with enthusiastic language and exclamation points whereas teaching science to college students may take on a more serious and professional tone, with fewer charged words and punctuation choices that are inherent to academia.

Sentence fluidity—whether sentences are long and rhythmic or short and succinct—also affects a piece of writing as it determines the way in which a piece is read. Children or audiences unfamiliar with a subject do better with short, succinct sentence structures as these break difficult concepts up into shorter points. A period, question mark, or exclamation point is literally a signal for the reader to stop and takes more time to process. Thus, longer, more complex sentences are more appropriate for adults or educated audiences as they can fit more information in between processing time.

The amount of **supporting detail** provided is also tailored to the audience. A text that introduces a new subject to its readers will focus more on broad ideas without going into greater detail whereas a text that focuses on a more specific subject is likely to provide greater detail about the ideas discussed.

Writing styles, like modes, are most effective when tailored to their audiences. Having awareness of an audience's demographic is one of the most crucial aspects of properly communicating an argument, a story, or a set of information.

Choosing the Most Appropriate Type of Writing

Before beginning any writing, it is imperative that a writer have a firm grasp on the message he or she wishes to convey and how he or she wants readers to be affected by the writing. For example, does the author want readers to be more informed about the subject? Does the writer want readers to agree with their opinion? Does the writer want readers to get caught up in an exciting narrative? The following steps are a guide to determining the appropriate type of writing for a task, purpose, and audience:

1. Identifying the purpose for writing the piece
2. Determining the audience
3. Adapting the writing mode, word choices, tone, and style to fit the audience and the purpose

It is important to distinguish between a work's purpose and its main idea. The essential difference between the two is that the *main idea* is what the author wants to communicate about the topic at hand whereas the *primary purpose* is why the author is writing in the first place. The primary purpose is what will determine the type of writing an author will choose to utilize, not the main idea, though the two are related. For example, if an author writes an article on the mistreatment of animals in factory farms and, at the end, suggests that people should convert to vegetarianism, the main idea is that vegetarianism would reduce the poor treatment of animals. The primary purpose is to convince the reader to stop eating animals. Since the primary purpose is to galvanize an audience into action, the author would choose the argumentative writing mode.

The next step is to consider to whom the author is appealing as this will determine the type of details to be included, the diction to be used, the tone to be employed, and the sentence structure to be used. An audience can be identified by considering the following questions:

- What is the purpose for writing the piece?
- To whom is it being written?

77

- What is their age range?
- Are they familiar with the material being presented, or are they just being newly introduced to it?
- Where are they from?
- Is the task at hand in a professional or casual setting?
- Is the task at hand for monetary gain?

These are just a few of the numerous considerations to keep in mind, but the main idea is to become as familiar with the audience as possible. Once the audience has been understood, the author can then adapt the writing style to align with the readers' education and interests. The audience is what determines the *rhetorical appeal* the author will use—ethos, pathos, or logos. *Ethos* is a rhetorical appeal to an audience's ethics and/or morals. Ethos is most often used in argumentative and informative writing modes. *Pathos* is an appeal to the audience's emotions and sympathies, and it is found in argumentative, descriptive, and narrative writing modes. *Logos* is an appeal to the audience's logic and reason and is used primarily in informative texts as well as in supporting details for argumentative pieces. Rhetorical appeals are discussed in depth in the informational texts and rhetoric section of the test.

If the author is trying to encourage global conversion to vegetarianism, he or she may choose to use all three rhetorical appeals to reach varying personality types. Those who are less interested in the welfare of animals but are interested in facts and science would relate more to logos. Animal lovers would relate better to an emotional appeal. In general, the most effective works utilize all three appeals.

Finally, after determining the writing mode and rhetorical appeal, the author will consider word choice, sentence structure, and tone, depending on the purpose and audience. The author may choose words that convey sadness or anger when speaking about animal welfare if writing to persuade, or he or she will stick to dispassionate and matter-of-fact tones, if informing the public on the treatment of animals in factory farms. If the author is writing to a younger or less-educated audience, he or she may choose to shorten and simplify sentence structures and word choice. If appealing to an audience with more expert knowledge on a particular subject, writers will more likely employ a style of longer sentences and more complex vocabulary.

Depending on the task, the author may choose to use a first person, second person, or third person point of view. First person and second person perspectives are inherently more casual in tone, including the author and the reader in the rhetoric, while third person perspectives are often seen in more professional settings.

Using Clear and Coherent Writing
Identifying Details that Develop a Main Idea

The main idea of a piece is the central topic or theme. To identify the **main idea**, a reader should consider these questions: "What's the point? What does the author want readers to take away from this text?" Everything within the selection should relate back to the main idea because it is the center of the organizational web of any written work. Particularly in articles and reports, the main idea often appears within the opening paragraphs to orient the reader to what the author wants to say about the subject. A sentence that expresses the main idea is known as a thesis sentence or *thesis statement*.

After the main idea has been introduced, *supporting details* are what develop the main idea—they make up the bulk of the work. Without supporting details, the main idea would simply be a statement, so

78

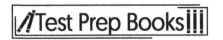

additional details are needed to give that statement weight and validity. Supporting details can often be identified by recognizing the key words that introduce them. The following example offers several supporting details, with key words underlined:

> Man did not evolve from apes. Though we share a common ancestor, humans and apes originated through very different evolutionary paths. There are several reasons why this is true. The <u>first</u> reason is that, logically, if humans evolved from apes, modern-day apes and humans would not coexist. Evolution occurs when a genetic mutation in a species ensures the survival over the rest of the species, allowing them to pass on their genes and create a new lineage of organisms. <u>Another</u> reason is that hominid fossils only fall into one of two categories—ape-like or human-like—and there are very strong differences between the two. Australopithecines, the hominid fossils originally believed to be ancestral to humans, are ape-like, indicated by their long arms, long and curved fingers, and funnel-shaped chests. Their hand bones suggest that they "knuckle-walked" like modern day chimpanzees and gorillas, something not found in *Homo sapien* fossils. <u>Finally</u>, there is no fossilized evidence to suggest a transition between the ape-like ancestor and the *Homo sapien*, indicating that a sudden mutation may have been responsible. These and many other reasons are indicative that humans and ape-like creatures are evolutionarily different.

The underlined words—*first, another,* and *finally*—are the key words that identify the supporting details. These details can be summarized as follows:

- Humans and apes could not coexist.
- Human-like and ape-like fossils are very different.
- No transition is seen between humans and ape-like ancestors.

The supporting details all relate to the central idea that "Man did not evolve from apes," which is the first sentence of the paragraph.

Even though supporting details are more specific than the main idea, they should nevertheless all be directly related to the main idea. Without sufficient supporting details, the writer's main idea will be too weak to be effective.

Organizing a Text Clearly and Coherently

There are five basic elements inherent in effective writing, and each will be discussed throughout the various subheadings of this section.

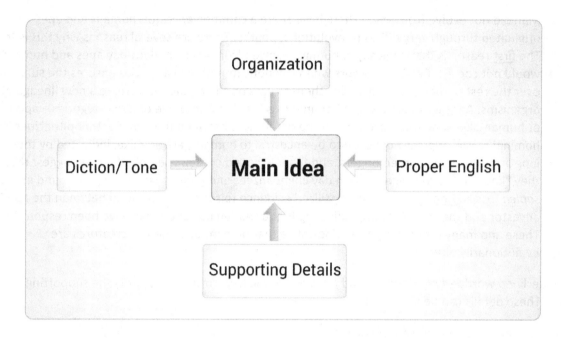

- *Main idea*: The driving message of the writing, clearly stated or implied
- *Clear organization*: The effective and purposeful arrangement of the content to support the main idea
- *Supporting details/evidence*: Content that gives appropriate depth and weight to the main idea of the story, argument, or information
- *Diction/tone*: The type of language, vocabulary, and word choice used to express the main idea, purposefully aligned to the audience and purpose
- *Adherence to conventions of English*: Correct spelling, grammar, punctuation, and sentence structure, allowing for clear communication of ideas

Using Varied and Effective Transitions

Transitions are the glue that holds the writing together. They function to purposefully incorporate new topics and supporting details in a smooth and coherent way. Usually, transitions are found at the beginnings of sentences, but they can also be located in the middle as a way to link clauses together. There are two types of clauses: independent and dependent as discussed in the language use and vocabulary section.

Transition words connect clauses within and between sentences for smoother writing. "I dislike apples. They taste like garbage." is choppier than "I dislike apples because they taste like garbage." Transitions demonstrate the relationship between ideas, allow for more complex sentence structures, and can alert the reader to which type of organizational format the author is using. For example, the above selection on human evolution uses the words *first, another*, and *finally* to indicate that the writer will be listing the reasons why humans and apes are evolutionarily different.

Transition words can be categorized based on the relationships they create between ideas:

- *General order*: signaling elaboration of an idea to emphasize a point—e.g., *for example, for instance, to demonstrate, including, such as, in other words, that is, in fact, also, furthermore, likewise, and, truly, so, surely, certainly, obviously, doubtless*
- *Chronological order*: referencing the time frame in which the main event or idea occurs—e.g., *before, after, first, while, soon, shortly thereafter, meanwhile*
- *Numerical order/order of importance*: indicating that related ideas, supporting details, or events will be described in a sequence, possibly in order of importance—e.g., *first, second, also, finally, another, in addition, equally important, less importantly, most significantly, the main reason, last but not least*
- *Spatial order*: referring to the space and location of something or where things are located in relation to each other—e.g., *inside, outside, above, below, within, close, under, over, far, next to, adjacent to*
- *Cause and effect order*: signaling a causal relationship between events or ideas—e.g., *thus, therefore, since, resulted in, for this reason, as a result, consequently, hence, for, so*
- *Compare and contrast order*: identifying the similarities and differences between two or more objects, ideas, or lines of thought—e.g., *like, as, similarly, equally, just as, unlike, however, but, although, conversely, on the other hand, on the contrary*
- *Summary order*: indicating that a particular idea is coming to a close—e.g., *in conclusion, to sum up, in other words, ultimately, above all*

Sophisticated writing also aims to avoid overuse of transitions and ensure that those used are meaningful. Using a variety of transitions makes the writing appear more lively and informed and helps readers follow the progression of ideas.

Justifying Stylistic Choices

Stylistic choices refer to elements such as a writer's diction, sentence structure, and use of figurative language. A writer's *diction* is their word choice and may be elevated, academic, conversational, humorous, or any other style. The choice of diction depends on the purpose of a piece of writing. A textbook or a research paper is likely to use academic diction whereas a blog post will use more conversational expressions.

Sentence structure also affects an author's writing style. Will he or she use short, staccato sentences or longer sentences with complex structure? Effective writing tends to incorporate both styles to increase reader interest or to punctuate ideas.

Figurative language includes the use of simile, metaphor, hyperbole, or allusion, to name but a few examples. Creative or descriptive writing is likely to incorporate more non-literal expressions than academic or informative writing will. Instructors should allow students to experiment with different styles of writing and understand how style affects expression and understanding.

Introducing, Developing, and Concluding a Text Effectively

Almost all coherent written works contain three primary parts: a beginning, middle, and end. The organizational arrangements differ widely across distinct writing modes. Persuasive and expository texts utilize an introduction, body, and conclusion whereas narrative works use an orientation, series of events/conflict, and a resolution.

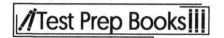

Every element within a written piece relates back to the main idea, and the beginning of a persuasive or expository text generally conveys the main idea or the purpose. For a narrative piece, the beginning is the section that acquaints the reader with the characters and setting, directing them to the purpose of the writing. The main idea in narrative may be implied or addressed at the end of the piece.

Depending on the primary purpose, the arrangement of the middle will adhere to one of the basic organizational structures described in the information texts and rhetoric section. They are cause and effect, problem and solution, compare and contrast, description/spatial, sequence, and order of importance.

The ending of a text is the metaphorical wrap-up of the writing. A solid ending is crucial for effective writing as it ties together loose ends, resolves the action, highlights the main points, or repeats the central idea. A conclusion ensures that readers come away from a text understanding the author's main idea. The table below highlights the important characteristics of each part of a piece of writing.

Structure	Argumentative/Informative	Narrative
Beginning	Introduction *Purpose, main idea*	Orientation *Introduces characters, setting, necessary background*
Middle	Body *Supporting details, reasons and evidence*	Events/Conflict *Story's events that revolve around a central conflict*
End	Conclusion *Highlights main points, summarizes and paraphrases ideas, reiterates the main idea*	Resolution *The solving of the central conflict*

Evaluation of Reasoning

Critical Thinking Skills

It's important to read any piece of writing critically. The goal is to discover the point and purpose of what the author is writing about through analysis. It's also crucial to establish the point or stance the author has taken on the topic of the piece. After determining the author's perspective, readers can then more effectively develop their own viewpoints on the subject of the piece.

It is important to distinguish between **fact and opinion** when reading a piece of writing. A fact is information that is true. If information can be disproven, it is not a fact. For example, water freezes at or below thirty-two degrees Fahrenheit. An argument stating that water freezes at seventy degrees Fahrenheit cannot be supported by data and is therefore not a fact. Facts tend to be associated with science, mathematics, and statistics. **Opinions** are information open for debate. Opinions are often tied to subjective concepts like feelings, desires, or manners. They can also be controversial.

Authors often use words like *think, feel, believe,* or *in my opinion* when expressing opinion, but these words won't always appear in an opinion piece, especially if it is formally written. An author's opinion may be backed up by facts, which gives it more credibility, but that opinion should not be taken as fact. A critical reader should be wary of an author's opinion, especially if it is only supported by other opinions.

Fact	Opinion
There are 9 innings in a game of baseball.	Baseball games run too long.
James Garfield was assassinated on July 2, 1881.	James Garfield was a good president.
McDonalds has stores in 118 countries.	McDonalds has the best hamburgers.

Critical readers examine the facts used to support an author's argument. They check the facts against other sources to be sure those facts are correct. They also check the validity of the sources used to be sure those sources are credible, academic, and/or peer reviewed. Consider that when an author uses another person's opinion to support their argument, even if it is an expert's opinion, it is still only an opinion and should not be taken as fact. A strong argument uses valid, measurable facts to support ideas. Even then, the reader may disagree with the argument as it may be rooted in their personal beliefs.

An authoritative argument may use the facts to sway the reader. In an example of global warming, many experts differ in their opinions of what alternative fuels can be used to aid in offsetting it. Because of this, a writer may choose to only use the information and expert opinion that supports their viewpoint.

If the argument is that wind energy is the best solution, the author will use facts that support this idea. That same author may leave out relevant facts on solar energy. The way the author uses facts can influence the reader, so it's important to consider the facts being used, how those facts are being presented, and what information might be left out.

Critical readers should also look for errors in the argument such as logical fallacies and bias. A **logical fallacy** is a flaw in the logic used to make the argument. Logical fallacies include slippery slope, straw man, and begging the question. Authors can also reflect **bias** if they ignore an opposing viewpoint or present their side in an unbalanced way. A strong argument considers the opposition and finds a way to refute it. Critical readers should look for an unfair or one-sided presentation of the argument and be skeptical, as a bias may be present. Even if this bias is unintentional, if it exists in the writing, the reader should be wary of the validity of the argument.

Readers should also look for the use of stereotypes. These are the overly simplified beliefs about a person, place, thing, etc. that is indiscriminately applied to a larger group. These can be positive but are usually negative in nature. When a reader comes across the use of stereotypes, they should take that into consideration as they analyze the author's argument. These should generally be avoided. Stereotypes reveal a flaw in the writer's thinking and may suggest a lack of knowledge or understanding about the subject.

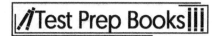

Identifying False Statements

A reader must also be able to identify any *logical fallacies*—logically flawed statements—that an author may make as those fallacies impact the validity and veracity of the author's claims.

Some of the more common fallacies are shown in the following chart.

Fallacy	Definition
Slippery Slope	A fallacy that is built on the idea that a particular action will lead to a series of events with negative results
Red Herring	The use of an observation or distraction to remove attention from the actual issue
Straw Man	An exaggeration or misrepresentation of an argument so that it is easier to refute
Post Hoc Ergo Propter Hoc	A fallacy that assumes an event to be the consequence of an earlier event merely because it came after it
Bandwagon	A fallacy that assumes because the majority of people feel or believe a certain way then it must be the right way
Ad Hominem	The use of a personal attack on the person or persons associated with a certain argument rather than focusing on the actual argument itself

Readers who are aware of the types of fallacious reasoning are able to weigh the credibility of the author's statements in terms of effective argument. Rhetorical text that contains a myriad of fallacious statements should be considered ineffectual and suspect.

Interpreting Textual Evidence

Literal and Figurative Meanings

It is important when evaluating texts to consider the use of both literal and figurative meanings. The words and phrases an author chooses to include in a text must be evaluated. How does the word choice affect the meaning and tone? By recognizing the use of literal and figurative language, a reader can more readily ascertain the message or purpose of a text. Literal word choice is the easiest to analyze as it represents the usual and intended way a word or phrase is used. While figurative language is typically associated with fiction and poetry, it can be found in informational texts as well. The reader must determine not only what is meant by the figurative language in context, but also how the author intended it to shape the overall text.

Inference

Inference refers to the reader's ability to understand the unwritten text, i.e., "read between the lines" in terms of an author's intent or message. The strategy asks that a reader not take everything he or she reads at face value but instead, add their own interpretation of what the author seems to be trying to convey. A reader's ability to make inferences relies on their ability to think clearly and logically about the text. It does not ask that the reader make wild speculation or guess about the material but demands that he or she be able to come to a sound conclusion about the material.

An author's use of less literal words and phrases requires readers to make more inference when they read. Since inference involves *deduction*—deriving conclusions from ideas assumed to be true—there's more room for interpretation. Still, critical readers who employ inference, if careful in their thinking, can still arrive at the logical, sound conclusions the author intends.

Textual Evidence

Once a reader has determined an author's thesis or main idea, he or she will need to understand how **textual evidence** supports interpretation of that thesis or main idea. Test takers will be asked direct questions regarding an author's main idea and may be asked to identify evidence that would support those ideas. This will require test takers to comprehend literal and figurative meanings within the text passage, be able to draw inferences from provided information, and be able to separate important evidence from minor supporting detail. It's often helpful to skim test questions and answer options prior to critically reading; however, test takers should avoid the temptation to solely look for the correct answers. Just trying to find the "right answer" may cause test takers to miss important supporting textual evidence. Making mental note of test questions is only helpful as a guide when reading.

After identifying an author's thesis or main idea, a test taker should look at the supporting details that the author provides to back up their assertions, identifying those additional pieces of information that help expand the thesis. From there, test takers should examine the additional information and related details for credibility, the author's use of outside sources, and be able to point to direct evidence that supports the author's claims. It's also imperative that test takers be able to identify what is strong support and what is merely additional information that is nice to know but not necessary. Being able to make this differentiation will help test takers effectively answer questions regarding an author's use of supporting evidence.

Examining and Conveying Ideas, Concepts, and Information Clearly and Accurately

Informational texts are a category of texts within the genre of nonfiction. Their intent is to inform, and while they do convey a point of view and may include literary devices, they do not utilize other literary elements, such as characters or plot. An informational text also reflects a *thesis*—an implicit or explicit statement of the text's intent and/or a *main idea*—the overarching focus and/or purpose of the text, generally implied. Some examples of informational texts are informative articles, instructional/how-to texts, factual reports, reference texts, and self-help texts.

Understanding Organizational Patterns and Structures

Organizational Structure within Informational Text

Informational text is specifically designed to relate factual information, and although it is open to a reader's interpretation and application of the facts, the structure of the presentation is carefully designed to lead the reader to a particular conclusion or central idea. When reading informational text,

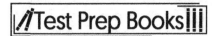

it is important that readers are able to understand its organizational structure as the structure often directly relates to an author's intent to inform and/or persuade the reader.

The first step in identifying the text's structure is to determine the thesis or main idea. The thesis statement and organization of a work are closely intertwined. *A thesis statement* indicates the writer's purpose and may include the scope and direction of the text. It may be presented at the beginning of a text or at the end, and it may be explicit or implicit.

Once a reader has a grasp of the thesis or main idea of the text, he or she can better determine its organizational structure. Test takers are advised to read informational text passages more than once in order to comprehend the material fully. It is also helpful to examine any text features present in the text including the table of contents, index, glossary, headings, footnotes, and visuals. The analysis of these features and the information presented within them, can offer additional clues about the central idea and structure of a text. The following questions should be asked when considering structure:

- How does the author assemble the parts to make an effective whole argument?
- Is the passage linear in nature and if so, what is the timeline or thread of logic?
- What is the presented order of events, facts, or arguments? Are these effective in contributing to the author's thesis?
- How can the passage be divided into sections? How are they related to each other and to the main idea or thesis?
- What key terms are used to indicate the organization?

Next, test takers should skim the passage, noting the first line or two of each body paragraph—the **topic sentences**—and the conclusion. Key *transitional terms*, such as *on the other hand*, *also*, *because*, *however*, *therefore*, *most importantly*, and *first*, within the text can also signal organizational structure. Based on these clues, readers should then be able to identify what type of organizational structure is being used. The following organizational structures are most common:

- *Problem/solution*—organized by an analysis/overview of a problem, followed by potential solution(s)
- *Cause/effect*—organized by the effects resulting from a cause or the cause(s) of a particular effect
- *Spatial order*—organized by points that suggest location or direction—e.g., top to bottom, right to left, outside to inside
- *Chronological/sequence order*—organized by points presented to indicate a passage of time or through purposeful steps/stages
- *Comparison/Contrast*—organized by points that indicate similarities and/or differences between two things or concepts
- *Order of importance*—organized by priority of points, often most significant to least significant or vice versa

Identifying Rhetorical Strategies

Rhetoric refers to an author's use of particular strategies, appeals, and devices to persuade an intended audience. The more effective the use of rhetoric, the more likely the audience will be persuaded.

Determining an Author's Point of View

A **rhetorical strategy**—also referred to as a *rhetorical mode*—is the structural way an author chooses to present their argument. Though the terms noted below are similar to the organizational structures noted earlier, these strategies do not imply that the entire text follows the approach. For example, a cause-and-effect organizational structure is solely that, nothing more. A persuasive text may use cause and effect as a strategy to convey a singular point. Thus, an argument may include several of the strategies as the author strives to convince their audience to take action or accept a different point of view. It's important that readers are able to identify an author's thesis and position on the topic in order to be able to identify the careful construction through which the author speaks to the reader. The following are some of the more common rhetorical strategies:

- *Cause and effect*—establishing a logical correlation or causation between two ideas
- *Classification/division*—the grouping of similar items together or division of something into parts
- *Comparison/contrast*—the distinguishing of similarities/differences to expand on an idea
- *Definition*—used to clarify abstract ideas, unfamiliar concepts, or to distinguish one idea from another
- *Description*—use of vivid imagery, active verbs, and clear adjectives to explain ideas
- *Exemplification*—the use of examples to explain an idea
- *Narration*—anecdotes or personal experience to present or expand on a concept
- *Problem/Solution*—presentation of a problem or problems, followed by proposed solution(s)

Rhetorical Strategies and Devices

A **rhetorical device** is the phrasing and presentation of an idea that reinforces and emphasizes a point in an argument. A rhetorical device is often quite memorable. One of the more famous uses of a rhetorical device is in John F. Kennedy's 1961 inaugural address: "Ask not what your country can do for you, ask what you can do for your country." The contrast of ideas presented in the phrasing is an example of the rhetorical device of antimetabole. Some other common examples are listed on the following page, but test takers should be aware that this is not a complete list.

Device	Definition	Example
Allusion	A reference to a famous person, event, or significant literary text as a form of significant comparison	"We are apt to shut our eyes against a painful truth, and listen to the song of that siren till she transforms us into beasts." Patrick Henry
Anaphora	The repetition of the same words at the beginning of successive words, phrases, or clauses, designed to emphasize an idea	"We shall not flag or fail. We shall go on to the end. We shall fight in France, we shall fight on the seas and oceans, we shall fight with growing confidence ... we shall fight in the fields and in the streets, we shall fight in the hills. We shall never surrender." Winston Churchill

87

Device	Definition	Example
Understatement	A statement meant to portray a situation as less important than it actually is to create an ironic effect	"The war in the Pacific has not necessarily developed in Japan's favor." Emperor Hirohito, surrendering Japan in World War II
Parallelism	A syntactical similarity in a structure or series of structures used for impact of an idea, making it memorable	"A penny saved is a penny earned." Ben Franklin
Rhetorical question	A question posed that is not answered by the writer though there is a desired response, most often designed to emphasize a point	"Can anyone look at our reduced standing in the world today and say, 'Let's have four more years of this?'" Ronald Reagan

Understanding Methods Used to Appeal to a Specific Audience

Rhetorical Appeals

In an argument or persuasive text, an author will strive to sway readers to an opinion or conclusion. To be effective, an author must consider their intended audience. Although an author may write text for a general audience, he or she will use methods of appeal or persuasion to convince that audience. Aristotle asserted that there were three methods or modes by which a person could be persuaded. These are referred to as *rhetorical appeals*.

The three main types of rhetorical appeals are shown in the following graphic.

Ethos, also referred to as an *ethical appeal*, is an appeal to the audience's perception of the writer as credible (or not), based on their examination of their ethics and who the writer is, their experience or incorporation of relevant information, or their argument. For example, authors may present testimonials to bolster their arguments. The reader who critically examines the veracity of the testimonials and the credibility of those giving the testimony will be able to determine if the author's use of testimony is valid to their argument. In turn, this will help the reader determine if the author's thesis is valid. An author's careful and appropriate use of technical language can create an overall knowledgeable effect and, in turn, act as a convincing vehicle when it comes to credibility. Overuse of technical language, however, may create confusion in readers and obscure an author's overall intent.

Pathos, also referred to as a *pathetic* or *emotional appeal*, is an appeal to the audience's sense of identity, self-interest, or emotions. A critical reader will notice when the author is appealing to pathos through anecdotes and descriptions that elicit an emotion such as anger or pity. Readers should also beware of factual information that uses generalization to appeal to the emotions. While it's tempting to believe an author is the source of truth in their text, an author who presents factual information as universally true, consistent throughout time, and common to all groups is using *generalization*. Authors who exclusively use generalizations without specific facts and credible sourcing are attempting to sway readers solely through emotion.

Logos, also referred to as a *logical appeal*, is an appeal to the audience's ability to see and understand the logic in a claim offered by the writer. A critical reader has to be able to evaluate an author's arguments for validity of reasoning and for sufficiency when it comes to argument.

Understanding Development of a Written Argument

Evaluating an Author's Purpose

A reader must be able to evaluate the argument or point the author is trying to make and determine if it is adequately supported. The first step is to determine the main idea. The main idea is what the author wants to say about a specific topic. The next step is to locate the supporting details. An author uses supporting details to illustrate the main idea. These are the details that provide evidence or examples to help make a point. Supporting details often appear in the form of quotations, paraphrasing, or analysis. Test takers should then examine the text to make sure the author connects details and analysis to the main point. These steps are crucial to understanding the text and evaluating how well the author presents their argument and evidence. The following graphic demonstrates the connection between the main idea and the supporting details.

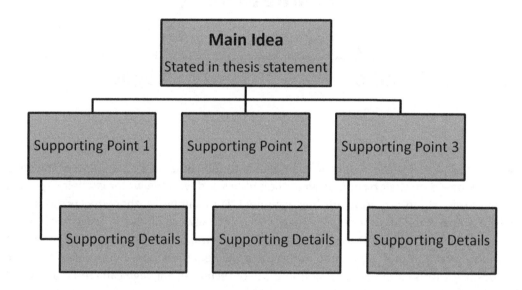

Evaluating Evidence

It is important to evaluate the author's supporting details to be sure that they are credible, provide evidence of the author's point, and directly support the main idea. Critical readers examine the facts used to support an author's argument and check those facts against other sources to be sure they are correct. They also check the validity of the sources used to be sure those sources are credible, academic, and/or peer reviewed. A strong argument uses valid, measurable facts to support ideas.

Electronic Resources

With print texts, it is easy to identify the authors and their credentials, as well as the publisher and their reputation. With electronic resources like websites, though, it can be trickier to assess the reliability of information. Students should be alert when gathering information from the Internet. Understanding the significance of website *domains*—which include identification strings of a site—can help. Website domains ending in *.edu* are educational sites and tend to offer more reliable research in their field. A *.org* ending tends to be used by nonprofit organizations and other community groups, *.com* indicates a privately-owned website, and a *.gov* site is run by the government. Websites affiliated with official organizations, research groups, or institutes of learning are more likely to offer relevant, fact-checked, and reliable information.

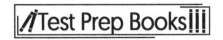

Writing Arguments Focused on Discipline-Specific Content

When it comes to writing discipline-specific content, the key is in understanding the characteristics of the specific discipline you are planning on writing about. Whether you are writing essays in high school, taking a broad range of college courses, or writing to communicate in a new career, there are many different disciplines that you will have to deal with. These disciplines are most likely one of the following:

- Business and Communication
- Humanities
- Social Sciences
- Sciences

It's important to remember that your basic five-paragraph essay that you write in high school won't cut it if you're expected to write a twenty-five-page proposal in your business class in college. Learning the expectations of the discipline you are writing for is key if in order to be successful in your writing. Here are some basic characteristics of each of the above disciplines:

Business and Communication

Business and communication writing, focuses on persuasive writing as well as informational documents. Although it's important to identify your audience in all writing situations, it is especially important in this discipline to create a list before you start writing of who will receive the document, what their status of knowledge or authority is on the subject, and how they are expected to receive the document you plan on writing. Will they be hostile to the information? If so, it's important to begin with a neutral stance. Are they on board with a business proposal you are writing? If so, focus on how to most efficiently get to the facts of what it will take to make the proposal work. Knowing your audience is key in this kind of writing. Also, it's important to pay attention to the length and organization of the document. Are they a busy executive? If so, writing an abstract to sum up the entirety of the proposal is a great idea. For organization, if the document is some kind of proposal, the most common structure to write in would be the problem-solution structure.

Humanities

Humanities is a broad field, containing various formats and styles you will have to choose from. If you are writing an essay for an English class, most likely this will be structured as an essay with a clear introduction containing a thesis statement, body paragraphs, and a conclusion regardless of whether it's a cause-and-effect essay or a comparison/contrast essay. Writing arguments are important in this genre, as rhetoric focuses on persuasive techniques such as audience persuasion using ethos, pathos, and logos. Sometimes the humanities involve creative works, in which organization and formatting will be up to you to decide. Whatever you are being asked to write, it's important to either research the topic and find credible sources, or ask your professor or mentor for examples of this type of writing.

Social Sciences

The social sciences field contains disciplines such as anthropology, sociology, history, and political science, among others. These disciplines are similar to the humanities in their organization; they will want straightforward writing containing an introduction, body paragraphs, and a conclusion. The social sciences are also dedicated to clear, informative writing. It's important to keep in mind to approach social science topics from a non-biased, objective tone, rather than a persuasive, personal tone that you

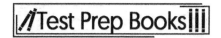

might take up in a humanities paper. Giving the most up-to-date information possible based on your content-base will establish you as a credible author and allow your readers to trust you.

Sciences

Writing in the sciences is much like other writing; it's important to identify your audience, present a clear, concise understanding of your topic, and to also remain objective in your findings. Science writing includes lab reports, peer-reviewed journal articles, grant proposals, and literature review articles. Credibility is extremely important in scientific writing, so it's imperative to use the correct styling and format when dealing with science writing. Most of the time, science writing uses APA style for publications, so it might be helpful to do research to find out exactly what APA-style writing entails.

Style Manual

A **style manual** is a comprehensive collection of guidelines for language use and document formatting. Some fields refer to a common style guide—e.g., the Associated Press or *AP Stylebook*, a standard in American journalism. Individual organizations may rely on their own house style. Regardless, the purpose of a style manual is to ensure uniformity across all documents. Style manuals explain things such as how to format titles, when to write out numbers or use numerals, and how to cite sources. Because there are many different style guides, students should know how and when to consult an appropriate guide. The Chicago Manual of Style is common in the publication of books and academic journals. The Modern Language Association style (MLA) is another commonly used academic style format, while the American Psychological Association style (APA) may be used for scientific publications. Familiarity with using a style guide is particularly important for students who are college bound or pursuing careers in academic or professional writing.

Narrating Historical Events and Describing Scientific Procedures/Experiments & Technical Processes

Writing informative or explanatory texts is helpful for anyone going into the social sciences, science, or technical field. As stated above, precision and conciseness are very important in this type of writing. Identifying the audience before the writing begins is also a helpful tip to guiding your writing toward the appropriate tone. Some examples of types of writing we will look at is narration of historical events, scientific procedures, and technical processes.

Narration of Historical Events

A trend in historical writing is writing in a narrative fashion about an event that happened in the past rather than an analytical document about a historical event. Historical narratives are either written in a traditional or modern narrative. Traditional narratives tend to focus more on the chronology of the event itself and does not pull in other contexts associated with that event. For example, a historical narrative written in the traditional format of the American Revolution would focus solely on events that happened within that world. Modern narratives focus more on causes of the event and are not afraid to bring in outside contexts to make sense of the event that is being narrated. For example, a modern form of the historical narrative dealing with the American Revolution may look at other revolutions around the same time as America in order to make sense of the collective social consciousness during that era.

Scientific Procedures/Experiments

Science procedures have specific directions regarding style and format. Most science procedures are written in APA-style format. This gives specific directions on how to write in-text citations, as well as what references will look like when the report is complete. Scientific procedures are also written in third person past tense. Third person means an objective tone, like the following:

> An experiment was conducted to see if helium balloons would rise in a zero-gravity chamber.

Rather than

> We did an experiment to see if helium balloons would rise in a zero-gravity chamber.

The first example is written in third person, while the second example is written in first person, because it uses "we."

Scientific procedures are also specific in that they usually include a set of steps you must adhere to. These include determining a problem, creating a hypothesis, designating what materials to use, explaining the procedure, recording the results, returning to the hypothesis, including any errors, and concluding with the analysis of the findings.

Technical Processes

Instructional and process reports explain how a thing is done. These documents are not limited only to technical fields. Your history professor can ask for a process report regarding the chronology of wars, or your writing professor can ask for a process report over how theory evolved over a period of time. Process reports may contain descriptive or prescriptive processes. Descriptive processes describe how something is done so that the audience can better grasp the content. Prescriptive processes are instructional, and they explain how something *should* be done so that someone else can read it and do it themselves. As in any other writing, it's important for process writing to be clear. Process writing is usually written in chronological order and has images or videos to accompany the material so that visual learners can understand the process as well.

Practice Quiz

1. Which of the following sentences has an error in capitalization?
   a. The East Coast has experienced very unpredictable weather this year.
   b. My Uncle owns a home in Florida, where he lives in the winter.
   c. I am taking English Composition II on campus this fall.
   d. There are several nice beaches we can visit on our trip to the Jersey Shore this summer.

2. Julia Robinson, an avid photographer in her spare time, was able to capture stunning shots of the local wildlife on her last business trip to Australia.
Which of the following is an adjective in the preceding sentence?
   a. Time
   b. Capture
   c. Avid
   d. Photographer

3. Which of the following sentences uses correct punctuation?
   a. Carole is not currently working; her focus is on her children at the moment.
   b. Carole is not currently working and her focus is on her children at the moment.
   c. Carole is not currently working, her focus is on her children at the moment.
   d. Carole is not currently working her focus is on her children at the moment.

4. Which of these examples is a compound sentence?
   a. Alex and Shane spent the morning coloring and later took a walk down to the park.
   b. After coloring all morning, Alex and Shane spent the afternoon at the park.
   c. Alex and Shane spent the morning coloring, and then they took a walk down to the park.
   d. After coloring all morning and spending part of the day at the park, Alex and Shane took a nap.

5. Which of these examples shows INCORRECT use of subject-verb agreement?
   a. Neither of the cars are parked on the street.
   b. Both of my kids are going to camp this summer.
   c. Any of your friends are welcome to join us on the trip in November.
   d. Each of the clothing options is appropriate for the job interview.

See answers on the next page.

Answer Explanations

1. B: In Choice *B* the word *Uncle* should not be capitalized because it is not functioning as a proper noun. If the word named a specific uncle, such as *Uncle Jerry*, then it would be considered a proper noun and should be capitalized. Choice *A* correctly capitalizes the proper noun *East Coast*. Choice *C* correctly capitalizes the name of a specific college course, which is considered a proper noun. Choice *D* correctly capitalizes the proper noun *Jersey Shore*.

2. C: In Choice *C*, *avid* is functioning as an adjective that modifies the word photographer. *Avid* describes the photographer Julia Robinson's style. The words *time* and *photographer* are functioning as nouns, and the word *capture* is functioning as a verb in the sentence. Other words functioning as adjectives in the sentence include *local*, *business*, and *spare*, as they all describe the nouns they precede.

3. A: Choice *A* is correct because it uses a semicolon to join the two independent clauses (clauses that could function as independent sentences). Choice *B* is incorrect because the conjunction is not preceded by a comma. A comma and conjunction should be used together to join independent clauses. Choice *C* is incorrect because a comma should only be used to join independent sentences when it also includes a coordinating conjunction such as *and* or *so*. Choice *D* does not use punctuation to join the independent clauses, so it is considered a fused (same as a run-on) sentence.

4. C: Choice *C* is a compound sentence because it joins two independent clauses with a comma and the coordinating conjunction *and*. The sentences in Choices *B* and *D* include one independent clause and one dependent clause, so they are complex sentences, not compound sentences. The sentence in Choice *A* has both a compound subject, *Alex and Shane*, and a compound verb, *spent and took*, but the entire sentence itself is one independent clause.

5. A: Choice *A* uses incorrect subject-verb agreement because the indefinite pronoun *neither* is singular and must use the singular verb form *is*. The pronoun *both* is plural and uses the plural verb form of *are*. The pronoun *any* can be either singular or plural. In this example, it is used as a plural, so the plural verb form is used. The pronoun *each* is singular and uses the singular verb form *is*.

Math

Geometry

Knowing Precise Definitions Relevant to Geometry

Algebraic equations can be used to describe geometric figures in the plane. The method for doing so is to use the **Cartesian coordinate plane**. The idea behind these Cartesian coordinates (named for mathematician and philosopher Descartes) is that from a specific point on the plane, known as the *center*, one can specify any other point by saying *how far to the right or left* and *how far up or down*.

The plane is covered with a grid. The two directions, right to left and bottom to top, are called **axes** (singular **axis**). When working with x- and y-variables, the x-variable corresponds to the right and left axis, and the y-variable corresponds to the up and down axis.

Any point on the grid is found by specifying how far to travel from the center along the x-axis and how far to travel along the y-axis. The ordered pair can be written as (x, y). A positive x-value means go to the right on the x-axis, while a negative x value means to go to the left. A positive y-value means to go up, while a negative value means to go down. Several points are shown as examples in the figure.

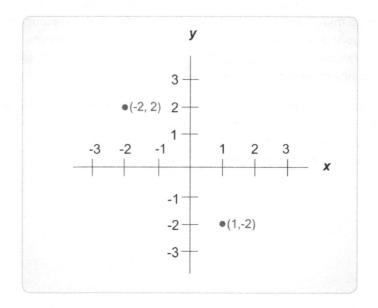

Cartesian Coordinate Plane

The coordinate plane can be divided into four **quadrants**. The upper-right part of the plane is called the **first quadrant**, where both x and y are positive. The **second quadrant** is the upper-left, where x is negative but y is positive. The **third quadrant** is the lower left, where both x and y are negative. Finally, the **fourth quadrant** is in the lower right, where x is positive but y is negative. These quadrants are often written with Roman numerals:

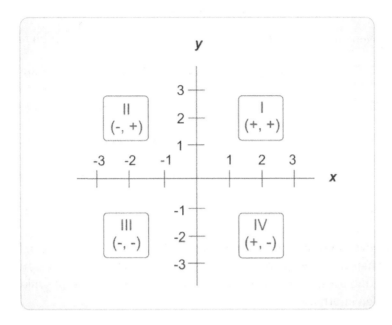

In addition to graphing individual points as shown above, the graph lines and curves in the plane can be graphed corresponding to equations. In general, if there is some equation involving x and y, then the **graph of that equation** consists of all the points (x, y) in the Cartesian coordinate plane, which satisfy this equation.

Given the equation $y = x + 2$, the point $(0, 2)$ is in the graph, since $2 = 0 + 2$ is a true equation. However, the point $(1, 4)$ will *not* be in the graph, because $4 = 1 + 2$ is false.

Straight Lines

The simplest equations to graph are the equations whose graphs are lines, called **linear equations**. Every linear equation can be rewritten algebraically so that it looks like $Ax + By = C$.

First, the ratio of the change in the y coordinate to the change in the x coordinate is constant for any two distinct points on the line. In any pair of points on a line, two points, (x_1, y_1) and (x_2, y_2)—where $x_1 \neq x_2$—the ratio $\frac{y_2 - y_1}{x_2 - x_1}$ will always be the same, even if another pair of points is used.

This ratio, $\frac{y_2 - y_1}{x_2 - x_1}$, is called the **slope of the line** and is often denoted with the letter m. If the slope is *positive*, then the line goes upward when moving to the right. If the slope is *negative*, then it moves downward when moving to the right. If the slope is 0, then the line is *horizontal*, and the y-coordinate is constant along the entire line. For lines where the x-coordinate is constant along the entire line, the slope is not defined, and these lines are called *vertical* lines.

The y-coordinate of the point where the line touches the y-axis is called the **y-intercept** of the line. It is often denoted by the letter b, used in the form of the linear equation $y = mx + b$. The x-coordinate of the point where the line touches the x-axis is called the **x-intercept**. It is also called the **zero of the line**.

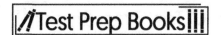

Suppose two lines have slopes m_1 and m_2. If the slopes are equal, $m_1 = m_2$, then the lines are **parallel**. Parallel lines never meet one another. If $m_1 = -\frac{1}{m_2}$, then the lines are called **perpendicular** or **orthogonal**. Their slopes can also be called opposite reciprocals of each other.

There are several convenient ways to write down linear equations. The common forms are listed here:

Standard Form: $Ax + By = C$, where the slope is given by $\frac{-A}{B}$, and the y-intercept is given by $\frac{C}{B}$.

Slope-Intercept Form: $y = mx + b$, where the slope is m, and the y-intercept is b.

Point-Slope Form: $y - y_1 = m(x - x_1)$, where m is the slope, and (x_1, y_1) is any point on the line.

Two-Point Form: $\frac{y - y_1}{x - x_1} = \frac{y_2 - y_1}{x_2 - x_1}$, where (x_1, y_1), and (x_2, y_2) are any two distinct points on the line.

Intercept Form: $\frac{x}{x_1} + \frac{y}{y_1} = 1$, where x_1 is the x-intercept, and y_1 is the y-intercept.

Depending upon the given information, different forms of the linear equation can be easier to write down than others. When given two points, the two-point form is easy to write down. If the slope and a single point is known, the point-slope form is easiest to start with. In general, which form to start with depends upon the given information.

Conics
The graph of an equation of the form $y = ax^2 + bx + c$ or $x = ay^2 + by + c$ is called a **parabola**.

The graph of an equation of the form $\frac{x^2}{a^2} - \frac{y^2}{b^2} = 1$ or $-\frac{x^2}{a^2} + \frac{y^2}{b^2} = 1$ is called a **hyperbola**.

The graph of an equation of the form $\frac{(x-x_0)^2}{a^2} + \frac{(y-y_0)^2}{b^2} = 1$ is called an **ellipse**. If $a = b$ then this is a circle with **radius** $r = \frac{1}{a}$.

Sets of Points in the Plane
The *midpoint* between two points, (x_1, y_1) and (x_2, y_2), is given by taking the average of the x-coordinates and the average of the y-coordinates:

$$\left(\frac{x_1 + x_2}{2}, \frac{y_1 + y_2}{2}\right)$$

The *distance* between two points, (x_1, y_1) and (x_2, y_2), is given by the **Pythagorean formula**:

$$\sqrt{(x_2 - x_1)^2 + (y_2 - y_1)^2}$$

To find the perpendicular distance between a line $Ax + By = C$ and a point (x_1, y_1) not on the line, we need to use the formula:

$$\frac{|Ax_1 + By_1 + C|}{\sqrt{A^2 + B^2}}$$

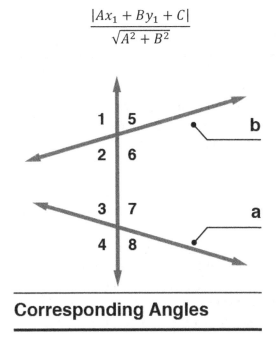

Corresponding Angles

Relationships between Angles

Supplementary angles add up to 180 degrees. **Vertical angles** are two nonadjacent angles formed by two intersecting lines. **Corresponding angles** are two angles in the same position whenever a straight line (known as a *transversal*) crosses two others. If the two lines are parallel, the corresponding angles are equal. **Alternate interior angles** are also a pair of angles formed when two lines are crossed by a transversal. They are opposite angles that exist inside of the two lines. In the corresponding angles diagram above, angles 2 and 7 are alternate interior angles, as well as angles 6 and 3.

Alternate exterior angles are opposite angles formed by a transversal but, in contrast to interior angles, exterior angles exist outside the two original lines. Therefore, angles 1 and 8 are alternate exterior angles and so are angles 5 and 4. Finally, **consecutive interior angles** are pairs of angles formed by a transversal. These angles are located on the same side of the transversal and inside the two original lines. Therefore, angles 2 and 3 are a pair of consecutive interior angles, and so are angles 6 and 7. These definitions are instrumental in solving many problems that involve determining relationships between angles.

Medians, Midpoints, and Altitudes

A **median** of a triangle is a line segment that connects a vertex to the midpoint on the other side of the triangle. A triangle has three medians, and their point of intersection is known as the **centroid**. An **altitude** is a line drawn from a vertex perpendicular to the opposite side. A triangle has three altitudes, and their point of intersection is known as the **orthocenter**. An altitude can actually exist outside, inside, or on the triangle depending on the placement of the vertex. Many problems involve these definitions. For example, given one endpoint of a line segment and the midpoint, the other endpoint can be determined by using the midpoint formula. In addition, area problems heavily depend on these definitions. For example, it can be proven that the median of a triangle divides it into two regions of equal areas. The actual formula for the area of a triangle depends on its altitude.

Special Triangles

An **isosceles triangle** contains at least two equal sides. Therefore, it must also contain two equal angles and, subsequently, contain two medians of the same length. An isosceles triangle can also be labelled as an **equilateral triangle** (which contains three equal sides and three equal angles) when it meets these conditions. In an equilateral triangle, the measure of each angle is always 60 degrees. Also, within an equilateral triangle, the medians are of the same length. A **scalene triangle** can never be an equilateral or an isosceles triangle because it contains no equal sides and no equal angles. Also, medians in a scalene triangle can't have the same length. However, a **right triangle**, which is a triangle containing a 90-degree angle, can be a scalene triangle.

There are two types of special right triangles. The *30-60-90 right triangle* has angle measurements of 30 degrees, 60 degrees, and 90 degrees. Because of the nature of this triangle, and through the use of the Pythagorean theorem, the side lengths have a special relationship. If x is the length opposite the 30-degree angle, the length opposite the 60-degree angle is $\sqrt{3}x$, and the hypotenuse has length $2x$. The *45-45-90 right triangle* is also special as it contains two angle measurements of 45 degrees. It can be proven that, if x is the length of the two equal sides, the hypotenuse is $x\sqrt{2}$. The properties of all of these special triangles are extremely useful in determining both side lengths and angle measurements in problems where some of these quantities are given and some are not.

Special Quadrilaterals

A special quadrilateral is one in which both pairs of opposite sides are parallel. This type of quadrilateral is known as a **parallelogram**. A parallelogram has six important properties:

- Opposite sides are congruent.
- Opposite angles are congruent.
- Within a parallelogram, consecutive angles are supplementary, so their measurements total 180 degrees.
- If one angle is a right angle, all of them have to be right angles.
- The diagonals of the angles bisect each other.
- These diagonals form two congruent triangles.

A parallelogram with four congruent sides is a **rhombus.** A quadrilateral containing only one set of parallel sides is known as a **trapezoid.** The parallel sides are known as bases, and the other two sides are known as legs. If the legs are congruent, the trapezoid can be labelled an **isosceles trapezoid.** An important property of an isosceles trapezoid is that its diagonals are congruent. Also, the median of a trapezoid is parallel to the bases, and its length is equal to half of the sum of the base lengths.

Quadrilateral Relationships

Rectangles, squares, and rhombuses are **polygons** with four sides. By definition, all rectangles are parallelograms, but only some rectangles are squares. However, some parallelograms are rectangles. Also, it's true that all squares are rectangles, and some rhombuses are squares. There are no rectangles, squares, or rhombuses that are trapezoids though, because they have more than one set of parallel sides.

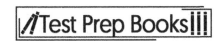

Diagonals and Angles

Diagonals are lines (excluding sides) that connect two vertices within a polygon. **Mutually bisecting diagonals** intersect at their midpoints. Parallelograms, rectangles, squares, and rhombuses have mutually bisecting diagonals. However, trapezoids don't have such lines. **Perpendicular diagonals** occur when they form four right triangles at their point of intersection. Squares and rhombuses have perpendicular diagonals, but trapezoids, rectangles, and parallelograms do not. Finally, **perpendicular bisecting** diagonals (also known as **perpendicular bisectors**) form four right triangles at their point of intersection, but this intersection is also the midpoint of the two lines. Both rhombuses and squares have perpendicular bisecting angles, but trapezoids, rectangles, and parallelograms do not. Knowing these definitions can help tremendously in problems that involve both angles and diagonals.

Polygons with More Than Four Sides

A **pentagon** is a five-sided figure. A six-sided shape is a **hexagon.** A seven-sided figure is classified as a **heptagon,** and an eight-sided figure is called an **octagon.** An important characteristic is whether a polygon is regular or irregular. If it's *regular*, the side lengths and angle measurements are all equal. An *irregular* polygon has unequal side lengths and angle measurements. Mathematical problems involving polygons with more than four sides usually involve side length and angle measurements. The sum of all internal angles in a polygon equals $180(n - 2)$ degrees, where n is the number of sides. Therefore, the total of all internal angles in a pentagon is 540 degrees because there are five sides so:

$$180(5 - 2) = 540 \text{ degrees}$$

Unfortunately, area formulas don't exist for polygons with more than four sides. However, their shapes can be split up into triangles, and the formula for area of a triangle can be applied and totaled to obtain the area for the entire figure.

Using Congruence and Similarity Criteria for Triangles

Similar Figures and Proportions

Sometimes, two figures are similar, meaning they have the same basic shape and the same interior angles, but they have different dimensions. If the ratio of two corresponding sides is known, then that ratio, or scale factor, holds true for all of the dimensions of the new figure.

Here is an example of applying this principle. Suppose that Lara is 5 feet tall and is standing 30 feet from the base of a light pole, and her shadow is 6 feet long. How high is the light on the pole? To figure this, it helps to make a sketch of the situation:

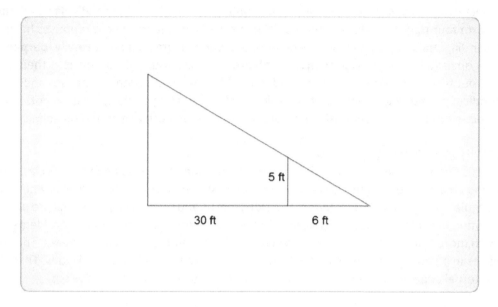

The light pole is the left side of the triangle. Lara is the 5-foot vertical line. Notice that there are two right triangles here, and that they have all the same angles as one another. Therefore, they form similar triangles. So, the ratio of proportionality between them must be determined.

The bases of these triangles are known. The small triangle, formed by Lara and her shadow, has a base of 6 feet. The large triangle formed by the light pole along with the line from the base of the pole out to the end of Lara's shadow is $30 + 6 = 36$ feet long. So, the ratio of the big triangle to the little triangle will be $\frac{36}{6} = 6$. The height of the little triangle is 5 feet. Therefore, the height of the big triangle will be $6 \times 5 = 30$ feet, meaning that the light is 30 feet up the pole.

Notice that the perimeter of a figure changes by the ratio of proportionality between two similar figures, but the area changes by the *square* of the ratio. This is because if the length of one side is doubled, the area is quadrupled.

As an example, suppose two rectangles are similar, but the edges of the second rectangle are three times longer than the edges of the first rectangle. The area of the first rectangle is 10 square inches. How much more area does the second rectangle have than the first?

To answer this, note that the area of the second rectangle is $3^2 = 9$ times the area of the first rectangle, which is 10 square inches. Therefore, the area of the second rectangle is going to be $9 \times 10 = 90$ square inches. This means it has $90 - 10 = 80$ square inches more area than the first rectangle.

As a second example, suppose X and Y are similar right triangles. The hypotenuse of X is 4 inches. The area of Y is $\frac{1}{4}$ the area of X. What is the hypotenuse of Y?

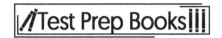

First, realize the area has changed by a factor of $\frac{1}{4}$. The area changes by a factor that is the *square* of the ratio of changes in lengths, so the ratio of the lengths is the square root of the ratio of areas. That means that the ratio of lengths must be is $\sqrt{\frac{1}{4}} = \frac{1}{2}$, and the hypotenuse of Y must be $\frac{1}{2} \times 4 = 2$ inches.

Volumes between similar solids change like the cube of the change in the lengths of their edges. Likewise, if the ratio of the volumes between similar solids is known, the ratio between their lengths is known by finding the cube root of the ratio of their volumes.

For example, suppose there are two similar rectangular pyramids X and Y. The base of X is 1 inch by 2 inches, and the volume of X is 8 inches. The volume of Y is 64 inches. What are the dimensions of the base of Y?

To answer this, first find the ratio of the volume of Y to the volume of X. This will be given by $\frac{64}{8} = 8$. Now the ratio of lengths is the cube root of the ratio of volumes, or $\sqrt[3]{8} = 2$. So, the dimensions of the base of Y must be 2 inches by 4 inches.

Proving Geometric Theorems
Proving Theorems About Lines and Angles
To prove any geometric theorem, the proven theorems must be linked in a logical order that flows from an original point to the desired result. Proving theorems about lines and angles is the basis of proving theorems that involve other shapes. A *transversal* is a line that passes through two lines at two points. Common theorems that need to be proved are: vertical angles are congruent; a transversal passing through two parallel lines forms two alternate interior angles that are congruent and two corresponding angles that are congruent; and points on a perpendicular bisector of a line segment are equidistant from the endpoints of the line segment.

Triangle Theorems
To prove **theorems** about triangles, basic definitions involving triangles (e.g., equilateral, isosceles, etc.) need to be known. Proven theorems concerning lines and angles can be applied to prove theorems about triangles. Common theorems to be proved include: the sum of all angles in a triangle equals 180 degrees; the sum of the lengths of two sides of a triangle is greater than the length of the third side; the base angles of an isosceles triangle are congruent; the line segment connecting the midpoint of two sides of a triangle is parallel to the third side and its length is half the length of the third side; and the medians of a triangle all meet at a single point.

Parallelogram Theorems
A **parallelogram** is a quadrilateral with parallel opposing sides. Within parallelograms, opposite sides and angles are congruent and the diagonals bisect each other. Known theorems about parallel lines, transversals, complementary angles, and congruent triangles can be used to prove theorems about parallelograms. Theorems that need to be proved include: opposite sides of a parallelogram are congruent; opposite angles are congruent; the diagonals bisect each other; and rectangles are parallelograms with congruent diagonals.

Determining Congruence
Two figures are **congruent** if there is a rigid motion that can map one figure onto the other. Therefore, all pairs of sides and angles within the image and pre-image must be congruent. For example, in

triangles, each pair of the three sides and three angles must be congruent. Similarly, in two four-sided figures, each pair of the four sides and four angles must be congruent.

Similarity

Two figures are *similar* if there is a combination of translations, reflections, rotations, and dilations, which maps one figure onto the other. The difference between congruence and similarity is that dilation can be used in similarity. Therefore, side lengths between each shape can differ. However, angle measure must be preserved within this definition. If two polygons differ in size so that the lengths of corresponding line segments differ by the same factor, but corresponding angles have the same measurement, they are similar.

Triangle Congruence

There are five theorems to show that triangles are congruent when it's unknown whether each pair of angles and sides are congruent. Each theorem is a shortcut that involves different combinations of sides and angles that must be true for the two triangles to be congruent. For example, *side-side-side (SSS)* states that if all sides are equal, the triangles are congruent. *Side-angle-side (SAS)* states that if two pairs of sides are equal and the included angles are congruent, then the triangles are congruent. Similarly, *angle-side-angle* (ASA) states that if two pairs of angles are congruent and the included side lengths are equal, the triangles are congruent.

Angle-angle-side (AAS) states that two triangles are congruent if they have two pairs of congruent angles and a pair of corresponding equal side lengths that aren't included. Finally, *hypotenuse-leg (HL)* states that if two right triangles have equal hypotenuses and an equal pair of shorter sides, then the triangles are congruent. An important item to note is that angle-angle-angle *(AAA)* is not enough information to have congruence. It's important to understand why these rules work by using rigid motions to show congruence between the triangles with the given properties. For example, three reflections are needed to show why *SAS* follows from the definition of congruence.

Similarity for Two Triangles

If two angles of one triangle are congruent with two angles of a second triangle, the triangles are similar. This is because, within any triangle, the sum of the angle measurements is 180 degrees. Therefore, if two are congruent, the third angle must also be congruent because their measurements are equal. Three congruent pairs of angles mean that the triangles are similar.

Proving Congruence and Similarity

The criteria needed to prove triangles are congruent involves both angle and side congruence. Both pairs of related angles and sides need to be of the same measurement to use congruence in a proof. The criteria to prove similarity in triangles involves proportionality of side lengths. Angles must be congruent in similar triangles; however, corresponding side lengths only need to be a constant multiple of each other. Once similarity is established, it can be used in proofs as well. Relationships in geometric figures other than triangles can be proven using triangle congruence and similarity. If a similar or congruent triangle can be found within another type of geometric figure, their criteria can be used to prove a relationship about a given formula. For instance, a rectangle can be broken up into two congruent triangles.

Transformations of a Plane

Given a figure drawn on a plane, many changes can be made to that figure, including **rotation**, **translation**, and **reflection**. Rotations turn the figure about a point, translations slide the figure, and

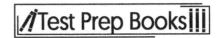

reflections flip the figure over a specified line. When performing these transformations, the original figure is called the *pre-image*, and the figure after transformation is called the *image*.

More specifically, *translation* means that all points in the figure are moved in the same direction by the same distance. In other words, the figure is slid in some fixed direction. Of course, while the entire figure is slid by the same distance, this does not change any of the measurements of the figures involved. The result will have the same distances and angles as the original figure.

In terms of Cartesian coordinates, a translation means a shift of each of the original points (x, y) by a fixed amount in the x and y directions, to become $(x + a, y + b)$.

Another procedure that can be performed is called *reflection*. To do this, a line in the plane is specified, called the **line of reflection**. Then, take each point and flip it over the line so that it is the same distance from the line but on the opposite side of it. This does not change any of the distances or angles involved, but it does reverse the order in which everything appears.

To reflect something over the x-axis, the points (x, y) are sent to $(x, -y)$. To reflect something over the y-axis, the points (x, y) are sent to the points $(-x, y)$. Flipping over other lines is not something easy to express in Cartesian coordinates. However, by drawing the figure and the line of reflection, the distance to the line and the original points can be used to find the reflected figure.

Example: Reflect this triangle with vertices $(-1, 0)$, $(2, 1)$, and $(2, 0)$ over the y-axis. The pre-image is shown below.

To do this, flip the x-values of the points involved to the negatives of themselves, while keeping the y-values the same. The image is shown here.

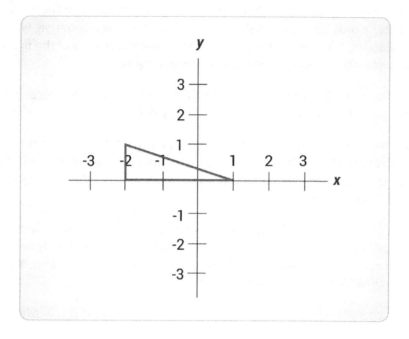

The new vertices will be $(1, 0)$, $(-2, 1)$, and $(-2, 0)$.

Another procedure that does not change the distances and angles in a figure is *rotation*. In this procedure, pick a center point, then rotate every vertex along a circle around that point by the same angle. This procedure is also not easy to express in Cartesian coordinates, and this is not a requirement on this test. However, as with reflections, it's helpful to draw the figures and see what the result of the rotation would look like. This transformation can be performed using a compass and protractor.

Each one of these transformations can be performed on the coordinate plane without changes to the original dimensions or angles.

If two figures in the plane involve the same distances and angles, they are called *congruent figures*. In other words, two figures are congruent when they go from one form to another through reflection, rotation, and translation, or a combination of these.

Remember that rotation and translation will give back a new figure that is identical to the original figure, but reflection will give back a mirror image of it.

To recognize that a figure has undergone a rotation, check to see that the figure has not been changed into a mirror image, but that its orientation has changed (that is, whether the parts of the figure now form different angles with the x- and y-axes).

To recognize that a figure has undergone a translation, check to see that the figure has not been changed into a mirror image, and that the orientation remains the same.

To recognize that a figure has undergone a reflection, check to see that the new figure is a mirror image of the old figure.

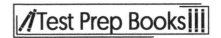

Keep in mind that sometimes a combination of translations, reflections, and rotations may be performed on a figure.

Dilation

A **dilation** is a transformation that preserves angles, but not distances. This can be thought of as stretching or shrinking a figure. If a dilation makes figures larger, it is called an *enlargement*. If a dilation makes figures smaller, it is called a *reduction*. The easiest example is to dilate around the origin. In this case, multiply the x- and y-coordinates by a *scale factor*, k, sending points (x, y) to (kx, ky).

As an example, draw a dilation of the following triangle, whose vertices will be the points $(-1, 0)$, $(1, 0)$, and $(1, 1)$.

For this problem, dilate by a scale factor of 2, so the new vertices will be $(-2, 0)$, $(2, 0)$, and $(2, 2)$.

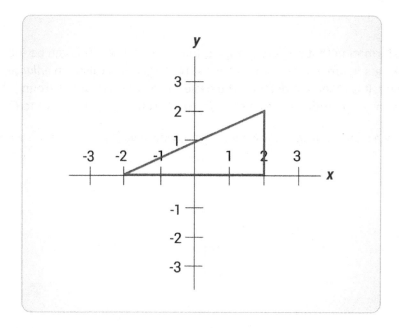

Note that after a dilation, the distances between the vertices of the figure will have changed, but the angles will remain the same. The two figures that are obtained by dilation, along with possibly translation, rotation, and reflection, are all *similar* to one another. Another way to think of this is that similar figures have the same number of vertices and edges, and their angles are all the same. Similar figures have the same basic shape, but are different in size.

Symmetry

Using the types of transformations above, if an object can undergo these changes and not appear to have changed, then the figure is symmetrical. If an object can be split in half by a line and flipped over that line to lie directly on top of itself, it is said to have **line symmetry**. An example of both types of figures is seen below.

Line of symmetry

If an object can be rotated about its center to any degree smaller than 360, and it lies directly on top of itself, the object is said to have **rotational symmetry**. An example of this type of symmetry is shown below. The pentagon has an order of 5.

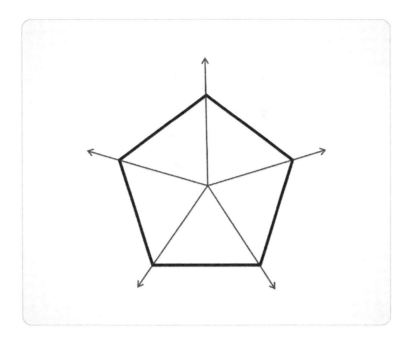

The rotational symmetry lines in the figure above can be used to find the angles formed at the center of the pentagon. Knowing that all of the angles together form a full circle, at 360 degrees, the figure can be split into 5 angles equally. By dividing the 360° by 5, each angle is 72°.

Given the length of one side of the figure, the perimeter of the pentagon can also be found using rotational symmetry. If one side length was 3 cm, that side length can be rotated onto each other side length four times. This would give a total of 5 side lengths equal to 3 cm. To find the perimeter, or distance around the figure, multiply 3 by 5. The perimeter of the figure would be 15 cm.

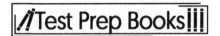
If a line cannot be drawn anywhere on the object to flip the figure onto itself or rotated less than or equal to 180 degrees to lay on top of itself, the object is asymmetrical. Examples of these types of figures are shown below.

Symmetric   Asymmetric

No line of symmetry

Using Volume Formulas to Solve Problems

Geometry in three dimensions is similar to geometry in two dimensions. The main new feature is that three points now define a unique **plane** that passes through each of them. Three dimensional objects can be made by putting together two-dimensional figures in different surfaces. Below, some of the possible three-dimensional figures will be provided, along with formulas for their volumes and surface areas.

A rectangular prism is a box whose sides are all rectangles meeting at 90° angles. Such a box has three dimensions: length, width, and height. If the length is x, the width is y, and the height is z, then the volume is given by $V = xyz$.

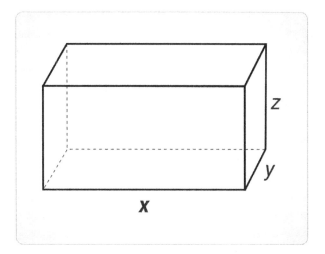

The surface area will be given by computing the surface area of each rectangle and adding them together. There are a total of six rectangles. Two of them have sides of length x and y, two have sides of length y and z, and two have sides of length x and z. Therefore, the total surface area will be given by:

$$SA = 2xy + 2yz + 2xz$$

A **rectangular pyramid** is a figure with a rectangular base and four triangular sides that meet at a single vertex. If the rectangle has sides of length x and y, then the volume will be given by:

$$V = \frac{1}{3}xyh$$

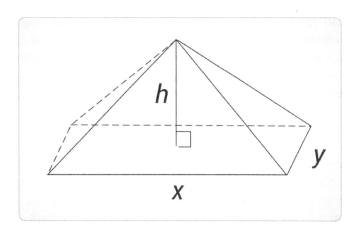

To find the surface area, the dimensions of each triangle need to be known. However, these dimensions can differ depending on the problem in question. Therefore, there is no general formula for calculating total surface area.

111

A **sphere** is a set of points all of which are equidistant from some central point. It is like a circle, but in three dimensions. The volume of a sphere of radius r is given by:

$$V = \frac{4}{3}\pi r^3$$

The surface area is given by:

$$A = 4\pi r^2$$

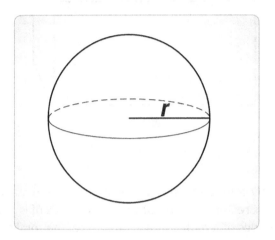

Applying Concepts of Density Based on Area and Volume in Modeling Situations

Real-World Geometry

Many real-world objects can be compared to geometric shapes. Describing certain objects using the measurements and properties of two- and three-dimensional shapes is an important part of geometry. For example, basic ideas such as angles and line segments can be seen in real-world objects. The corner of any room is an angle, and the intersection of a wall with the floor is like a line segment. Building upon this idea, entire objects can be related to both two- and three-dimensional shapes. An entire room can be thought of as square, rectangle, or a sum of a few three-dimensional shapes. Knowing what properties and measures are needed to make decisions in real life is why geometry is such a useful branch of mathematics. One obvious relationship between a real-life situation and geometry exists in construction. For example, to build an addition onto a house, several geometric measurements will be used.

Density

The **density** of a substance is the ratio of mass to area or volume. It's a relationship between the mass and how much space the object actually takes up. Knowing which units to use in each situation is crucial. Population density is an example of a real-life situation that's modeled by using density concepts. It involves calculating the ratio of the number of people to the number of square miles. The amount of material needed per a specific unit of area or volume is another application. For example, estimating the number of BTUs per cubic foot of a home is a measurement that relates to heating or cooling the house based on the desired temperature and the house's size.

Solving Design Problem

Design problems are an important application of geometry (e.g., building structures that satisfy physical constraints and/or minimize costs). These problems involve optimizing a situation based on what's given and required. For example, determining what size barn to build, given certain dimensions and a specific budget, uses both geometric properties and other mathematical concepts. Equations are formed using geometric definitions and the given constraints. In the end, such problems involve solving a system of equations and rely heavily on a strong background in algebra. **Typographic grid systems** also help with such design problems. A grid made up of intersecting straight or curved lines can be used as a visual representation of the structure being designed. This concept is seen in the blueprints used throughout the graphic design process.

The Pythagorean Theorem

The Pythagorean theorem is an important concept in geometry. It states that for right triangles, the sum of the squares of the two shorter sides will be equal to the square of the longest side (also called the **hypotenuse**). The longest side will always be the side opposite to the 90° angle. If this side is called c, and the other two sides are a and b, then the Pythagorean theorem states that:

$$c^2 = a^2 + b^2$$

Since lengths are always positive, this also can be written as:

$$c = \sqrt{a^2 + b^2}$$

A diagram to show the parts of a triangle using the Pythagorean theorem is below.

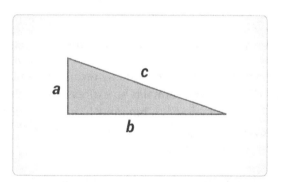

As an example of the theorem, suppose that Shirley has a rectangular field that is 5 feet wide and 12 feet long, and she wants to split it in half using a fence that goes from one corner to the opposite corner. How long will this fence need to be? To figure this out, note that this makes the field into two right triangles, whose hypotenuse will be the fence dividing it in half. Therefore, the fence length will be given by:

$$\sqrt{5^2 + 12^2} = \sqrt{169} = 13 \text{ feet long}$$

113

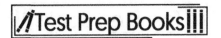 Math

Expressions and Equations

Algebraic Expressions

Algebraic expressions look similar to equations, but they do not include the equal sign. Algebraic expressions are comprised of numbers, variables, and mathematical operations. Some examples of algebraic expressions are:

$$8x + 7y - 12z, 3a^2$$

and

$$5x^3 - 4y^4$$

Algebraic expressions consist of variables, numbers, and operations. A **term** of an expression is any combination of numbers and/or variables, and terms are separated by addition and subtraction. For example, the expression $5x^2 - 3xy + 4 - 2$ consists of 4 terms: $5x^2$, $-3xy$, $4y$, and -2. Note that each term includes its given sign (+ or −). The **variable** part of a term is a letter that represents an unknown quantity. The coefficient of a term is the number by which the variable is multiplied. For the term $4y$, the variable is y and the coefficient is 4. Terms are identified by the power (or exponent) of its variable.

A number without a variable is referred to as a **constant**. If the variable is to the first power (x^1 or simply x), it is referred to as a **linear** term. A term with a variable to the second power (x^2) is **quadratic** and a term to the third power (x^3) is **cubic**. Consider the expression:

$$x^3 + 3x - 1$$

The constant is -1. The linear term is $3x$. There is no quadratic term. The cubic term is x^3.

An algebraic expression can also be classified by how many terms exist in the expression. Any like terms should be combined before classifying. A **monomial** is an expression consisting of only one term. Examples of monomials are: 17, $2x$, and $-5ab^2$. A **binomial** is an expression consisting of two terms separated by addition or subtraction. Examples include $2x - 4$ and $-3y^2 + 2y$. A **trinomial** consists of 3 terms. For example, $5x^2 - 2x + 1$ is a trinomial.

Algebraic expressions and equations can be used to represent real-life situations and model the behavior of different variables. For example, $2x + 5$ could represent the cost to play games at an arcade. In this case, 5 represents the price of admission to the arcade and 2 represents the cost of each game played. To calculate the total cost, use the number of games played for x, multiply it by 2, and add 5.

Adding and Subtracting Linear Algebraic Expressions

An algebraic expression is simplified by combining like terms. A term is a number, variable, or product of a number, and variables separated by addition and subtraction. For the algebraic expression:

$$3x^2 - 4x + 5 - 5x^2 + x - 3$$

the terms are $3x^2$, $-4x$, 5, $-5x^2$, x, and -3. **Like terms** have the same variables raised to the same powers (exponents). The like terms for the previous example are $3x^2$ and $-5x^2$, $-4x$ and x, 5 and -3.

114

To combine like terms, the coefficients (numerical factor of the term including sign) are added, and the variables and their powers are kept the same. Note that if a coefficient is not written, it is an implied coefficient of 1 ($x = 1x$). The previous example will simplify to $-2x^2 - 3x + 2$.

When adding or subtracting algebraic expressions, each expression is written in parentheses. The negative sign is distributed when necessary, and like terms are combined. Consider the following:

$$\text{add } 2a + 5b - 2 \text{ to } a - 2b + 8c - 4$$

The sum is set as follows:

$$(a - 2b + 8c - 4) + (2a + 5b - 2)$$

In front of each set of parentheses is an implied positive one, which, when distributed, does not change any of the terms. Therefore, the parentheses are dropped and like terms are combined:

$$a - 2b + 8c - 4 + 2a + 5b - 2$$

$$3a + 3b + 8c - 6$$

Consider the following problem:

$$\text{Subtract } 2a + 5b - 2 \text{ from } a - 2b + 8c - 4$$

The difference is set as follows:

$$(a - 2b + 8c - 4) - (2a + 5b - 2)$$

The implied one in front of the first set of parentheses will not change those four terms. However, distributing the implied -1 in front of the second set of parentheses will change the sign of each of those three terms:

$$a - 2b + 8c - 4 - 2a - 5b + 2$$

Combining like terms yields the simplified expression:

$$-a - 7b + 8c - 2$$

Multiplying Algebraic Expressions

The **distributive property** states that multiplying a sum (or difference) by a number produces the same result as multiplying each value in the sum (or difference) by the number and adding (or subtracting) the products. Using mathematical symbols, the distributive property states $a(b + c) = ab + ac$. The expression $4(3 + 2)$ is simplified using the order of operations. Simplifying inside the parentheses first produces 4×5, which equals 20. The expression $4(3 + 2)$ can also be simplified using the distributive property:

$$4(3 + 2)$$

$$4 \times 3 + 4 \times 2$$

$$12 + 8$$

$$20$$

Consider the following example:

$$4(3x - 2)$$

The expression cannot be simplified inside the parentheses because $3x$ and -2 are not like terms, and therefore cannot be combined. However, the expression can be simplified by using the distributive property and multiplying each term inside of the parentheses by the term outside of the parentheses: $12x - 8$. The resulting equivalent expression contains no like terms, so it cannot be further simplified.

Consider the expression:

$$(3x + 2y + 1) - (5x - 3) + 2(3y + 4)$$

Again, there are no like terms, but the distributive property is used to simplify the expression. Note there is an implied one in front of the first set of parentheses and an implied -1 in front of the second set of parentheses. Distributing the one, -1, and 2 produces:

$$1(3x) + 1(2y) + 1(1) - 1(5x) - 1(-3) + 2(3y) + 2(4)$$

$$3x + 2y + 1 - 5x + 3 + 6y + 8$$

This expression contains like terms that are combined to produce the simplified expression:

$$-2x + 8y + 12$$

Algebraic expressions are tested to be equivalent by choosing values for the variables and evaluating both expressions. For example, $4(3x - 2)$ and $12x - 8$ are tested by substituting 3 for the variable x and calculating to determine if equivalent values result.

Evaluating Algebraic Expressions

To evaluate the expression, the given values for the variables are substituted (or replaced) and the expression is simplified using the order of operations. Parentheses should be used when substituting. Consider the following: Evaluate $a - 2b + ab$ for $a = 3$ and $b = -1$. To evaluate, any variable a is replaced with 3 and any variable b with -1, producing:

$$(3) - 2(-1) + (3)(-1)$$

Next, the order of operations is used to calculate the value of the expression, which is 2.

116

Here's another example:

$$Evaluate \ a - 2b + ab \ for \ a = 3 \ and \ b = -1$$

To evaluate an expression, the given values should be substituted for the variables and simplified using the order of operations. In this case:

$$(3) - 2(-1) + (3)(-1)$$

Parentheses are used when substituting.

Given an algebraic expression, students may be asked to simplify the expression. For example:

$$Simplify \ 5x^2 - 10x + 2 - 8x^2 + x - 1.$$

Simplifying algebraic expressions requires combining like terms. A term is a number, variable, or product of a number and variables separated by addition and subtraction. The terms in the above expression are: $5x^2$, $-10x$, 2, $-8x^2$, x, and -1. Like terms have the same variables raised to the same powers (exponents). To combine like terms, the coefficients (numerical factor of the term including sign) are added, while the variables and their powers are kept the same. The example above simplifies to:

$$-3x^2 - 9x + 1$$

Let's try two more.

Evaluate $\frac{1}{2}x^2 - 3, x = 4$.

The first step is to substitute in 4 for x in the expression:

$$\frac{1}{2}(4)^2 - 3$$

Then, the order of operations is used to simplify.

The exponent comes first, $\frac{1}{2}(16) - 3$, then the multiplication, $8 - 3$, and then, after subtraction, the solution is 5.

Evaluate $4|5 - x| + 2y, x = 4, y = -3$.

The first step is to substitute 4 in for x and -3 in for y in the expression:

$$4|5 - 4| + 2(-3)$$

Then, the absolute value expression is simplified, which is:

$$|5 - 4| = |1| = 1$$

The expression is $4(1) + 2(-3)$ which can be simplified using the order of operations.

First is the multiplication, $4 + (-6)$; then addition yields an answer of -2.

Creating Algebraic Expressions

A linear expression is a statement about an unknown quantity expressed in mathematical symbols. The statement "five times a number added to forty" can be expressed as $5x + 40$. A linear equation is a statement in which two expressions (at least one containing a variable) are equal to each other. The statement "five times a number added to forty is equal to ten" can be expressed as $5x + 40 = 10$.

Real world scenarios can also be expressed mathematically. Suppose a job pays its employees $300 per week and $40 for each sale made. The weekly pay is represented by the expression $40x + 300$ where x is the number of sales made during the week.

Consider the following scenario: Bob had $20 and Tom had $4. After selling 4 ice cream cones to Bob, Tom has as much money as Bob. The cost of an ice cream cone is an unknown quantity and can be represented by a variable (x). The amount of money Bob has after his purchase is four times the cost of an ice cream cone subtracted from his original $20 → $20 - 4x$. The amount of money Tom has after his sale is four times the cost of an ice cream cone added to his original $4 → $4x + 4$. After the sale, the amount of money that Bob and Tom have is equal → $20 - 4x = 4x + 4$.

When expressing a verbal or written statement mathematically, it is key to understand words or phrases that can be represented with symbols. The following are examples:

Symbol	Phrase
$+$	added to, increased by, sum of, more than
$-$	decreased by, difference between, less than, take away
x	multiplied by, 3 (4, 5 ...) times as large, product of
$\div$	divided by, quotient of, half (third, etc.) of
$=$	is, the same as, results in, as much as
x, t, n, etc.	a number, unknown quantity, value of

One-Variable Linear Equations and Inequalities

Linear equations and **linear inequalities** are both comparisons of two algebraic expressions. However, unlike equations in which the expressions are equal, linear inequalities compare expressions that may be unequal. Linear equations typically have one value for the variable that makes the statement true. Linear inequalities generally have an infinite number of values that make the statement true.

When solving a linear equation, the desired result requires determining a numerical value for the unknown variable. If given a linear equation involving addition, subtraction, multiplication, or division, working backwards isolates the variable. Addition and subtraction are inverse operations, as are multiplication and division. Therefore, they can be used to cancel each other out.

For example, solve $4(t - 2) + 2t - 4 = 2(9 - 2t)$

Distributing: $4t - 8 + 2t - 4 = 18 - 4t$

Combining like terms: $6t - 12 = 18 - 4t$

Adding $4t$ to each side to move the variable: $10t - 12 = 18$

Adding 12 to each side to isolate the variable: $10t = 30$

118

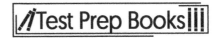

Dividing each side by 10 to isolate the variable: $t = 3$

The answer can be checked by substituting the value for the variable into the original equation, ensuring that both sides calculate to be equal.

Linear inequalities express the relationship between unequal values. More specifically, they describe in what way the values are unequal. A value can be greater than ($>$), less than ($<$), greater than or equal to ($\geq$), or less than or equal to ($\leq$) another value. $5x + 40 > 65$ is read as *five times a number added to forty is greater than sixty-five.*

When solving a linear inequality, the solution is the set of all numbers that make the statement true. The inequality $x + 2 \geq 6$ has a solution set of 4 and every number greater than 4 (4.01; 5; 12; 107; etc.). Adding 2 to 4 or any number greater than 4 results in a value that is greater than or equal to 6. Therefore, $x \geq 4$ is the solution set.

To algebraically solve a linear inequality, follow the same steps as those for solving a linear equation. The inequality symbol stays the same for all operations *except* when multiplying or dividing by a negative number. If multiplying or dividing by a negative number while solving an inequality, the relationship reverses (the sign flips). In other words, $>$ switches to $<$ and vice versa. Multiplying or dividing by a positive number does not change the relationship, so the sign stays the same. An example is shown below.

Solve $-2x - 8 \leq 22$ for the value of x.

Add 8 to both sides to isolate the variable:

$$-2x \leq 30$$

Divide both sides by -2 to solve for x:

$$x \geq -15$$

Solutions of a linear equation or a linear inequality are the values of the variable that make a statement true. In the case of a linear equation, the solution set (list of all possible solutions) typically consists of a single numerical value. To find the solution, the equation is solved by isolating the variable. For example, solving the equation $3x - 7 = -13$ produces the solution $x = -2$. The only value for x which produces a true statement is -2. This can be checked by substituting -2 into the original equation to check that both sides are equal. In this case,

$$3(-2) - 7 = -13 \rightarrow -13 = -13$$

Therefore, -2 is a solution.

Although linear equations generally have one solution, this is not always the case. If there is no value for the variable that makes the statement true, there is no solution to the equation. Consider the equation $x + 3 = x - 1$. There is no value for x in which adding 3 to the value produces the same result as subtracting one from the value. Conversely, if any value for the variable makes a true statement, the equation has an infinite number of solutions. Consider the equation:

$$3x + 6 = 3(x + 2)$$

119

Any number substituted for x will result in a true statement (both sides of the equation are equal).

By manipulating equations like the two above, the variable of the equation will cancel out completely. If the remaining constants express a true statement (ex. $6 = 6$), then all real numbers are solutions to the equation. If the constants left express a false statement (ex. $3 = -1$), then no solution exists for the equation.

Solving a linear inequality requires all values that make the statement true to be determined. For example, solving $3x - 7 \geq -13$ produces the solution $x \geq -2$. This means that -2 and any number greater than -2 produces a true statement. Solution sets for linear inequalities will often be displayed using a number line. If a value is included in the set ($\geq$ or $\leq$), a shaded dot is placed on that value and an arrow extending in the direction of the solutions. For a variable $>$ or $\geq$ a number, the arrow will point right on a number line, the direction where the numbers increase. If a variable is $<$ or $\leq$ a number, the arrow will point left on a number line, which is the direction where the numbers decrease. If the value is not included in the set ($>$ or $<$), an open (unshaded) circle on that value is used with an arrow in the appropriate direction.

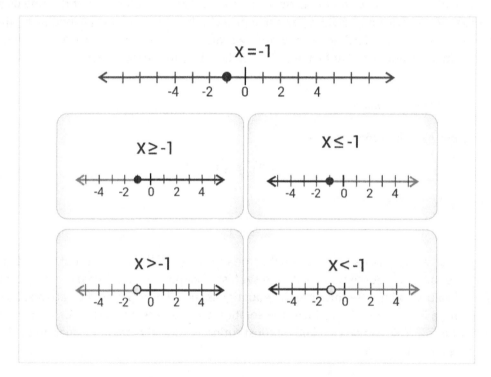

Similar to linear equations, a linear inequality may have a solution set consisting of all real numbers or can contain no solution. When solved algebraically, a linear inequality in which the variable cancels out and results in a true statement (ex. $7 \geq 2$) has a solution set of all real numbers. A linear inequality in which the variable cancels out and results in a false statement (ex. $7 \leq 2$) has no solution.

Linear Inequalities in One Variable

Linear inequalities and linear equations are both comparisons of two algebraic expressions. However, unlike equations in which the expressions are equal to each other, **linear inequalities** compare expressions that are unequal. Linear equations typically have one value for the variable that makes the statement true. Linear inequalities generally have an infinite number of values that make the statement true.

Linear inequalities are a concise mathematical way to express the relationship between unequal values. More specifically, they describe in what way the values are unequal. A value could be greater than ($>$); less than ($<$); greater than or equal to ($\geq$); or less than or equal to ($\leq$) another value. The statement "five times a number added to forty is more than sixty-five" can be expressed as $5x + 40 > 65$. Common words and phrases that express inequalities are:

Symbol	Phrase
$<$	is under, is below, smaller than, beneath
$>$	is above, is over, bigger than, exceeds
$\leq$	no more than, at most, maximum
$\geq$	no less than, at least, minimum

Solving Linear Inequalities

When solving a linear inequality, the solution is the set of all numbers that makes the statement true. The inequality $x + 2 \geq 6$ has a solution set of 4 and every number greater than 4 (4.0001, 5, 12, 107, etc.). Adding 2 to 4 or any number greater than 4 would result in a value that is greater than or equal to 6. Therefore, $x \geq 4$ would be the solution set.

Solution sets for linear inequalities often will be displayed using a number line. If a value is included in the set ($\geq$ or $\leq$), there is a shaded dot placed on that value and an arrow extending in the direction of the solutions. For a variable $>$ or $\geq$ a number, the arrow would point right on the number line (the direction where the numbers increase); and if a variable is $<$ or $\leq$ a number, the arrow would point left (where the numbers decrease). If the value is not included in the set ($>$ or $<$), an open circle on that value would be used with an arrow in the appropriate direction.

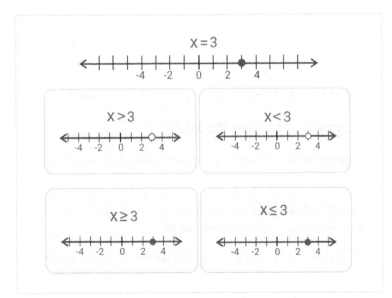

Students may be asked to write a linear inequality given a graph of its solution set. To do so, they should identify whether the value is included (shaded dot or open circle) and the direction in which the arrow is pointing.

In order to algebraically solve a linear inequality, the same steps should be followed as in solving a linear equation. The inequality symbol stays the same for all operations EXCEPT when multiplying or dividing by a negative number. If multiplying or dividing by a negative number while solving an inequality, the relationship reverses (the sign flips). Multiplying or dividing by a positive does not change the relationship, so the sign stays the same. In other words, $>$ switches to $<$ and vice versa. An example is shown below.

Solve $-2(x + 4) \leq 22$ for the value of x.

First, distribute -2 to the binomial by multiplying:

$$-2x - 8 \leq 22$$

Next, add 8 to both sides to isolate the variable:

$$-2x \leq 30$$

Divide both sides by -2 to solve for x:

$$x \geq -15$$

Systems of Two Linear Equations in Two Variables

A system of two linear equations in two variables is a set of equations that use the same variables, usually x and y. Here's a sample problem:

> An Internet provider charges an installation fee and a monthly charge. It advertises that two months of its offering costs $100 and six months costs $200. Find the monthly charge and the installation fee.

The two unknown quantities (variables) are the monthly charge and the installation fee. There are two different statements given relating the variables: two months added to the installation fee is $100; and six months added to the installation fee is $200. Using the variable x as the monthly charge and y as the installation fee, the statements can be written as the following: $2x + y = 100$; $6x + y = 200$. These two equations taken together form a system modeling the given scenario.

Systems of Linear Inequalities in Two Variables

A system of linear inequalities consists of two linear inequalities making comparisons between two variables. Students may be given a scenario and asked to express it as a system of inequalities:

> A consumer study calls for at least 60 adult participants. It cannot use more than 25 men. Express these constraints as a system of inequalities.

This can be modeled by the system: $x + y \geq 60$; $x \leq 25$, where x represents the number of men and y represents the number of women. A solution to the system is an ordered pair that makes both inequalities true when substituting the values for x and y.

Ratios and Proportional Relationships

Ratios and Proportional Relationships

Ratios are used to show the relationship between two quantities. The ratio of oranges to apples in the grocery store may be 3 to 2. That means that for every 3 oranges, there are 2 apples. This comparison can be expanded to represent the actual number of oranges and apples, such as 36 oranges to 24 apples. Another example may be the number of boys to girls in a math class. If the ratio of boys to girls is given as 2 to 5, that means there are 2 boys to every 5 girls in the class. Ratios can also be compared if the units in each ratio are the same. The ratio of boys to girls in the math class can be compared to the ratio of boys to girls in a science class by stating which ratio is higher and which is lower.

Rates are used to compare two quantities with different units. **Unit rates** are the simplest form of rate. With unit rates, the denominator in the comparison of two units is one. For example, if someone can type at a rate of 1,000 words in 5 minutes, then their unit rate for typing is $\frac{1,000}{5} = 200$ words in one minute or 200 words per minute. Any rate can be converted into a unit rate by dividing to make the denominator one. 1,000 words in 5 minutes has been converted into the unit rate of 200 words per minute.

Ratios and rates can be used together to convert rates into different units. For example, if someone is driving 50 kilometers per hour, that rate can be converted into miles per hour by using a ratio known as the **conversion factor**. Since the given value contains kilometers and the final answer needs to be in miles, the ratio relating miles to kilometers needs to be used. There are 0.62 miles in 1 kilometer. This, written as a ratio and in fraction form, is:

$$\frac{0.62 \text{ miles}}{1 \text{ km}}$$

To convert 50 km/hour into miles per hour, the following conversion needs to be set up:

$$\frac{50 \text{ km}}{\text{hour}} \times \frac{0.62 \text{ miles}}{1 \text{ km}} = 31 \text{ miles per hour}$$

The ratio between two similar geometric figures is called the **scale factor**. For example, a problem may depict two similar triangles, A and B. The scale factor from the smaller triangle A to the larger triangle B is given as 2 because the length of the corresponding side of the larger triangle, 16, is twice the corresponding side on the smaller triangle, 8. This scale factor can also be used to find the value of a missing side, x, in triangle A. Since the scale factor from the smaller triangle (A) to larger one (B) is 2, the larger corresponding side in triangle B (given as 25) can be divided by 2 to find the missing side in A ($x = 12.5$). The scale factor can also be represented in the equation $2A = B$ because two times the lengths of A gives the corresponding lengths of B. This is the idea behind similar triangles.

Unit Rate

Unit rate word problems will ask to calculate the rate or quantity of something in a different value. For example, a problem might say that a car drove a certain number of miles in a certain number of minutes and then ask how many miles per hour the car was traveling. These questions involve solving proportions. Consider the following examples:

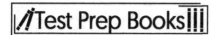

1) Alexandra made $96 during the first 3 hours of her shift as a temporary worker at a law office. She will continue to earn money at this rate until she finishes in 5 more hours. How much does Alexandra make per hour? How much will Alexandra have made at the end of the day?

This problem can be solved in two ways. The first is to set up a proportion, as the rate of pay is constant. The second is to determine her hourly rate, multiply the 5 hours by that rate, and then add the $96.

To set up a proportion, put the money already earned over the hours already worked on one side of an equation. The other side has x over 8 hours (the total hours worked in the day). It looks like this:

$$\frac{96}{3} = \frac{x}{8}$$

Now, cross-multiply to get $768 = 3x$. To get x, divide by 3, which leaves $x = 256$. Alternatively, as x is the numerator of one of the proportions, multiplying by its denominator will reduce the solution by one step. Thus, Alexandra will make $256 at the end of the day. To calculate her hourly rate, divide the total by 8, giving $32 per hour.

Alternatively, it is possible to figure out the hourly rate by dividing $96 by 3 hours to get $32 per hour. Now her total pay can be figured by multiplying $32 per hour by 8 hours, which comes out to $256.

2) Jonathan is reading a novel. So far, he has read 215 of the 335 total pages. It takes Jonathan 25 minutes to read 10 pages, and the rate is constant. How long does it take Jonathan to read one page? How much longer will it take him to finish the novel? Express the answer in time.

To calculate how long it takes Jonathan to read one page, divide the 25 minutes by 10 pages to determine the page per minute rate. Thus, it takes 2.5 minutes to read one page.

Jonathan must read 120 more pages to complete the novel. (This is calculated by subtracting the pages already read from the total.) Now, multiply his rate per page by the number of pages. Thus:

$$120 \times 2.5 = 300$$

Expressed in time, 300 minutes is equal to 5 hours.

3) At a hotel, $\frac{4}{5}$ of the 120 rooms are booked for Saturday. On Sunday, $\frac{3}{4}$ of the rooms are booked. On which day are more of the rooms booked, and by how many more?

The first step is to calculate the number of rooms booked for each day. Do this by multiplying the fraction of the rooms booked by the total number of rooms.

$$\text{Saturday: } \frac{4}{5} \times 120 = \frac{4}{5} \times \frac{120}{1} = \frac{480}{5} = 96 \text{ rooms}$$

$$\text{Sunday: } \frac{3}{4} \times 120 = \frac{3}{4} \times \frac{120}{1} = \frac{360}{4} = 90 \text{ rooms}$$

Thus, more rooms were booked on Saturday by 6 rooms.

4) In a veterinary hospital, the veterinarian-to-pet ratio is $1 : 9$. The ratio is always constant. If there are 45 pets in the hospital, how many veterinarians are currently in the veterinary hospital?

Set up a proportion to solve for the number of veterinarians: $\frac{1}{9} = \frac{x}{45}$

Cross-multiplying results in $9x = 45$, which works out to 5 veterinarians.

Alternatively, as there are always 9 times as many pets as veterinarians, it is possible to divide the number of pets (45) by 9. This also arrives at the correct answer of 5 veterinarians.

5) At a general practice law firm, 30% of the lawyers work solely on tort cases. If 9 lawyers work solely on tort cases, how many lawyers work at the firm?

First, solve for the total number of lawyers working at the firm, which will be represented here with x. The problem states that 9 lawyers work solely on torts cases, and they make up 30% of the total lawyers at the firm. Thus, 30% multiplied by the total, x, will equal 9. Written as equation, this is:

$$30\% \times x = 9$$

It's easier to deal with the equation after converting the percentage to a decimal, leaving $0.3x = 9$. Thus, $x = \frac{9}{0.3} = 30$ lawyers working at the firm.

6) Xavier was hospitalized with pneumonia. He was originally given 35 mg of antibiotics. Later, after his condition continued to worsen, Xavier's dosage was increased to 60 mg. What was the percent increase of the antibiotics? Round the percentage to the nearest tenth.

An increase or decrease in percentage can be calculated by dividing the difference in amounts by the original amount and multiplying by 100. Written as an equation, the formula is:

$$\frac{new\ quantity - old\ quantity}{old\ quantity} \times 100$$

Here, the question states that the dosage was increased from 35 mg to 60 mg, so these are plugged into the formula to find the percentage increase.

$$\frac{60 - 35}{35} \times 100 = \frac{25}{35} \times 100$$

$$0.7142 \times 100 = 71.4\%$$

Analyzing Proportional Relationships and Using Them

Much like a scale factor can be written using an equation like $2A = B$, a **relationship** is represented by the equation $Y = kX$. X and Y are proportional because as values of X increase, the values of Y also increase. A relationship that is inversely proportional can be represented by the equation $Y = \frac{k}{X}$, where the value of Y decreases as the value of x increases and vice versa.

Proportional reasoning can be used to solve problems involving ratios, percentages, and averages. Ratios can be used in setting up proportions and solving them to find unknowns. For example, if a student completes an average of 10 pages of math homework in 3 nights, how long would it take the student to complete 22 pages? Both ratios can be written as fractions. The second ratio would contain the unknown.

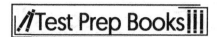

The following proportion represents this problem, where x is the unknown number of nights:

$$\frac{10 \text{ pages}}{3 \text{ nights}} = \frac{22 \text{ pages}}{x \text{ nights}}$$

Solving this proportion entails cross-multiplying and results in the following equation:

$$10x = 22 \times 3$$

Simplifying and solving for x results in the exact solution: $x = 6.6$ nights. The result would be rounded up to 7 because the homework would actually be completed on the 7th night.

The following problem uses ratios involving percentages:

If 20% of the class is girls and 30 students are in the class, how many girls are in the class?

To set up this problem, it is helpful to use the common proportion:

$$\frac{\%}{100} = \frac{is}{of}$$

Within the proportion, % is the percentage of girls, 100 is the total percentage of the class, *is* is the number of girls, and *of* is the total number of students in the class. Most percentage problems can be written using this language. To solve this problem, the proportion should be set up as $\frac{20}{100} = \frac{x}{30}$, and then solved for x. Cross-multiplying results in the equation $20 \times 30 = 100x$, which results in the solution $x = 6$. There are 6 girls in the class.

Ratios can be used to solve problems that concern length, volume, and other units. For example, a problem may ask for the volume of a cone to be found that has a radius, $r = 7$ m and a height, $h = 16$ m. Referring to the formulas provided on the test, the volume of a cone is given as: $V = \pi r^2 \frac{h}{3}$, where r is the radius, and h is the height. Plugging $r = 7$ and $h = 16$ into the formula, the following is obtained:

$$V = \pi(7^2)\frac{16}{3}$$

Therefore, the volume of the cone is found to be approximately 821 m³. Sometimes, answers in different units are sought. If this problem wanted the answer in liters, 821 m³ would need to be converted. Using the equivalence statement $1 \text{ m}^3 = 1{,}000$ L, the following ratio would be used to solve for liters:

$$821 \text{ m}^3 \times \frac{1{,}000 \text{ L}}{1 \text{ m}^3}$$

Cubic meters in the numerator and denominator cancel each other out, and the answer is converted to 821,000 liters, or 8.21×10^5 L.

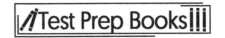

Other conversions can also be made between different given and final units. If the temperature in a pool is 30°C, what is the temperature of the pool in degrees Fahrenheit? To convert these units, an equation is used relating Celsius to Fahrenheit. The following equation is used:

$$T_{°F} = 1.8T_{°C} + 32$$

Plugging in the given temperature and solving the equation for T yields the result:

$$T_{°F} = 1.8(30) + 32 = 86°F$$

Units in both the metric system and U.S. customary system are widely used.

Here are some more examples of how to solve for proportions:

1) $\frac{75\%}{90\%} = \frac{25\%}{x}$

To solve for x, the fractions must be cross multiplied:

$$(75\%x = 90\% \times 25\%)$$

To make things easier, let's convert the percentages to decimals:

$$(0.9 \times 0.25 = 0.225 = 0.75x)$$

To get rid of x's coefficient, each side must be divided by that same coefficient to get the answer:

$$x = 0.3$$

The question could ask for the answer as a percentage or fraction in lowest terms, which are 30% and $\frac{3}{10}$, respectively.

2) $\frac{x}{12} = \frac{30}{96}$

Cross-multiply: $96x = 30 \times 12$

Multiply: $96x = 360$

Divide: $x = 360 \div 96$

Answer: $x = 3.75$

3) $\frac{0.5}{3} = \frac{x}{6}$

Cross-multiply: $3x = 0.5 \times 6$

Multiply: $3x = 3$

Divide: $x = 3 \div 3$

Answer: $x = 1$

You may have noticed there's a faster way to arrive at the answer. If there is an obvious operation being performed on the proportion, the same operation can be used on the other side of the proportion to solve for x. For example, in the first practice problem, 75% became 25% when divided by 3, and upon doing the same to 90%, the correct answer of 30% would have been found with much less legwork. However, these questions aren't always so intuitive, so it's a good idea to work through the steps, even if the answer seems apparent from the outset.

Statistics and Probability

Representing Data with Plots on the Real Number Line

Interpretation of Tables, Charts, and Graphs
Data can be represented in many ways. It is important to be able to organize the data into categories that could be represented using one of these methods. Equally important is the ability to read these types of diagrams and interpret their meaning.

Data in Tables
One of the most common ways to express data is in a table. The primary reason for plugging data into a table is to make interpretation more convenient. It's much easier to look at the table than to analyze results in a narrative paragraph. When analyzing a table, pay close attention to the title, variables, and data.

Let's analyze a theoretical antibiotic study. The study has 6 groups, named A through F, and each group receives a different dose of medicine. The results of the study are listed in the table below.

Results of Antibiotic Studies		
Group	**Dosage of Antibiotics in milligrams (mg)**	**Efficacy (% of participants cured)**
A	0 mg	20%
B	20 mg	40%
C	40 mg	75%
D	60 mg	95%
E	80 mg	100%
F	100 mg	100%

Tables generally list the title immediately above the data. The title should succinctly explain what is listed below. Here, "Results of Antibiotic Studies" informs the audience that the data pertains to the results of a scientific study on antibiotics.

Identifying the variables at play is one of the most important parts of interpreting data. Remember, the independent variable is intentionally altered, and its change is independent of the other variables. Here, the dosage of antibiotics administered to the different groups is the independent variable. The study is intentionally manipulating the strength of the medicine to study the related results. Efficacy is the dependent variable since its results *depend* on a different variable, the dose of antibiotics. Generally, the independent variable will be listed before the dependent variable in tables.

128

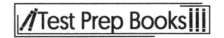

Also, pay close attention to the variables' labels. Here, the dose is expressed in milligrams (mg) and efficacy in percentages (%). Keep an eye out for questions referencing data in a different unit measurement, or questions asking for a raw number when only the percentage is listed.

Now that the nature of the study and variables at play have been identified, the data itself needs be interpreted. Group A did not receive any of the medicine. As discussed earlier, Group A is the control, as it reflects the amount of people cured in the same timeframe without medicine. It's important to see that efficacy positively correlates with the dosage of medicine. A question using this study might ask for the lowest dose of antibiotics to achieve 100% efficacy. Although Group E and Group F both achieve 100% efficacy, it's important to note that Group E reaches 100% with a lower dose.

Data in Graphs

Graphs provide a visual representation of data. The variables are placed on the two axes. The bottom of the graph is referred to as the horizontal axis or X-axis. The left-hand side of the graph is known as the vertical axis or Y-axis. Typically, the independent variable is placed on the X-axis, and the dependent variable is located on the Y-axis. Sometimes, the X-axis is a timeline, and the dependent variables for different trials or groups have been measured throughout points in time; time is still an independent variable but is not always immediately thought of as the independent variable being studied.

The most common types of graphs are the bar graph and the line graph.

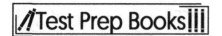

The **bar graph** above expresses the data from the table entitled "Results of Antibiotic Studies." To interpret the data for each group in the study, look at the top of their bars and read the corresponding efficacy on the *Y*-axis.

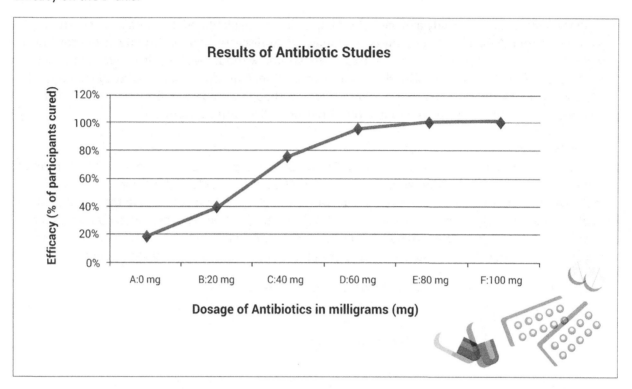

Here, the same data is expressed on a *line graph*. The points on the line correspond with each data entry. Reading the data on the line graph works like the bar graph. The data trend is measured by the slope of the line.

Data in Other Charts
Chart is a broad term that refers to a variety of ways to represent data.

To graph relations, the *Cartesian plane* is used. This means to think of the plane as being given a grid of squares, with one direction being the x-axis and the other direction the y-axis. Generally, the independent variable is placed along the horizontal axis, and the dependent variable is placed along the vertical axis. Any point on the plane can be specified by saying how far to go along the x-axis and how far along the y-axis with a pair of numbers (x, y). Specific values for these pairs can be given names such as $C = (-1, 3)$. Negative values mean to move left or down; positive values mean to move right or up. The point where the axes cross one another is called the *origin*. The origin has coordinates $(0, 0)$ and is usually called O when given a specific label. An illustration of the Cartesian plane, along with the plotted points $(2, 1)$ and $(-1, -1)$, is below.

A **line plot** is a diagram that shows quantity of data along a number line. It is a quick way to record data in a structure similar to a bar graph without needing to do the required shading of a bar graph. Here is an example of a line plot:

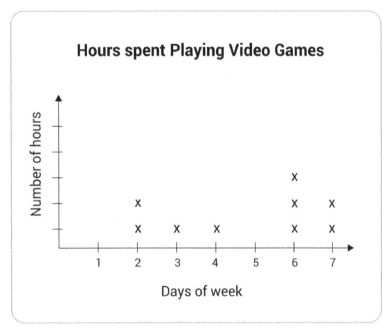

A **tally chart** is a diagram in which tally marks are utilized to represent data. Tally marks are a means of showing a quantity of objects within a specific classification. Here is an example of a tally chart:

Number of days with rain	Number of weeks
0	‖
1	⧄
2	⧄	
3	⧄ ‖‖
4	⧄ ⧄ ⧄
5	⧄
6	⧄	
7	‖‖

Data is often recorded using fractions, such as half a mile, and understanding fractions is critical because of their popular use in real-world applications. Also, it is extremely important to label values with their units when using data. For example, regarding length, the number 2 is meaningless unless it is attached to a unit. Writing 2 cm shows that the number refers to the length of an object.

A **picture graph** is a diagram that shows pictorial representation of data being discussed. The symbols used can represent a certain number of objects. Notice how each fruit symbol in the following graph represents a count of two fruits. One drawback of picture graphs is that they can be less accurate if each symbol represents a large number. For example, if each banana symbol represented ten bananas, and students consumed 22 bananas, it may be challenging to draw and interpret two and one-fifth bananas as a frequency count of 22.

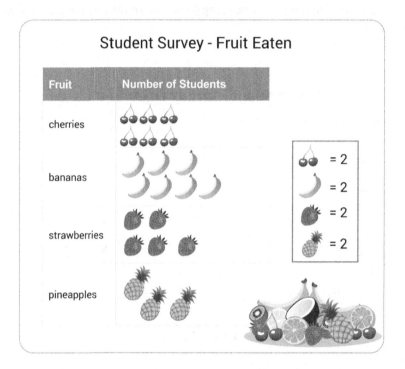

A circle graph, also called a pie chart, shows categorical data with each category representing a percentage of the whole data set. To make a circle graph, the percent of the data set for each category must be determined. To do so, the frequency of the category is divided by the total number of data points and converted to a percent. For example, if 80 people were asked what their favorite sport is and

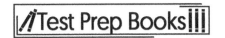

20 responded basketball, basketball makes up 25% of the data ($\frac{20}{80} = 0.25 = 25\%$). Each category in a data set is represented by a *slice* of the circle proportionate to its percentage of the whole.

FAVORITE SPORT

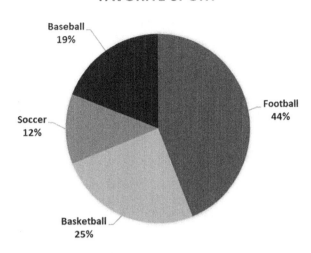

A **scatter plot** displays the relationship between two variables. Values for the independent variable, typically denoted by x, are paired with values for the dependent variable, typically denoted by y. Each set of corresponding values are written as an ordered pair (x, y). To construct the graph, a coordinate grid is labeled with the x-axis representing the independent variable and the y-axis representing the dependent variable. Each ordered pair is graphed.

Like a scatter plot, a line graph compares two variables that change continuously, typically over time. Paired data values (ordered pair) are plotted on a coordinate grid with the x- and y-axis representing the two variables. A line is drawn from each point to the next, going from left to right. A double line graph simply displays two sets of data that contain values for the same two variables. The double line

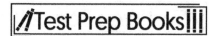

graph below displays the profit for given years (two variables) for Company A and Company B (two data sets).

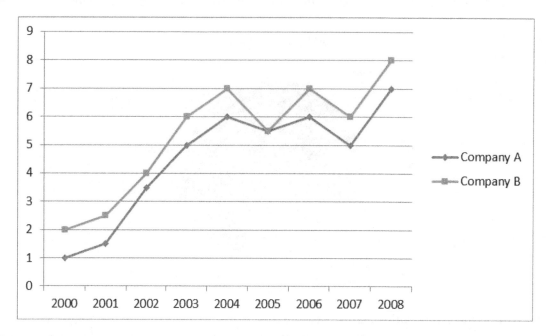

Choosing the appropriate graph to display a data set depends on what type of data is included in the set and what information must be shown.

Scatter plots and line graphs can be used to display data consisting of two variables. Examples include height and weight, or distance and time. A correlation between the variables is determined by examining the points on the graph. Line graphs are used if each value for one variable pairs with a distinct value for the other variable. Line graphs show relationships between variables.

Interpreting Competing Data

Be careful of questions with competing studies. These questions will ask the student to interpret which of two studies shows the greater amount or the higher rate of change between two results.

Here's an example. A research facility runs studies on two different antibiotics: Drug A and Drug B. The Drug A study includes 1,000 participants and cures 600 people. The Drug B study includes 200 participants and cures 150 people. Which drug is more successful?

The first step is to determine the percentage of each drug's rate of success. Drug A was successful in curing 60% of participants, while Drug B achieved a 75% success rate. Thus, Drug B is more successful based on these studies, even though it cured fewer people.

Sample size and experiment consistency should also be considered when answering questions based on competing studies. Is one study significantly larger than the other? In the antibiotics example, the Drug A study is five times larger than Drug B. Thus, Drug B's higher efficacy (desired result) could be a result of the smaller sample size, rather than the quality of drug.

Consistency between studies is directly related to sample size. Let's say the research facility elects to conduct more studies on Drug B. In the next study, there are 400 participants, and 200 are cured. The success rate of the second study is 50%. The results are clearly inconsistent with the first study, which

134

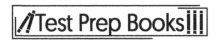

means more testing is needed to determine the drug's efficacy. A hallmark of mathematical or scientific research is repeatability. Studies should be consistent and repeatable, with an appropriately large sample size, before drawing extensive conclusions.

Histograms and Box Plots

To construct a **histogram**, the range of the data points is divided into equal intervals. The frequency for each interval is then determined, which reveals how many points fall into each interval. A graph is constructed with the vertical axis representing the frequency and the horizontal axis representing the intervals. The lower value of each interval should be labeled along the horizontal axis. Finally, for each interval, a bar is drawn from the lower value of each interval to the lower value of the next interval with a height equal to the frequency of the interval. Because of the intervals, histograms do not have any gaps between bars along the horizontal axis.

To construct a **box (or box-and-whisker) plot**, the five-number summary for the data set is calculated as follows: the second quartile (Q_2) is the median of the set. The first quartile (Q_1) is the median of the values below Q_2. The third quartile (Q_3) is the median of the values above Q_2. The upper extreme is the highest value in the data set if it is not an outlier (greater than 1.5 times the interquartile range $Q_3 - Q_1$). The lower extreme is the least value in the data set if it is not an outlier (more than 1.5 times lower than the interquartile range). To construct the box-and-whisker plot, each value is plotted on a number line, along with any outliers. The *box* consists of Q_1 and Q_3 as its *top* and *bottom* and Q_2 as the dividing line inside the box. The *whiskers* extend from the lower extreme to Q_1 and from Q_3 to the upper extreme.

Box Plot

Choice of Graphs to Display Data

Choosing the appropriate graph to display a data set depends on what type of data is included in the set and what information must be displayed. Histograms and box plots can be used for data sets consisting of individual values across a wide range. Examples include test scores and incomes. Histograms and box plots will indicate the center, spread, range, and outliers of a data set. A histogram will show the shape of the data set, while a box plot will divide the set into quartiles (25% increments), allowing for comparison between a given value and the entire set.

Scatter plots and line graphs can be used to display data consisting of two variables. Examples include height and weight, or distance and time. A correlation between the variables is determined by examining the points on the graph. Line graphs are used if each value for one variable pairs with a distinct value for the other variable. Line graphs show relationships between variables.

Line plots, bar graphs, and circle graphs are all used to display categorical data, such as surveys. Line plots and bar graphs both indicate the frequency of each category within the data set. A line plot is used when the categories consist of numerical values. For example, the number of hours of TV watched by individuals is displayed on a line plot. A bar graph is used when the categories consists of words. For

135

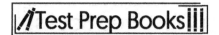
example, the favorite ice cream of individuals is displayed with a bar graph. A circle graph can be used to display either type of categorical data. However, unlike line plots and bar graphs, a circle graph does not indicate the frequency of each category. Instead, the circle graph represents each category as its percentage of the whole data set.

Interpreting Differences in Shape, Center, and Spread

A set of data can be described in terms of its center, spread, shape and any unusual features. The center of a data set can be measured by its mean, median, or mode. The spread of a data set refers to how far the data points are from the center (mean or median). The spread can be measured by the range or by the quartiles and interquartile range. A data set with all its data points clustered around the center will have a small spread. A data set covering a wide range of values will have a large spread.

When a data set is displayed as a histogram or frequency distribution plot, the shape indicates if a sample is normally distributed, symmetrical, or has measures of skewness or kurtosis. When graphed, a data set with a normal distribution will resemble a bell curve.

If the data set is symmetrical, each half of the graph when divided at the center is a mirror image of the other. If the graph has fewer data points to the right, the data is skewed right. If it has fewer data points to the left, the data is skewed left.

Right-Skewed   Symmetric   Left-Skewed

Kurtosis is a measure of whether the data is heavy-tailed with a high number of outliers, or light-tailed with a low number of outliers.

A description of a data set should include any unusual features such as gaps or outliers. A gap is a span within the range of the data set containing no data points. An outlier is a data point with a value either extremely large or extremely small when compared to the other values in the set.

136

Normal Distribution

A **normal distribution** of data follows the shape of a bell curve. In a normal distribution, the data set's median, mean, and mode are equal. Therefore, 50 percent of its values are less than the mean and 50 percent are greater than the mean. Data sets that follow this shape can be generalized using normal distributions. Normal distributions are described as **frequency distributions** in which the data set is plotted as percentages rather than true data points. A **relative frequency distribution** is one where the y-axis is between zero and 1, which is the same as 0% to 100%.

Within a standard deviation, 68 percent of the values are within 1 standard deviation of the mean, 95 percent of the values are within 2 standard deviations of the mean, and 99.7 percent of the values are within 3 standard deviations of the mean. The number of standard deviations that a data point falls from the mean is called the *z-score*. The formula for the z-score is $Z = \frac{x-\mu}{\sigma}$, where μ is the mean, σ is the standard deviation, and x is the data point. This formula is used to fit any data set that resembles a normal distribution to a standard normal distribution in a process known as **standardizing**. Here is a normal distribution with labelled z-scores:

Normal Distribution with Labelled Z-Scores

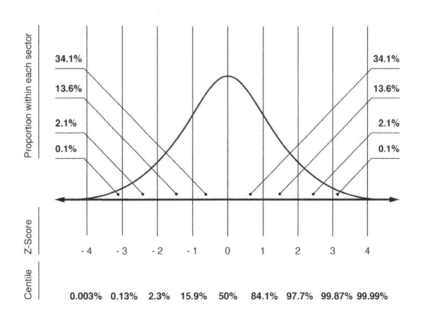

Population percentages can be estimated using normal distributions. For example, the probability that a data point will be less than the mean, or that the z-score will be less than 0, is 50%. Similarly, the probability that a data point will be within 1 standard deviation of the mean, or that the z-score will be between -1 and 1, is about 68.2%. When using a z-table, the left column states how many standard deviations (to one decimal place) away from the mean the point is, and the row heading states the second decimal place. The entries in the table corresponding to each column and row give the probability, which is equal to the area.

137

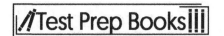

Measures of Center and Range

The center of a set of data (statistical values) can be represented by its mean, median, or mode. These are sometimes referred to as measures of central tendency. The mean is the average of the data set. The mean can be calculated by adding the data values and dividing by the sample size (the number of data points). Suppose a student has test scores of 93, 84, 88, 72, 91, and 77. To find the mean, or average, the scores are added and the sum is divided by 6 because there are 6 test scores:

$$\frac{93 + 84 + 88 + 72 + 91 + 77}{6} = \frac{505}{6} = 84.17$$

Given the mean of a data set and the sum of the data points, the sample size can be determined by dividing the sum by the mean. Suppose you are told that Kate averaged 12 points per game and scored a total of 156 points for the season. The number of games that she played (the sample size or the number of data points) can be determined by dividing the total points (sum of data points) by her average (mean of data points): $\frac{156}{12} = 13$. Therefore, Kate played in 13 games this season.

If given the mean of a data set and the sample size, the sum of the data points can be determined by multiplying the mean and sample size. Suppose you are told that Tom worked 6 days last week for an average of 5.5 hours per day. The total number of hours worked for the week (sum of data points) can be determined by multiplying his daily average (mean of data points) by the number of days worked (sample size): $5.5 \times 6 = 33$. Therefore, Tom worked a total of 33 hours last week.

The median of a data set is the value of the data point in the middle when the sample is arranged in numerical order. To find the median of a data set, the values are written in order from least to greatest. The lowest and highest values are simultaneously eliminated, repeating until the value in the middle remains. Suppose the salaries of math teachers are: $35,000; $38,500; $41,000; $42,000; $42,000; $44,500; $49,000. The values are listed from least to greatest to find the median. The lowest and highest values are eliminated until only the middle value remains. Repeating this step three times reveals a median salary of $42,000. If the sample set has an even number of data points, two values will remain after all others are eliminated. In this case, the mean of the two middle values is the median. Consider the following data set: 7, 9, 10, 13, 14, 14. Eliminating the lowest and highest values twice leaves two values, 10 and 13, in the middle. The mean of these values $\left(\frac{10+13}{2}\right)$ is the median. Therefore, the set has a median of 11.5.

The mode of a data set is the value that appears most often. A data set may have a single mode, multiple modes, or no mode. If different values repeat equally as often, multiple modes exist. If no value repeats, no mode exists. Consider the following data sets:

- A: 7, 9, 10, 13, 14, 14
- B: 37, 44, 33, 37, 49, 44, 51, 34, 37, 33, 44
- C: 173, 154, 151, 168, 155

Set A has a mode of 14. Set B has modes of 37 and 44. Set C has no mode.

The range of a data set is the difference between the highest and the lowest values in the set. The range can be considered the span of the data set. To determine the range, the smallest value in the set is subtracted from the largest value. The ranges for the data sets A, B, and C above are calculated as follows: A: $14 - 7 = 7$; B: $51 - 33 = 18$; C: $173 - 151 = 22$.

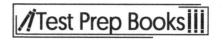

Best Description of a Set of Data

Measures of central tendency, namely mean, median, and mode, describe characteristics of a set of data. Specifically, they are intended to represent a *typical* value in the set by identifying a central position of the set. Depending on the characteristics of a specific set of data, different measures of central tendency are more indicative of a typical value in the set.

When a data set is grouped closely together with a relatively small range and the data is spread out somewhat evenly, the mean is an effective indicator of a typical value in the set. Consider the following data set representing the height of sixth grade boys in inches: 61 inches, 54 inches, 58 inches, 63 inches, 58 inches. The mean of the set is 58.8 inches. The data set is grouped closely (the range is only 9 inches) and the values are spread relatively evenly (three values below the mean and two values above the mean). Therefore, the mean value of 58.8 inches is an effective measure of central tendency in this case.

When a data set contains a small number of values either extremely large or extremely small when compared to the other values, the mean is not an effective measure of central tendency. Consider the following data set representing annual incomes of homeowners on a given street: $71,000; $74,000; $75,000; $77,000; $340,000. The mean of this set is $127,400. This figure does not indicate a typical value in the set, which contains four out of five values between $71,000 and $77,000. The median is a much more effective measure of central tendency for data sets such as these. Finding the middle value diminishes the influence of outliers, or numbers that may appear out of place, like the $340,000 annual income. The median for this set is $75,000 which is much more typical of a value in the set.

The mode of a data set is a useful measure of central tendency for categorical data when each piece of data is an option from a category. Consider a survey of 31 commuters asking how they get to work with results summarized below.

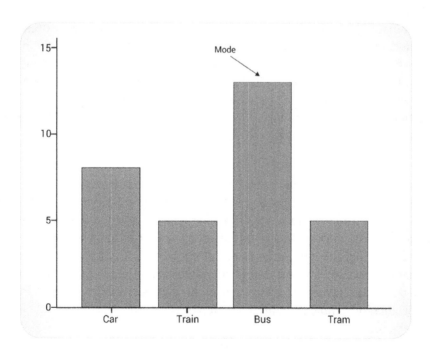

The mode for this set represents the value, or option, of the data that repeats most often. This indicates that the bus is the most popular method of transportation for the commuters.

Effects of Changes in Data

Changing all values of a data set in a consistent way produces predictable changes in the measures of the center and range of the set. A linear transformation changes the original value into the new value by either adding a given number to each value, multiplying each value by a given number, or both. Adding (or subtracting) a given value to each data point will increase (or decrease) the mean, median, and any modes by the same value. However, the range will remain the same due to the way that range is calculated. Multiplying (or dividing) a given value by each data point will increase (or decrease) the mean, median, and any modes, and the range by the same factor.

Consider the following data set, call it set P, representing the price of different cases of soda at a grocery store: $4.25, $4.40, $4.75, $4.95, $4.95, $5.15. The mean of set P is $4.74. The median is $4.85. The mode of the set is $4.95. The range is $0.90. Suppose the state passes a new tax of $0.25 on every case of soda sold. The new data set, set T, is calculated by adding $0.25 to each data point from set P. Therefore, set T consists of the following values: $4.50, $4.65, $5.00, $5.20, $5.20, $5.40. The mean of set T is $4.99. The median is $5.10. The mode of the set is $5.20. The range is $.90. The mean, median and mode of set T is equal to $0.25 added to the mean, median, and mode of set P. The range stays the same.

Now suppose, due to inflation, the store raises the cost of every item by 10 percent. Raising costs by 10 percent is calculated by multiplying each value by 1.1. The new data set, set I, is calculated by multiplying each data point from set T by 1.1. Therefore, set I consists of the following values: $4.95, $5.12, $5.50, $5.72, $5.72, $5.94. The mean of set I is $5.49. The median is $5.61. The mode of the set is $5.72. The range is $0.99. The mean, median, mode, and range of set I is equal to 1.1 multiplied by the mean, median, mode, and range of set T because each increased by a factor of 10 percent.

Comparing Data

Data sets can be compared by looking at the center and spread of each set. Measures of central tendency involve median, mean, midrange, and mode. The **mode** of a data set is the data value or values that appears the most frequently. The **midrange** is equal to the maximum value plus the minimum value divided by two. The **median** is the value that is halfway into each data set; it splits the data into two intervals. The **mean** is the sum of all data values divided by the number of data points. Two completely different sets of data can have the same mean. For example, a data set having values ranging from 0 to 100 and a data set having values ranging from 44 to 46 could both have means equal to 50.

The first data set would have a much wider range, which is known as the **spread** of the data. It measures how varied the data is within each set. Spread can be defined further as either interquartile range or standard deviation. The **interquartile range (IQR)** is the range of the middle fifty percent of the data set. The **standard deviation**, s, quantifies the amount of variation with respect to the mean. A lower standard deviation shows that the data set does not differ much from the mean. A larger standard deviation shows that the data set is spread out farther away from the mean. The formula used for standard deviation depends on whether it's being used for a population or a sample (a subset of a population). The formula for sample standard deviation is:

$$s = \sqrt{\frac{\sum(x - \bar{x})^2}{n - 1}}$$

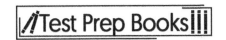

In this formula, s represents the standard deviation value, x is each value in the data set, $\bar{x}$ is the sample mean, and n is the total number of data points in the set. Note that sample standard deviations use *one less than the total* in the denominator. The population standard deviation formula is similar:

$$\sigma = \sqrt{\frac{\Sigma(x - \mu)^2}{N}}$$

For population standard deviations, sigma (σ) represents the standard deviation, x represents each value in the data set, mu (μ) is the population mean, and N is the total number of data points for the population. The square of the standard deviation is known as the **variance** of the data set. A data set can have outliers, and measures of central tendency that are not affected by outliers are the mode and median. Those measures are labeled as resistant measures of center.

Summarizing Categorical Data

Two-Way Frequency Tables

Data that isn't described using numbers is known as **categorical data.** For example, age is numerical data but hair color is categorical data. Categorical data is summarized using two-way frequency tables. A **two-way frequency table** counts the relationship between two sets of categorical data. There are rows and columns for each category, and each cell represents frequency information that shows the actual data count between each combination.

For example, the graphic on the left-side below is a two-way frequency table showing the number of girls and boys taking language classes in school. Entries in the middle of the table are known as the **joint frequencies**. For example, the number of girls taking French class is 12, which is a joint frequency. The totals are the **marginal frequencies**. For example, the total number of boys is 20, which is a marginal frequency. If the frequencies are changed into percentages based on totals, the table is known as a **two-way relative frequency table**. Percentages can be calculated using the table total, the row totals, or the column totals. Here's the process of obtaining the two-way relative frequency table using the table total:

Two-Way Frequency Table

	Spanish	French	German	Total
Boys	10	2	8	**20**
Girls	15	12	3	**30**
Total	**25**	**14**	**11**	**50**

Joint frequencies
Marginal frequencies

Divide all tables entries by the table total (50)

Two-Way Relative Frequency Table (with respect to table total)

	Spanish	French	German	Total
Boys	0.2	0.04	0.16	**0.40**
Girls	0.3	0.24	0.06	**0.60**
Total	**0.5**	**0.28**	**0.22**	**1.00**

The middle entries are known as **joint probabilities** and the totals are **marginal probabilities.** In this data set, it appears that more girls than boys take Spanish class. However, that might not be the case

141

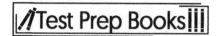

because more girls than boys were surveyed, and the results might be misleading. To avoid such errors, **conditional relative frequencies** are used. The relative frequencies are calculated based on a row or column.

Here are the conditional relative frequencies using column totals:

Two-Way Frequency Table

	Spanish	French	German	Total
Boys	10	2	8	20
Girls	15	12	3	30
Total	25	14	11	50

Divide each column entry by that column's total →

Two-Way Relative Frequency Table (with respect to table total)

	Spanish	French	German	Total
Boys	0.4	0.14	0.73	0.4
Girls	0.6	0.86	0.27	0.6
Total	1.00	1.00	1.00	1.00

Data Conclusions

Two-way frequency tables can help in making many conclusions about the data. If either the row or column of conditional relative frequencies differs between each row or column of the table, then an association exists between the two categories. For example, in the above tables, the majority of boys are taking German while the majority of girls are taking French. If the frequencies are equal across the rows, there is no association, and the variables are labelled as independent. It's important to note that the association does exist in the above scenario, though these results may not occur the next semester when students are surveyed.

Plotting Variables

A **scatter plot** is a way to visually represent the relationship between two variables. Each variable has its own axis, and usually the independent variable is plotted on the horizontal axis while the dependent variable is plotted on the vertical axis. Data points are plotted in a process that's similar to how ordered pairs are plotted on an xy-plane. Once all points from the data set are plotted, the scatter plot is finished. Below is an example of a scatter plot that's plotting the quality and price of an item. Note that price is the independent variable and quality is the dependent variable:

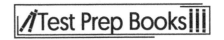

In this example, the quality of the item increases as the price increases.

Interpreting the Slope and the Intercept of a Linear Model in the Context of the Data

Linear Regression

Regression lines are a way to calculate a relationship between the independent variable and the dependent variable. A straight line means that there's a linear trend in the data. Technology can be used to find the equation of this line (e.g., a graphing calculator or Microsoft Excel®). In either case, all of the data points are entered, and a line is "fit" that best represents the shape of the data. Other functions used to model data sets include quadratic and exponential models.

Estimating Data Points

Regression lines can be used to estimate data points not already given. For example, if an equation of a line is found that fit the temperature and beach visitor data set, its input is the average daily temperature and its output is the projected number of visitors. Thus, the number of beach visitors on a 100-degree day can be estimated. The output is a data point on the regression line, and the number of daily visitors is expected to be greater than on a 96-degree day because the regression line has a positive slope.

Plotting and Analyzing Residuals

Once the function is found that fits the data, its accuracy can be calculated. Therefore, how well the line fits the data can be determined. The difference between the actual dependent variable from the data set and the estimated value located on the regression line is known as a *residual*. Therefore, the residual is known as the predicted value $\hat{y}$ minus the actual value y. A residual is calculated for each data point and can be plotted on the scatterplot. If all the residuals appear to be approximately the same distance from the regression line, the line is a good fit. If the residuals seem to differ greatly across the board, the line isn't a good fit.

Interpreting the Regression Line

The formula for a regression line is $y = mx + b$, where m is the slope and b is the y-intercept. Both the slope and y-intercept are found in the **Method of Least Squares**, which is the process of finding the equation of the line through minimizing residuals. The slope represents the rate of change in y as x gets larger. Therefore, because y is the dependent variable, the slope actually provides the predicted values given the independent variable. The y-intercept is the predicted value for when the independent variable equals zero. In the temperature example, the y-intercept is the expected number of beach visitors for a very cold average daily temperature of zero degrees.

Correlation Coefficient

The **correlation coefficient** (r) measures the association between two variables. Its value is between -1 and 1, where -1 represents a perfect negative linear relationship, 0 represents no relationship, and 1 represents a perfect positive linear relationship. A **negative linear relationship** means that as x-values increase, y-values decrease. A **positive linear relationship** means that as x-values increase, y-values increase. The formula for computing the correlation coefficient is:

$$r = \frac{n(\sum xy) - (\sum x)(\sum y)}{\sqrt{n(\sum x^2) - (\sum x)^2}\sqrt{n(\sum y^2) - (\sum y)^2}}$$

143

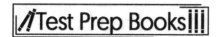

n is the number of data points

Both Microsoft Excel® and a graphing calculator can evaluate this easily once the data points are entered. A correlation greater than 0.8 or less than -0.8 is classified as "strong" while a correlation between -0.5 and 0.5 is classified as "weak."

Data Gathering Techniques

The three most common types of data gathering techniques are sample surveys, experiments, and observational studies. **Sample surveys** involve collecting data from a random sample of people from a desired population. The measurement of the variable is only performed on this set of people. To have accurate data, the sampling must be unbiased and random. For example, surveying students in an advanced calculus class on how much they enjoy math classes is not a useful sample if the population should be all college students based on the research question.

An **experiment** is the method by which a hypothesis is tested using a controlled process called the scientific method. A cause and the effect of that cause are measured, and the hypothesis is accepted or rejected. Experiments are usually completed in a controlled environment where the results of a control population are compared to the results of a test population. The groups are selected using a randomization process in which each group has a representative mix of the population being tested. Finally, an **observational study** is similar to an experiment. However, this design is used when circumstances prevent or do not allow for a designated control group and experimental group (e.g., lack of funding or unrealistic expectations). Instead, existing control and test populations must be used, so this method has a lack of randomization.

Population Mean and Proportion

Both the population mean and proportion can be calculated using data from a sample. The **population mean** (μ) is the average value of the parameter for the entire population. Due to size constraints, finding the exact value of μ is impossible, so the mean of the sample population is used as an estimate instead. The larger the sample size, the closer the sample mean gets to the population mean. An alternative to finding μ is to find the **proportion** of the population, which is the part of the population with the given characteristic. The proportion can be expressed as a decimal, a fraction, or a percentage, and can be given as a single value or a range of values. Because the population mean and proportion are both estimates, there's a **margin of error**, which is the difference between the actual value and the expected value.

T-Tests

A **randomized experiment** is used to compare two treatments by using statistics involving a *t-test*, which tests whether two data sets are significantly different from one another. To use a *t*-test, the test statistic must follow a normal distribution. The first step of the test involves calculating the *t*-value, which is given as:

$$t = \frac{\overline{x_1} - \overline{x_2}}{s_{\bar{x}_1 - \bar{x}_2}}$$

$\bar{x}_1$ and $\bar{x}_2$ are the averages of the two samples. Also,

$$s_{\bar{x}_1 - \bar{x}_2} = \sqrt{\frac{s_1^2}{n_1} + \frac{s_2^2}{n_2}}$$

144

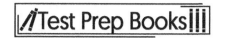

s_1 and s_2 are the standard deviations of each sample and n_1 and n_2 are their respective sample sizes. The **degrees of freedom** for two samples are calculated as the following (rounded to the lowest whole number).

$$df = \frac{(n_1 - 1) + (n_2 - 1)}{2}$$

Also, a significance level α must be chosen, where a typical value is $\alpha = 0.05$. Once everything is compiled, the decision is made to use either a **one-tailed test** or a **two-tailed test**. If there's an assumed difference between the two treatments, a one-tailed test is used. If no difference is assumed, a two-tailed test is used.

Analyzing Test Results

Once the type of test is determined, the **t-value**, significance level, and degrees of freedom are applied to the published table showing the **t distribution**. The row is associated with degrees of freedom and each column corresponds to the probability. The t-value can be exactly equal to one entry or lie between two entries in a row. For example, consider a t-value of 1.7 with degrees of freedom equal to 30. This **test statistic** falls between the p-values of 0.05 and 0.025. For a one-tailed test, the corresponding p-value lies between 0.05 and 0.025. For a two-tailed test, the p-values need to be doubled so the corresponding p-value falls between 0.1 and 0.05. Once the probability is known, this range is compared to α. If $p < \alpha$, the hypothesis is rejected. If $p > \alpha$, the hypothesis isn't rejected. In a two-tailed test, this scenario means the hypothesis is accepted that there's no difference in the two treatments. In a one-tailed test, the hypothesis is accepted, indicating that there's a difference in the two treatments.

Evaluating Completed Tests

In addition to applying statistical techniques to actual testing, evaluating completed tests is another important aspect of statistics. Reports can be read that already have conclusions, and the process can be evaluated using learned concepts. For example, deciding if a sample being used is appropriate. Other things that can be evaluated include determining if the samples are randomized or the results are significant. Once statistical concepts are understood, the knowledge can be applied to many applications.

Distinguishing Between Correlation and Causation

In an experiment, variables are the key to analyzing data, especially when data is in a graph or table. Variables can represent anything, including objects, conditions, events, and amounts of time.

Covariance is a general term referring to how two variables move in relation to each other. Take for example an employee that gets paid by the hour. For them, hours worked and total pay have a positive covariance. As hours worked increases, so does pay.

Constant variables remain unchanged by the scientist across all trials. Because they are held constant for all groups in an experiment, they aren't being measured in the experiment, and they are usually ignored. Constants can either be controlled by the scientist directly like the nutrition, water, and sunlight given to plants, or they can be selected by the scientist specifically for an experiment like using a certain animal species or choosing to investigate only people of a certain age group.

Independent variables are also controlled by the scientist, but they are the same only for each group or trial in the experiment. Each group might be composed of students that all have the same color of car or each trial may be run on different soda brands. The independent variable of an experiment is what is being indirectly tested because it causes change in the dependent variables.

Dependent variables experience change caused by the independent variable and are what is being measured or observed. For example, college acceptance rates could be a dependent variable of an experiment that sorted a large sample of high school students by an independent variable such as test scores. In this experiment, the scientist groups the high school students by the independent variable (test scores) to see how it affects the dependent variable (their college acceptance rates).

Note that most variables can be held constant in one experiment, but also serve as the independent variable or a dependent variable in another. For example, when testing how well a fertilizer aids plant growth, its amount of sunlight should be held constant for each group of plants, but if the experiment is being done to determine the proper amount of sunlight a plant should have, the amount of sunlight is an independent variable because it is necessarily changed for each group of plants.

Correlation

An **X-Y diagram**, also known as a **scatter diagram**, visually displays the relationship between two variables. The independent variable is placed on the **x-axis**, or horizontal axis, and the dependent variable is placed on the **y-axis**, or vertical axis.

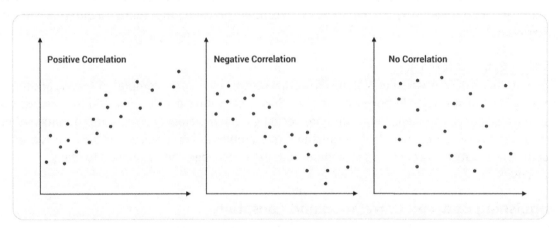

As shown in the figures above, an X-Y diagram may result in positive, negative, or no correlation between the two variables. In the first scatter plot, as the Y factor increases, the X factor increases as well. The opposite is true as well: as the X factor increases the Y factor also increases. Thus, there is a positive correlation because one factor appears to positively affect the other factor

Correlation Versus Causation

It's important to note, however, that a positive **correlation** between two variables doesn't equate to a cause-and-effect relationship. For example, a positive correlation between labor hours and units produced may not equate to a cause-and-effect relationship between the two. Any instance of correlation only indicates how likely the presence of one variable is in the instance of another. The variables should be further analyzed to determine which, if any, other variables (i.e., quality of employee work) may contribute to the positive correlation.

Correlation and causation have two different meanings. If two values are correlated, there is an association between them. However, correlation doesn't necessarily mean that one variable causes the other. **Causation** (or "cause and effect") occurs when one variable causes the other. Average daily temperature and number of beachgoers are correlated and have causation. If the temperature increases, the change in weather causes more people to go to the beach. However, alcoholism and smoking are correlated but don't have causation. The more someone drinks the more likely they are to smoke, but drinking alcohol doesn't cause someone to smoke.

The Number System

Rational Numbers

All real numbers can be separated into two groups: rational and irrational numbers. **Rational numbers** are any numbers that can be written as a fraction, such as $\frac{1}{3}$, $\frac{7}{4}$, and -25. Alternatively, **irrational numbers** are those that cannot be written as a fraction, such as numbers with never-ending, non-repeating decimal values. Many irrational numbers result from taking roots, such as $\sqrt{2}$ or $\sqrt{3}$. An irrational number may be written as:

$$34.5684952\ldots$$

The ellipsis (...) represents the line of numbers after the decimal that does not repeat and is never-ending.

When rational and irrational numbers interact, there are different types of number outcomes. For example, when adding or multiplying two rational numbers, the result is a rational number. No matter what two fractions are added or multiplied together, the result can always be written as a fraction. The following expression shows two rational numbers multiplied together:

$$\frac{3}{8} \times \frac{4}{7} = \frac{12}{56}$$

The product of these two fractions is another fraction that can be simplified to $\frac{3}{14}$.

As another interaction, rational numbers added to irrational numbers will always result in irrational numbers. No part of any fraction can be added to a never-ending, non-repeating decimal to make a rational number. The same result is true when multiplying a rational and irrational number. Taking a fractional part of a never-ending, non-repeating decimal will always result in another never-ending, non-repeating decimal. An example of the product of rational and irrational numbers is shown in the following expression: $2 \times \sqrt{7}$.

The last type of interaction concerns two irrational numbers, where the sum or product may be rational or irrational depending on the numbers being used. The following expression shows a rational sum from two irrational numbers:

$$\sqrt{3} + \left(6 - \sqrt{3}\right) = 6$$

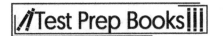

The product of two irrational numbers can be rational or irrational. A rational result can be seen in the following expression:

$$\sqrt{2} \times \sqrt{8} = \sqrt{2 \times 8} = \sqrt{16} = 4$$

An irrational result can be seen in the following:

$$\sqrt{3} \times \sqrt{2} = \sqrt{6}$$

Structure of the Number System

The mathematical number system is made up of two general types of numbers: real and complex. **Real numbers** are both irrational and rational numbers, while **complex numbers** are those composed of both a real number and an imaginary one. Imaginary numbers are the result of taking the square root of -1, and $\sqrt{-1} = i$.

The real number system is often explained using a Venn diagram similar to the one below. After a number has been labeled as a real number, further classification occurs when considering the other groups in this diagram. If a number is a never-ending, non-repeating decimal, it falls in the irrational category. Otherwise, it is rational. More information on these types of numbers is provided in the previous section. Furthermore, if a number does not have a fractional part, it is classified as an integer, such as -2, 75, or zero. Whole numbers are an even smaller group that only includes positive integers and zero. The last group of natural numbers is made up of only positive integers, such as 2, 56, or 12.

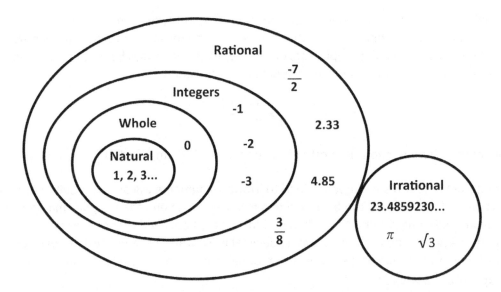

Real numbers can be compared and ordered using the number line. If a number falls to the left on the real number line, it is less than a number on the right. For example, $-2 < 5$ because -2 falls to the left of zero, and 5 falls to the right. Numbers to the left of zero are negative while those to the right are positive.

Complex numbers are made up of the sum of a real number and an imaginary number. Some examples of complex numbers include $6 + 2i$, $5 - 7i$, and $-3 + 12i$. Adding and subtracting complex numbers is similar to collecting like terms. The real numbers are added together, and the imaginary numbers are

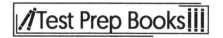
added together. For example, if the problem asks to simplify the expression $6 + 2i - 3 + 7i$, the 6 and (-3) are combined to make 3, and the $2i$ and $7i$ combine to make $9i$. Multiplying and dividing complex numbers is similar to working with exponents.

One rule to remember when multiplying is that $i \times i = -1$. For example, if a problem asks to simplify the expression $4i(3 + 7i)$, the $4i$ should be distributed throughout the 3 and the $7i$. This leaves the final expression $12i - 28$. The 28 is negative because $i \times i$ results in a negative number. The last type of operation to consider with complex numbers is the conjugate. The **conjugate** of a complex number is a technique used to change the complex number into a real number. For example, the conjugate of $4 - 3i$ is $4 + 3i$. Multiplying $(4 - 3i)(4 + 3i)$ results in $16 + 12i - 12i + 9$, which has a final answer of $16 + 9 = 25$.

The order of operations—PEMDAS—simplifies longer expressions with real or imaginary numbers. Each operation is listed in the order of how they should be completed in a problem containing more than one operation. Parentheses can also mean grouping symbols, such as brackets and absolute value. Then, exponents are calculated. Multiplication and division should be completed from left to right, and addition and subtraction should be completed from left to right.

Simplification of another type of expression occurs when radicals are involved. Root is another word for radical. For example, the following expression is a radical that can be simplified: $\sqrt{24x^2}$. First, the number must be factored out to the highest perfect square. Any perfect square can be taken out of a radical. Twenty-four can be factored into 4 and 6, and 4 can be taken out of the radical. $\sqrt{4} = 2$ can be taken out, and 6 stays underneath. If $x > 0$, x can be taken out of the radical because it is a perfect square. The simplified radical is $2x\sqrt{6}$. An approximation can be found using a calculator.

There are also properties of numbers that are true for certain operations. The **commutative** property allows the order of the terms in an expression to change while keeping the same final answer. Both addition and multiplication can be completed in any order and still obtain the same result. However, order does matter in subtraction and division. The **associative** property allows any terms to be "associated" by parentheses and retain the same final answer. For example,

$$(4 + 3) + 5 = 4 + (3 + 5)$$

Both addition and multiplication are associative; however, subtraction and division do not hold this property. The **distributive** property states that:

$$a(b + c) = ab + ac$$

It is a property that involves both addition and multiplication, and the a is distributed onto each term inside the parentheses.

Absolute Value

The distance that a number is from zero is called its **absolute value**. For example, both 3 and -3 are three spaces from zero. Thus, both -3 and 3 have an absolute value of 3 since they're both three spaces away from zero.

An absolute number is written by placing | | around the number. So, |3| and |−3| both equal 3, as that's their common absolute value.

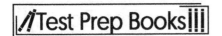

Functions

Understanding Functions

First, it's important to understand the definition of a **relation**. Given two variables, x and y, which stand for unknown numbers, a *relation* between x and y is an object that splits all of the pairs (x, y) into those for which the relation is true and those for which it is false. For example, consider the relation of $x^2 = y^2$. This relationship is true for the pair $(1, 1)$ and for the pair $(-2, 2)$, but false for $(2, 3)$. Another example of a relation is $x \leq y$. This is true whenever x is less than or equal to y.

A **function** is a special kind of relation where, for each value of x, there is only a single value of y that satisfies the relation. So, $x^2 = y^2$ is *not* a function because in this case, if x is 1, y can be either 1 or -1: the pair $(1, 1)$ and $(1, -1)$ both satisfy the relation. More generally, for this relation, any pair of the form $(a, \pm a)$ will satisfy it. On the other hand, consider the following relation:

$$y = x^2 + 1$$

This is a function because for each value of x, there is a unique value of y that satisfies the relation. Notice, however, there are multiple values of x that give us the same value of y. This is perfectly acceptable for a function. Therefore, y is a function of x.

To determine if a relation is a function, check to see if every x-value has a unique corresponding y-value.

A function can be viewed as an object that has x as its input and outputs a unique y-value. It is sometimes convenient to express this using **function notation**, where the function itself is given a name, often f. To emphasize that f takes x as its input, the function is written as $f(x)$. In the above example, the equation could be rewritten as:

$$f(x) = x^2 + 1$$

To write the value that a function yields for some specific value of x, that value is put in place of x in the function notation. For example, $f(3)$ means the value that the function outputs when the input value is 3. If $f(x) = x^2 + 1$, then:

$$f(3) = 3^2 + 1 = 10$$

A function can also be viewed as a table of pairs (x, y), which lists the value for y for each possible value of x.

The set of all possible values for x in $f(x)$ is called the **domain** of the function, and the set of all possible outputs is called the **range** of the function. Note that usually the domain is assumed to be all real numbers, except those for which the expression for $f(x)$ is not defined, unless the problem specifies otherwise. An example of how a function might not be defined is in the case of $f(x) = \frac{1}{x+1}$, which is not defined when $x = -1$ (which would require dividing by zero). Therefore, in this case the domain would be all real numbers except $x = -1$.

If y is a function of x, then x is the **independent variable** and y is the **dependent variable**. This is because in many cases, the problem will start with some value of x and then see how y changes depending on this starting value.

Domain and Range

The **domain** and **range** of a function can be found visually by its plot on the coordinate plane. In the function $f(x) = x^2 - 3$, for example, the domain is all real numbers because the parabola stretches as far left and as far right as it can go, with no restrictions. This means that any input value from the real number system will yield an answer in the real number system. For the range, the inequality $y \geq -3$ would be used to describe the possible output values because the parabola has a minimum at $y = -3$. This means there will not be any real output values less than -3 because -3 is the lowest value it reaches on the y-axis.

These same answers for domain and range can be found by observing a table. The table below shows that from input values $x = -1$ to $x = 1$, the output results in a minimum of -3. On each side of $x = 0$, the numbers increase, showing that the range is all real numbers greater than or equal to -3.

x (domain/input)	y (range/output)
-2	1
-1	-2
0	-3
-1	-2
2	1

Using Function Notation

A function is called **algebraic** if it is built up from polynomials by adding, subtracting, multiplying, dividing, and taking radicals. This means that, for example, the variable can never appear in an exponent. Thus, polynomials and rational functions are algebraic, but exponential functions are not algebraic. It turns out that logarithms and trigonometric functions are not algebraic either.

A function of the form $f(x) = a_n x^n + a_{n-1} x^{n-1} + a_{n-2} x^{n-2} + \ldots + a_1 x + a_0$ is called a **polynomial function**. The value of n is called the **degree of the polynomial**. In the case where $n = 1$, it is called a **linear function**. In the case where $n = 2$, it is called a **quadratic function**. In the case where $n = 3$, it is called a **cubic function**.

When n is even, the polynomial is called *even*, and not all real numbers will be in its range. When n is odd, the polynomial is called *odd*, and the range includes all real numbers.

The graph of a quadratic function $f(x) = ax^2 + bx + c$ will be a parabola. To see whether or not the parabola opens up or down, it's necessary to check the coefficient of x^2, which is the value a.

If the coefficient is positive, then the parabola opens upward. If the coefficient is negative, then the parabola opens downward.

The quantity $D = b^2 - 4ac$ is called the **discriminant** of the parabola. If the discriminant is positive, then the parabola has two real zeros. If the discriminant is negative, then it has no real zeros.

If the discriminant is zero, then the parabola's highest or lowest point is on the x-axis, and it has a single real zero.

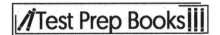

The highest or lowest point of the parabola is called the **vertex**. The coordinates of the vertex are given by the point $(-\frac{b}{2a}, -\frac{D}{4a})$. The roots of a quadratic function can be found with the quadratic formula, which is:

$$x = \frac{-b \pm \sqrt{b^2 - 4ac}}{2a}$$

A **rational function** is a function $f(x) = \frac{p(x)}{q(x)}$, where p and q are both polynomials. The domain of f will be all real numbers except the (real) roots of q.

At these roots, the graph of f will have a **vertical asymptote**, unless they are also roots of p. Here is an example to consider:

$$p(x) = p_n x^n + p_{n-1} x^{n-1} + p_{n-2} x^{n-2} + \ldots + p_1 x + p_0$$

$$q(x) = q_m x^m + q_{m-1} x^{m-1} + q_{m-2} x^{m-2} + \ldots + q_1 x + q_0$$

When the degree of p is less than the degree of q, there will be a horizontal asymptote of $y = 0$. If p and q have the same degree, there will be a horizontal asymptote of $y = \frac{p_n}{q_n}$. If the degree of p is exactly one greater than the degree of q, then f will have an oblique asymptote along the line:

$$y = \frac{p_n}{q_{n-1}} x + \frac{p_{n-1}}{q_{n-1}}$$

Not all equations in x and y can be written in the form $y = f(x)$. An equation can be written in such a form if it satisfies the **vertical line test**: no vertical line meets the graph of the equation at more than a single point. In this case, y is said to be a **function of x**. If a vertical line meets the graph in two places, then this equation cannot be written in the form $y = f(x)$.

The graph of a function $f(x)$ is the graph of the equation $y = f(x)$. Thus, it is the set of all pairs (x, y) where $y = f(x)$. In other words, it is all pairs $(x, f(x))$. The x-intercepts are called the **zeros of the function**. The y-intercept is given by $f(0)$.

If, for a given function f, the only way to get $f(a) = f(b)$ is for $a = b$, then f is *one-to-one*. Often, even if a function is not one-to-one on its entire domain, it is one-to-one by considering a restricted portion of the domain.

A function $f(x) = k$ for some number k is called a **constant function**. The graph of a constant function is a horizontal line.

The function $f(x) = x$ is called the **identity function**. The graph of the identity function is the diagonal line pointing to the upper right at 45 degrees, $y = x$.

Given two functions, $f(x)$ and $g(x)$, new functions can be formed by adding, subtracting, multiplying, or dividing the functions. Any algebraic combination of the two functions can be performed, including one function being the exponent of the other. If there are expressions for f and g, then the result can be found by performing the desired operation between the expressions. So, if $f(x) = x^2$ and $g(x) = 3x$, then:

$$f \cdot g(x) = x^2 \times 3x = 3x^3$$

152

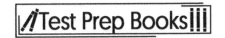

Given two functions, $f(x)$ and $g(x)$, where the domain of g contains the range of f, the two functions can be combined together in a process called *composition*. The function—"g composed of f"—is written:

$$(g \circ f)(x) = g(f(x))$$

This requires the input of x into f, then taking that result and plugging it in to the function g.

If f is one-to-one, then there is also the option to find the function $f^{-1}(x)$, called the **inverse of f**. Algebraically, the inverse function can be found by writing y in place of $f(x)$, and then solving for x. The inverse function also makes this statement true:

$$f^{-1}(f(x)) = x$$

Computing the inverse of a function f entails the following procedure:

Given $f(x) = x^2$, with a domain of $x \geq 0$, $x = y^2$ is written down to find the inverse. The square root of both sides is determined to solve for y.

Normally, this would mean $\pm\sqrt{x} = y$. However, the domain of f does not include the negative numbers, so the negative option needs to be eliminated.

The result is $y = \sqrt{x}$, so $f^{-1}(x) = \sqrt{x}$, with a domain of $x \geq 0$.

A function is called **monotone** if it is either always increasing or always decreasing. For example, the functions $f(x) = 3x$ and $f(x) = -x^5$ are monotone.

An *even function* looks the same when flipped over the y-axis:

$$f(x) = f(-x)$$

The following image shows a graphic representation of an even function.

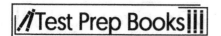

An **odd function** looks the same when flipped over the y-axis and then flipped over the x-axis:

$$f(x) = -f(-x)$$

The following image shows an example of an odd function.

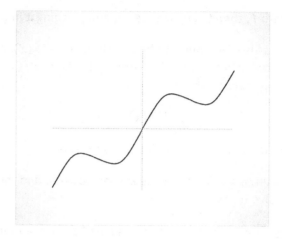

To evaluate functions, plug in the given value everywhere the variable appears in the expression for the function. For example, find $g(-2)$ where:

$$g(x) = 2x^2 - \frac{4}{x}$$

To complete the problem, plug in -2 in the following way:

$$g(-2) = 2(-2)^2 - \frac{4}{-2}$$

$$2 \cdot 4 + 2 = 8 + 2 = 10$$

Interpreting Key Features of Graphs and Tables

Scatter plots can be used to determine whether a correlation exists between two variables. The horizontal (x) axis represents the independent variable and the vertical (y) axis represents the dependent variable. If when graphed, the points model a linear, quadratic, or exponential relationship, then a correlation is said to exist. If so, a line of best-fit or curve of best-fit can be drawn through the points, with the points relatively close on either side. Writing the equation for the line or curve allows for predicting values for the variables. Suppose a scatterplot displays the value of an investment as a function of years after investing. By writing an equation for the line or curve and substituting a value for one variable into the equation, the corresponding value for the other variable can be calculated.

Linear Models

If the points of a scatterplot model a linear relationship, a line of best-fit is drawn through the points. If the line of best-fit has a positive slope (y-values increase as x-values increase), then the variables have a positive correlation. If the line of best-fit has a negative slope (y-values decrease as x-values increase),

Math

![Test Prep Books]

then a negative correlation exists. A positive or negative correlation can also be categorized as strong or weak, depending on how closely the points are grouped around the line of best-fit.

Given a line of best-fit, its equation can be written by identifying: the slope and y-intercept; a point and the slope; or two points on the line.

Quadratic Models
A quadratic function can be written in the form:

$$y = ax^2 + bx + c$$

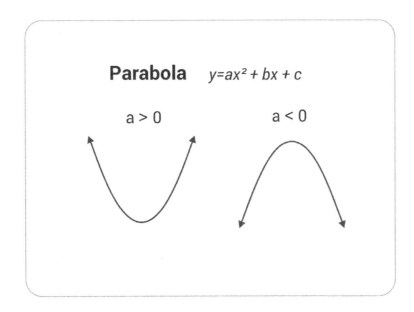

The u-shaped graph of a quadratic function is called a parabola. The graph can either open up or open down (upside down u). The graph is symmetric about a vertical line, called the axis of symmetry. Corresponding points on the parabola are directly across from each other (same y-value) and are the same distance from the axis of symmetry (on either side). The axis of symmetry intersects the parabola at its vertex. The y-value of the vertex represents the minimum or maximum value of the function. If the graph opens up, the value of a in its equation is positive, and the vertex represents the minimum of the function. If the graph opens down, the value of a in its equation is negative, and the vertex represents the maximum of the function.

Given a curve of best-fit that models a quadratic relationship, the equation of the parabola can be written by identifying the vertex of the parabola and another point on the graph. The values for the vertex (h, k) and the point (x, y) should be substituted into the vertex form of a quadratic function, $y = a(x - h)^2 + k$, to determine the value of a. To write the equation of a quadratic function with a vertex of $(4, 7)$ and containing the point $(8, 3)$, the values for h, k, x, and y should be substituted into the vertex form of a quadratic function, resulting in:

$$3 = a(8 - 4)^2 + 7$$

Solving for a, yields $a = -\frac{1}{4}$. Therefore, the equation of the function can be written as:

$$y = -\frac{1}{4}(x - 4)^2 + 7$$

The vertex form can be manipulated in order to write the quadratic function in standard form.

Exponential Models

An **exponential curve** can be used as a curve of best-fit for a scatterplot. The general form for an exponential function is $y = ab^x$ where b must be a positive number and cannot equal 1. When the value of b is greater than 1, the function models exponential growth (as x increases, y increases). When the value of b is less than 1, the function models exponential decay (as x increases, y decreases). If a is positive, the graph consists of points above the x-axis; if a is negative, the graph consists of points below the x-axis. An asymptote is a line that a graph approaches.

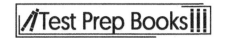

Given a curve of best-fit modeling an exponential function, its equation can be written by identifying two points on the curve. To write the equation of an exponential function containing the ordered pairs $(2, 2)$ and $(3, 4)$, the ordered pair $(2, 2)$ should be substituted in the general form and solved for a:

$$2 = a \times b^2 \rightarrow a = \frac{2}{b^2}$$

The ordered pair $(3, 4)$ and $\frac{2}{b^2}$ should be substituted in the general form and solved for b:

$$4 = \frac{2}{b^2} \times b^3 \rightarrow b = 2$$

Then, 2 should be substituted for b in the equation for a and then solved for a:

$$a = \frac{2}{2^2} \rightarrow a = \frac{1}{2}$$

Knowing the values of a and b, the equation can be written as:

$$y = \frac{1}{2} \times 2^x$$

Solving Line Problems

Two lines are parallel if they have the same slope and a different intercept. Two lines are perpendicular if the product of their slope equals -1. Parallel lines never intersect unless they are the same line, and perpendicular lines intersect at a right angle. If two lines aren't parallel, they must intersect at one point. Determining equations of lines based on properties of parallel and perpendicular lines appears in word problems. To find an equation of a line, both the slope and a point the line goes through are necessary.

Therefore, if an equation of a line is needed that's parallel to a given line and runs through a specified point, the slope of the given line and the point are plugged into the point-slope form of an equation of a line. Secondly, if an equation of a line is needed that's perpendicular to a given line running through a specified point, the negative reciprocal of the slope of the given line and the point are plugged into the point-slope form. Also, if the point of intersection of two lines is known, that point will be used to solve the set of equations. Therefore, to solve a system of equations, the point of intersection must be found. If a set of two equations with two unknown variables has no solution, the lines are parallel.

Calculating and Interpreting the Average Rate of Change of a Function

Rate of change for any line calculates the steepness of the line over a given interval. Rate of change is also known as the slope or rise/run. The rates of change for nonlinear functions vary depending on the interval being used for the function. The rate of change over one interval may be zero, while the next interval may have a positive rate of change. The equation plotted on the graph below, $y = x^2$, is a quadratic function and non-linear.

The average rate of change from points $(0, 0)$ to $(1, 1)$ is 1 because the vertical change is 1 over the horizontal change of 1. For the next interval, $(1, 1)$ to $(2, 4)$, the average rate of change is 3 because the slope is $\frac{3}{1}$.

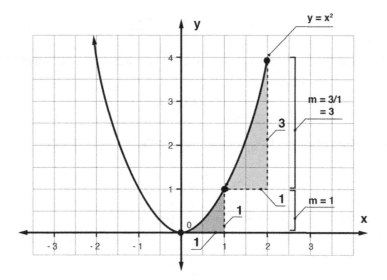

The rate of change for a linear function is constant and can be determined based on a few representations. One method is to place the equation in slope-intercept form:

$$y = mx + b$$

Thus, m is the slope, and b is the y-intercept. In the graph below, the equation is $y = x + 1$, where the slope is 1 and the y-intercept is 1. For every vertical change of 1 unit, there is a horizontal change of 1 unit. The x-intercept is -1, which is the point where the line crosses the x-axis.

Graph Functions Expressed Symbolically

To graph relations and functions, the **Cartesian plane** is used. This means to think of the plane as being given a grid of squares, with one direction being the x-axis and the other direction the y-axis. Generally, the independent variable is placed along the horizontal axis, and the dependent variable is placed along the vertical axis. Any point on the plane can be specified by saying how far to go along the x-axis and how far along the y-axis with a pair of numbers (x, y). Specific values for these pairs can be given names such as $C = (-1, 3)$. Negative values mean to move left or down; positive values mean to move right or up. The point where the axes cross one another is called the *origin*. The origin has coordinates $(0, 0)$ and is usually called O when given a specific label. An illustration of the Cartesian plane, along with the plotted points $(2, 1)$ and $(-1, -1)$, is below.

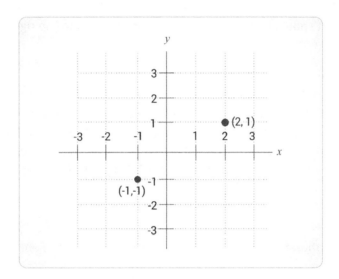

Relations also can be graphed by marking each point whose coordinates satisfy the relation. If the relation is a function, then there is only one value of y for any given value of x. This leads to the **vertical line test**: if a relation is graphed, then the relation is a function if any possible vertical line drawn anywhere along the graph would only touch the graph of the relation in no more than one place. Conversely, when graphing a function, then any possible vertical line drawn will not touch the graph of the function at any point or will touch the function at just one point. This test is made from the definition of a function, where each x-value must be mapped to one and only one y-value.

Understanding Connections Between Algebraic and Graphical Representations

The solution set to a linear equation in two variables can be represented visually by a line graphed on the coordinate plane. Every point on this line represents an ordered pair (x, y), which makes the equation true. The process for graphing a line depends on the form in which its equation is written: slope-intercept form or standard form.

Graphing a Line in Slope-Intercept Form

When an equation is written in slope-intercept form, $y = mx + b$, m represents the slope of the line and b represents the y-intercept. The y-intercept is the value of y when $x = 0$ and the point at which the graph of the line crosses the y-axis. The slope is the rate of change between the variables, expressed as a fraction. The fraction expresses the change in y compared to the change in x. If the slope is an integer, it should be written as a fraction with a denominator of 1. For example, 5 would be written as $\frac{5}{1}$.

To graph a line given an equation in slope-intercept form, the y-intercept should first be plotted. For example, to graph $y = -\frac{2}{3}x + 7$, the y-intercept of 7 would be plotted on the y-axis (vertical axis) at the point $(0, 7)$. Next, the slope would be used to determine a second point for the line. Note that all that is necessary to graph a line is two points on that line. The slope will indicate how to get from one point on the line to another. The slope expresses vertical change (y) compared to horizontal change (x) and therefore is sometimes referred to as $\frac{rise}{run}$. The numerator indicates the change in the y-value (move up for positive integers and move down for negative integers), and the denominator indicates the change in the x-value. For the previous example, using the slope of $-\frac{2}{3}$, from the first point at the y-intercept, the second point should be found by counting down 2 and to the right 3. This point would be located at $(3, 5)$.

Graphing a Line in Standard Form

When an equation is written in **standard form**, $Ax + By = C$, it is easy to identify the x- and y-intercepts for the graph of the line. Just as the y-intercept is the point at which the line intercepts the y-axis, the x-intercept is the point at which the line intercepts the x-axis. At the y-intercept, $x = 0$; and at the x-intercept, $y = 0$. Given an equation in standard form, $x = 0$ should be used to find the y-intercept. Likewise, $y = 0$ should be used to find the x-intercept. For example, to graph $3x + 2y = 6$, 0 for y results in:

$$3x + 2(0) = 6$$

Solving for y yields $x = 2$; therefore, an ordered pair for the line is $(2, 0)$. Substituting 0 for x results in:

$$3(0) + 2y = 6$$

160

Solving for y yields $y = 3$; therefore, an ordered pair for the line is $(0, 3)$. The two ordered pairs (the x- and y-intercepts) can be plotted, and a straight line through them can be constructed.

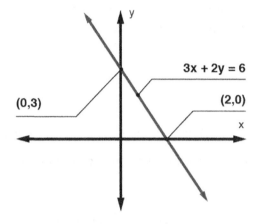

T - chart

x	y
0	3
2	0

Intercepts

x - intercept : (2,0)

y - intercept : (0,3)

Writing the Equation of a Line Given its Graph
Given the graph of a line, its equation can be written in two ways. If the y-intercept is easily identified (is an integer), it and another point can be used to determine the slope. When determining $\frac{change\ in\ y}{change\ in\ x}$ from one point to another on the graph, the distance for $\frac{rise}{run}$ is being figured. The equation should be written in slope-intercept form, $y = mx + b$, with m representing the slope and b representing the y-intercept.

The equation of a line can also be written by identifying two points on the graph of the line. To do so, the slope is calculated and then the values are substituted for the slope and either of the ordered pairs into the point-slope form of an equation.

Vertical, Horizontal, Parallel, and Perpendicular Lines
For a vertical line, the value of x remains constant (for all ordered pairs (x, y) on the line, the value of x is the same); therefore, the equations for all vertical lines are written in the form $x = number$. For example, a vertical line that crosses the x-axis at -2 would have an equation of $x = -2$. For a horizontal line, the value of y remains constant; therefore, the equations for all horizontal lines are written in the form $y = number$.

Parallel lines extend in the same exact direction without ever meeting. Their equations have the same slopes and different y-intercepts. For example, given a line with an equation of $y = -3x + 2$, a parallel line would have a slope of -3 and a y-intercept of any value other than 2. Perpendicular lines intersect to form a right angle. Their equations have slopes that are opposite reciprocal (the sign is changed and the fraction is flipped; for example, $-\frac{2}{3}$ and $\frac{3}{2}$) and y-intercepts that may or may not be the same. For

161

example, given a line with an equation of $y = \frac{1}{2}x + 7$, a perpendicular line would have a slope of $-\frac{2}{1}$ and any value for its y-intercept.

Using Properties of Exponents to Interpret Expressions for Exponential Functions

An **exponential function** is a function of the form $f(x) = b^x$, where b is a positive real number other than 1. In such a function, b is called the *base*.

The *domain* of an exponential function is all real numbers, and the *range* is all positive real numbers. There will always be a horizontal asymptote of $y = 0$ on one side. If b is greater than 1, then the graph will be increasing moving to the right. If b is less than 1, then the graph will be decreasing moving to the right. Exponential functions are one-to-one. The basic exponential function graph will go through the point $(0, 1)$.

Example
Solve $5^{x+1} = 25$.

Get the x out of the exponent by rewriting the equation $5^{x+1} = 5^2$ so that both sides have a base of 5.

Since the bases are the same, the exponents must be equal to each other.

This leaves $x + 1 = 2$ or $x = 1$.

To check the answer, the x-value of 1 can be substituted back into the original equation.

Solving Logarithmic and Exponential Functions
To solve an equation involving exponential expressions, the goal is to isolate the exponential expression. Once this process is completed, the logarithm—with the base equaling the base of the exponent of both sides—needs to be taken to get an expression for the variable. If the base is e, the natural log of both sides needs to be taken.

To solve an equation with logarithms, the given equation needs to be written in exponential form, using the fact that $\log_b y = x$ means $b^x = y$, and then solved for the given variable. Lastly, properties of logarithms can be used to simplify more than one logarithmic expression into one.

When working with logarithmic functions, it is important to remember the following properties. Each one can be derived from the definition of the logarithm as the inverse to an exponential function:

$$\log_b 1 = 0$$

$$\log_b b = 1$$

$$\log_b b^p = p$$

$$\log_b MN = \log_b M + \log_b N$$

$$\log_b \frac{M}{N} = \log_b M - \log_b N$$

$$\log_b M^p = p \log_b M$$

162

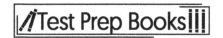

When solving equations involving exponentials and logarithms, the following fact should be used:

If f is a one-to-one function, $a = b$ is equivalent to $f(a) = f(b)$.

Using this, together with the fact that logarithms and exponentials are inverses, allows manipulations of the equations to isolate the variable.

Example
Solve $4 = \ln(x - 4)$.

Using the definition of a logarithm, the equation can be changed to:

$$e^4 = e^{\ln(x-4)}$$

The functions on the right side cancel with a result of:

$$e^4 = x - 4$$

This then gives:

$$x = 4 + e^4$$

Exponential Expressions
Exponential expressions can also be rewritten, just as quadratic equations. Properties of exponents must be understood. Multiplying two exponential expressions with the same base involves adding the exponents:

$$a^m a^n = a^{m+n}$$

Dividing two exponential expressions with the same base involves subtracting the exponents:

$$\frac{a^m}{a^n} = a^{m-n}$$

Raising an exponential expression to another exponent includes multiplying the exponents:

$$(a^m)^n = a^{mn}$$

The zero power always gives a value of 1: $a^0 = 1$. Raising either a product or a fraction to a power involves distributing that power:

$$(ab)^m = a^m b^m \text{ and } \left(\frac{a}{b}\right)^m = \frac{a^m}{b^m}$$

Finally, raising a number to a negative exponent is equivalent to the reciprocal including the positive exponent:

$$a^{-m} = \frac{1}{a^m}$$

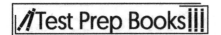

Math

Comparing Properties of Two Functions Represented in a Different Ways

Mathematical functions such as polynomials, rational functions, radical functions, absolute value functions, and piecewise-defined functions can be utilized to approximate, or model, real-life phenomena. For example, a function can be built that approximates the average amount of snowfall on a given day of the year in Chicago. This example could be as simple as a polynomial. Modeling situations using such functions has limitations; the most significant issue is the error that exists between the exact amount and the approximate amount. Typically, the model will not give exact values as outputs. However, choosing the type of function that provides the best fit of the data will reduce this error. Technology can be used to model situations. For example, given a set of data, the data can be inputted into tools such as graphing calculators or spreadsheet software that output a function with a good fit. Some examples of polynomial modeling are linear, quadratic, and cubic regression.

Representing Exponential and Logarithmic Functions

The **logarithmic function** with base b is denoted $y = \log_b x$. Its base must be greater than 0 and not equal to 1, and the domain is all $x > 0$. The exponential function with base b is denoted $y = b^x$. Exponential and logarithmic functions with base b are inverses. By definition, if $y = \log_b x$, $x = b^y$. Because exponential and logarithmic functions are inverses, the graph of one is obtained by reflecting the other over the line $y = x$. A common base used is e, and in this case $y = e^x$ and its inverse $y = \log_e x$ is commonly written as the natural logarithmic function $y = \ln x$.

Here is the graph of both functions:

The Graphs of Exponential and Logarithmic Functions are Inverses

$y = e^x$

(*)

$y = x$

$y = \log_e x = \ln x$

(*)

(*) These functions are reflected over the line **y = x**

164

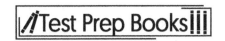

Graphing Functions

The x-intercept of the logarithmic function $y = \log_b x$ with any base is always the ordered pair $(1, 0)$. By the definition of inverse, the point $(0, 1)$ always lies on the exponential function $y = b^x$. This is true because any real number raised to the power of 0 equals 1. Therefore, the exponential function only has a y-intercept. The exponential function also has a horizontal asymptote of the x-axis as x approaches negative infinity. Because the graph is reflected over the line $y = x$, to obtain the graph of the logarithmic function, the asymptote is also reflected. Therefore, the logarithmic function has a one-sided vertical asymptote at $y = 0$. These asymptotes can be seen in the above graphs of $y = e^x$ and $y = \ln x$.

Solving Logarithmic and Exponential Functions

To solve an equation involving exponential expressions, the goal is to isolate the exponential expression. Once this process is completed, the logarithm—with the base equaling the base of the exponent of both sides—needs to be taken to get an expression for the variable. If the base is e, the natural log of both sides needs to be taken.

To solve an equation with logarithms, the given equation needs to be written in exponential form, using the fact that $\log_b a = x$ means $b^x = y$, and then solved for the given variable. Lastly, properties of logarithms can be used to simplify more than one logarithmic expression into one.

Some equations involving exponential and logarithmic functions can be solved algebraically, or analytically. To solve an equation involving exponential functions, the goal is to isolate the exponential expression. Then, the logarithm of both sides is found in order to yield an expression for the variable. Laws of Logarithms will be helpful at this point.

To solve an equation with logarithms, the equation needs to be rewritten in exponential form. The definition that $\log_b x = y$ means $b^y = x$ needs to be used. Then, one needs to solve for the given variable. Properties of logarithms can be used to simplify multiple logarithmic expressions into one.

Other methods can be used to solve equations containing logarithmic and exponential functions. Graphs and graphing calculators can be used to see points of intersection. In a similar manner, tables can be used to find points of intersection. Also, numerical methods can be utilized to find approximate solutions.

Exponential Growth and Decay

Exponential growth and decay are important concepts in modeling real-world phenomena. The growth and decay formula is $A(t) = Pe^{rt}$, where the independent variable t represents temperature, P represents an initial quantity, r represents the rate of increase or decrease, and $A(t)$ represents the amount of the quantity at time t. If $r > 0$, the equation models exponential growth and a common application is population growth. If $r < 0$, the equation models exponential decay and a common application is radioactive decay. Exponential and logarithmic solving techniques are necessary to work with the growth and decay formula.

Logarithmic Scales

A **logarithmic scale** is a scale of measurement that uses the logarithm of the given units instead of the actual given units. Each tick mark on such a scale is the product of the previous tick mark multiplied by a number. The advantage of using such a scale is that if one is working with large measurements, this technique reduces the scale into manageable quantities that are easier to read. The **Richter magnitude**

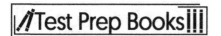

Math

scale is the famous logarithmic scale used to measure the intensity of earthquakes, and the decibel scale is commonly used to measure sound level in electronics.

Using Exponential and Logarithmic Functions in Finance Problems

Modeling within finance also involves exponential and logarithmic functions. Compound interest results when the bank pays interest on the original amount of money – the principal – and the interest that has accrued. The compound interest equation is $A(t) = P\left(1 + \frac{r}{n}\right)^{nt}$, where P is the principal, r is the interest rate, n is the number of times per year the interest is compounded, and t is the time in years. The result, $A(t)$, is the final amount after t years. Mathematical problems of this type that are frequently encountered involve receiving all but one of these quantities and solving for the missing quantity. The solving process then involves employing properties of logarithmic and exponential functions. Interest can also be compounded continuously. This formula is given as:

$$A(t) = Pe^{rt}$$

If $1,000 was compounded continuously at a rate of 2% for 4 years, the result would be:

$$A(4) = 1,000e^{0.02 \cdot 4} = \$1,083$$

Rate of Change Proportional to the Current Quantity

Many quantities grow or decay as fast as exponential functions. Specifically, if such a quantity grows or decays at a rate proportional to the quantity itself, it shows exponential behavior. If a data set is given with such specific characteristics, the initial amount and an amount at a specific time, t, can be plugged into the exponential function $A(t) = Pe^{rt}$ for A and P. Using properties of exponents and logarithms, one can then solve for the rate, r. This solution yields enough information to have the entire model, which can allow for an estimation of the quantity at any time, t, and the ability to solve various problems using that model.

Writing a Function that Describes a Relationship Between Two Quantities

Different types of functions behave in different ways. A function is defined to be increasing over a subset of its domain if for all $x_1 \geq x_2$ in that interval:

$$f(x_1) \geq f(x_2)$$

Also, a function is decreasing over an interval if for all $x_1 \geq x_2$ in that interval:

$$f(x_1) \leq f(x_2)$$

A point in which a function changes from increasing to decreasing can also be labeled as the **maximum value** of a function if it is the largest point the graph reaches on the y-axis. A point in which a function changes from decreasing to increasing can be labeled as the minimum value of a function if it is the smallest point the graph reaches on the y-axis. Maximum values are also known as **extreme values**. The graph of a continuous function does not have any breaks or jumps in the graph. This description is not true of all functions. A radical function, for example, $f(x) = \sqrt{x}$, has a restriction for the domain and range because there are no real negative inputs or outputs for this function. The domain can be stated as $x \geq 0$, and the range is $y \geq 0$.

166

A piecewise-defined function also has a different appearance on the graph. In the following function, there are three equations defined over different intervals. It is a function because there is only one y-value for each x-value, passing the Vertical Line Test. The domain is all real numbers less than or equal to 6. The range is all real numbers greater than zero. From left to right, the graph decreases to zero, then increases to almost 4, and then jumps to 6.

From input values greater than 2, the input decreases just below 8 to 4, and then stops.

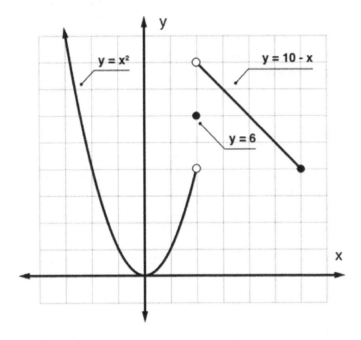

Logarithmic and exponential functions also have different behavior than other functions. These two types of functions are inverses of each other. The *inverse* of a function can be found by switching the place of x and y, and solving for y. When this is done for the exponential equation, $y = 2^x$, the function $y = \log_2 x$ is found. The general form of a *logarithmic function* is $y = \log_b x$, which says b raised to the y power equals x.

167

The thick black line on the graph above represents the logarithmic function:

$$y = \log_2 x$$

This curve passes through the point $(1, 0)$, just as all log functions do, because any value $b^0 = 1$. The graph of this logarithmic function starts very close to zero, but does not touch the y-axis. The output value will never be zero by the definition of logarithms. The thinner gray line seen above represents the exponential function $y = 2^x$. The behavior of this function is opposite the logarithmic function because the graph of an inverse function is the graph of the original function flipped over the line $y = x$. The curve passes through the point $(0, 1)$ because any number raised to the zero power is one. This curve also gets very close to the x-axis but never touches it because an exponential expression never has an output of zero. The x-axis on this graph is called a horizontal asymptote. An *asymptote* is a line that represents a boundary for a function. It shows a value that the function will get close to, but never reach.

Functions can also be described as being even, odd, or neither. If $f(-x) = f(x)$, the function is even. For example, the function $f(x) = x^2 - 2$ is even. Plugging in $x = 2$ yields an output of $y = 2$. After changing the input to $x = -2$, the output is still $y = 2$. The output is the same for opposite inputs. Another way to observe an even function is by the symmetry of the graph. If the graph is symmetrical about the axis, then the function is even. If the graph is symmetric about the origin, then the function is odd. Algebraically, if $f(-x) = -f(x)$, the function is odd.

Also, a function can be described as periodic if it repeats itself in regular intervals. Common periodic functions are trigonometric functions. For example, $y = \sin x$ is a periodic function with period 2π because it repeats itself every 2π units along the x-axis.

Building a Linear Function that Models a Linear Relationship Between Two Quantities

Linear relationships between two quantities can be expressed in two ways: function notation or as a linear equation with two variables. The relationship is referred to as linear because its graph is represented by a line. For a relationship to be linear, both variables must be raised to the first power only.

Function/Linear Equation Notation

A relation is a set of input and output values that can be written as ordered pairs. A function is a relation in which each input is paired with exactly one output. The domain of a function consists of all inputs, and the range consists of all outputs. Graphing the ordered pairs of a linear function produces a straight line. An example of a function would be $f(x) = 4x + 4$, read "f of x is equal to four times x plus four." In this example, the input would be x and the output would be $f(x)$. Ordered pairs would be represented as $(x, f(x))$. To find the output for an input value of 3, 3 would be substituted for x into the function as follows: $f(3) = 4(3) + 4$, resulting in $f(3) = 16$. Therefore, the ordered pair:

$$(3, f(3)) = (3, 16)$$

Note $f(x)$ is a function of x denoted by f. Functions of x could be named $g(x)$, read "g of x"; $p(x)$, read "p of x"; etc.

A linear function could also be written in the form of an equation with two variables. Typically, the variable x represents the inputs and the variable y represents the outputs. The variable x is considered the independent variable and y the dependent variable. The above function would be written as:

$$y = 4x + 4$$

Ordered pairs are written in the form (x, y).

Writing Linear Equations in Two Variables

When writing linear equations in two variables, the process depends on the information given. Questions will typically provide the slope of the line and its y-intercept, an ordered pair and the slope, or two ordered pairs.

Given the Slope and Y-Intercept

Linear equations are commonly written in slope-intercept form, $y = mx + b$, where m represents the slope of the line and b represents the y-intercept. The slope is the rate of change between the variables, usually expressed as a whole number or fraction. The y-intercept is the value of y when $x = 0$ (the point where the line intercepts the y-axis on a graph). Given the slope and y-intercept of a line, the values are substituted for m and b into the equation. A line with a slope of $\frac{1}{2}$ and y-intercept of -2 would have an equation $y = \frac{1}{2}x - 2$.

Given an Ordered Pair and the Slope

The **point-slope form of a line**, $y - y_1 = m(x - x_1)$, is used to write an equation when given an ordered pair (point on the equation's graph) for the function and its rate of change (slope of the line). The values for the slope, m, and the point (x_1, y_1) are substituted into the point-slope form to obtain the equation of the line. A line with a slope of 3 and an ordered pair $(4, -2)$ would have an equation $y - (-2) = 3(x - 4)$. If a question specifies that the equation be written in slope-intercept form, the equation should be manipulated to isolate y:

Solve: $y - (-2) = 3(x - 4)$

Distribute: $y + 2 = 3x - 12$

Subtract 2 from both sides: $y = 3x - 14$

Given Two Ordered Pairs

Given two **ordered pairs** for a function, (x_1, y_1) and (x_2, y_2), it is possible to determine the rate of change between the variables (slope of the line). To calculate the slope of the line, m, the values for the ordered pairs should be substituted into the formula:

$$m = \frac{y_2 - y_1}{x_2 - x_1}$$

The expression is substituted to obtain a whole number or fraction for the slope. Once the slope is calculated, the slope and either of the ordered pairs should be substituted into the point-slope form to obtain the equation of the line.

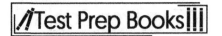

Building a Function for a Given Situation

Functions can be built out of the context of a situation. For example, the relationship between the money paid for a gym membership and the months that someone has been a member can be described through a function. If the one-time membership fee is $40 and the monthly fee is $30, then the function can be written:

$$f(x) = 30x + 40$$

The x-value represents the number of months the person has been part of the gym, while the output is the total money paid for the membership. The table below shows this relationship. It is a representation of the function because the initial cost is $40 and the cost increases each month by $30.

x (months)	y (money paid to gym)
0	40
1	70
2	100
3	130

Functions can also be built from existing functions. For example, a given function $f(x)$ can be transformed by adding a constant, multiplying by a constant, or changing the input value by a constant. The new function $g(x) = f(x) + k$ represents a vertical shift of the original function. In $f(x) = 3x - 2$, a vertical shift 4 units up would be:

$$g(x) = 3x - 2 + 4 = 3x + 2$$

Multiplying the function times a constant k represents a vertical stretch, based on whether the constant is greater than or less than 1. The following function represents a stretch:

$$g(x) = kf(x)$$

$$4(3x - 2) = 12x - 8$$

Changing the input x to a constant, forms the function:

$$g(x) = f(x + k)$$

$$3(x + 4) - 2 = 3x + 12 - 2$$

$$3x + 10$$

This represents a horizontal shift to the left 4 units. If $(x - 4)$ was plugged into the function, it would represent a horizontal shift.

A composition function can also be formed by plugging one function into another. In function notation, this is written:

$$(f \circ g)(x) = f(g(x))$$

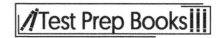

For two functions $f(x) = x^2$ and $g(x) = x - 3$, the composition function becomes:

$$f\big(g(x)\big) = (x - 3)^2$$

$$x^2 - 6x + 9$$

The composition of functions can also be used to verify if two functions are inverses of each other. Given the two functions $f(x) = 2x + 5$ and $g(x) = \frac{x-5}{2}$, the composition function can be found $(f \circ g)(x)$. Solving this equation yields:

$$f\big(g(x)\big) = 2\left(\frac{x - 5}{2}\right) + 5$$

$$x - 5 + 5 = x$$

It is also true that:

$$g\big(f(x)\big) = x$$

Since the composition of these two functions gives a simplified answer of x, this verifies that $f(x)$ and $g(x)$ are inverse functions. The domain of $f(g(x))$ is the set of all x-values in the domain of $g(x)$ such that $g(x)$ is in the domain of $f(x)$. Basically, both $f(g(x))$ and $g(x)$ have to be defined.

To build an inverse of a function, $f(x)$ needs to be replaced with y, and the x and y values need to be switched. Then, the equation can be solved for y. For example, given the equation $y = e^{2x}$, the inverse can be found by rewriting the equation $x = e^{2y}$. The natural logarithm of both sides is taken down, and the exponent is brought down to form the equation:

$$\ln(x) = \ln(e)\, 2y$$

$\ln(e) = 1$, which yields the equation $\ln(x) = 2y$. Dividing both sides by 2 yields the inverse equation

$$\frac{\ln(x)}{2} = y = f^{-1}(x)$$

The domain of an inverse function is the range of the original function, and the range of an inverse function is the domain of the original function. Therefore, an ordered pair (x, y) on either a graph or a table corresponding to $f(x)$ means that the ordered pair (y, x) exists on the graph of $f^{-1}(x)$. Basically, if $f(x) = y$, then $f^{-1}(y) = x$. For a function to have an inverse, it must be one-to-one. That means it must pass the **Horizontal Line Test**, and if any horizontal line passes through the graph of the function twice, a function is not one-to-one. The domain of a function that is not one-to-one can be restricted to an interval in which the function is one-to-one, to be able to define an inverse function.

Functions can also be formed from combinations of existing functions.

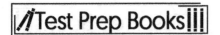

Given $f(x)$ and $g(x)$, the following can be built:

$$f + g$$

$$f - g$$

$$fg$$

$$\frac{f}{g}$$

The domains of $f + g$, $f - g$, and fg are the intersection of the domains of f and g. The domain of $\frac{f}{g}$ is the same set, excluding those values that make $g(x) = 0$.

For example, if:

$$f(x) = 2x + 3$$

$$g(x) = x + 1$$

then

$$\frac{f}{g} = \frac{2x + 3}{x + 1}$$

Its domain is all real numbers except -1.

Understanding When a Quantity Grows or Decays in a Consistent Manner

Linear relationships describe the way two quantities change with respect to each other. The relationship is defined as linear because a line is produced if all the sets of corresponding values are graphed on a coordinate grid. When expressing the linear relationship as an equation, the equation is often written in the form $y = mx + b$ (slope-intercept form) where m and b are numerical values and x and y are variables (for example, $y = 5x + 10$). Given a linear equation and the value of either variable (x or y), the value of the other variable can be determined.

Suppose a teacher is grading a test containing 20 questions with 5 points given for each correct answer, adding a curve of 10 points to each test. This linear relationship can be expressed as the equation $y = 5x + 10$ where x represents the number of correct answers, and y represents the test score. To determine the score of a test with a given number of correct answers, the number of correct answers is substituted into the equation for x and evaluated. For example, for 10 correct answers, 10 is substituted for x:

$$y = 5(10) + 10 \rightarrow y = 60$$

Therefore, 10 correct answers will result in a score of 60. The number of correct answers needed to obtain a certain score can also be determined. To determine the number of correct answers needed to score a 90, 90 is substituted for y in the equation (y represents the test score) and solved:

$$90 = 5x + 10$$

$$80 = 5x \rightarrow 16 = x$$

172

Therefore, 16 correct answers are needed to score a 90.

Linear relationships may be represented by a table of 2 corresponding values. Certain tables may determine the relationship between the values and predict other corresponding sets. Consider the table below, which displays the money in a checking account that charges a monthly fee:

Month	0	1	2	3	4
Balance	$210	$195	$180	$165	$150

An examination of the values reveals that the account loses $15 every month (the month increases by one and the balance decreases by 15). This information can be used to predict future values. To determine what the value will be in month 6, the pattern can be continued, and it can be concluded that the balance will be $120. To determine which month the balance will be $0, $210 is divided by $15 (since the balance decreases $15 every month), resulting in month 14.

Similar to a table, a graph can display corresponding values of a linear relationship.

The graph above represents the relationship between distance traveled and time. To find the distance traveled in 80 minutes, the mark for 80 minutes is located at the bottom of the graph. By following this mark directly up on the graph, the corresponding point for 80 minutes is directly across from the 160-kilometer mark. This information indicates that the distance travelled in 80 minutes is 160 kilometers. To predict information not displayed on the graph, the way in which the variables change with respect to one another is determined. In this case, distance increases by 40 kilometers as time increases by 20 minutes. This information can be used to continue the data in the graph or convert the values to a table.

Interpreting the Parameters in a Linear or Exponential Function

Three common functions used to model different relationships between quantities are linear, quadratic, and exponential functions. Linear functions are the simplest of the three, and the independent variable x has an exponent of 1. Written in the most common form, $y = mx + b$, the coefficient of x indicates how fast the function grows at a constant rate, and the b-value denotes the starting point. A quadratic function has an exponent of 2 on the independent variable x. Standard form for this type of function is $y = ax^2 + bx + c$, and the graph is a parabola. These type functions grow at a changing rate. An exponential function has an independent variable in the exponent $y = ab^x$. The graph of these types of

173

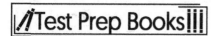

functions is described as *growth* or *decay*, based on whether the base, b, is greater than or less than 1. These functions are different from quadratic functions because the base stays constant. A common base is base e.

The following three functions model a linear, quadratic, and exponential function respectively: $y = 2x$, $y = x^2$, and $y = 2^x$. Their graphs are shown below. The first graph, modeling the linear function, shows that the growth is constant over each interval. With a horizontal change of 1, the vertical change is 2. It models constant positive growth. The second graph shows the quadratic function, which is a curve that is symmetric across the y-axis. The growth is not constant, but the change is mirrored over the axis. The last graph models the exponential function, where the horizontal change of 1 yields a vertical change that increases more and more with each iteration of horizontal change. The exponential graph gets very close to the x-axis, but never touches it, meaning there is an asymptote there. The y-value can never be zero because the base of 2 can never be raised to an input value that yields an output of zero.

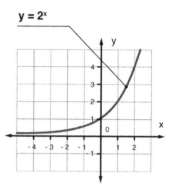

The three tables below show specific values for three types of functions. The third column in each table shows the change in the y-values for each interval. The first table shows a constant change of 2 for each equal interval, which matches the slope in the equation $y = 2x$. The second table shows an increasing change, but it also has a pattern. The increase is changing by 2 more each time, so the change is quadratic. The third table shows the change as factors of the base, 2. It shows a continuing pattern of factors of the base.

$y = 2x$		
x	y	Δy
1	2	
2	4	2
3	6	2
4	8	2
5	10	2

$y = x^2$		
x	y	Δy
1	1	
2	4	3
3	9	5
4	16	7
5	25	9

$y = 2^x$		
x	y	Δy
1	2	
2	4	2
3	8	4
4	16	8
5	32	16

Given a table of values, the type of function can be determined by observing the change in y over equal intervals. For example, the tables below model two functions. The changes in interval for the x-values is 1 for both tables. For the first table, the y-values increase by 5 for each interval. Since the change is constant, the situation can be described as a linear function. The equation would be:

$$y = 5x + 3$$

For the second table, the change for y is 20, 100, and 500, respectively. The increases are multiples of 5, meaning the situation can be modeled by an exponential function. The equation below models this situation:

$$y = 5^x + 3$$

$y = 5x + 3$	
x	y
1	8
2	13
3	18
4	23

$y = 5^x + 3$	
x	y
1	8
2	28
3	128
4	628

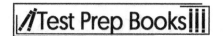

Quadratic equations can be used to model real-world area problems. For example, a farmer may have a rectangular field that he needs to sow with seed. The field has length $x + 8$ and width $2x$. The formula for area should be used: $A = lw$. Therefore:

$$A = (x + 8) * 2x = 2x^2 + 16x$$

The possible values for the length and width can be shown in a table, with input x and output A. If the equation was graphed, the possible area values can be seen on the y-axis for given x-values.

Exponential growth and decay can be found in real-world situations. For example, if a piece of notebook paper is folded 25 times, the thickness of the paper can be found. To model this situation, a table can be used. The initial point is one-fold, which yields a thickness of 2 papers. For the second fold, the thickness is 4. Since the thickness doubles each time, the table below shows the thickness for the next few folds. Notice the thickness changes by the same factor each time. Since this change for a constant interval of folds is a factor of 2, the function is exponential. The equation for this is $y = 2^x$. For twenty-five folds, the thickness would be 33,554,432 papers.

x (folds)	y (paper thickness)
0	1
1	2
2	4
3	8
4	16
5	32

One exponential formula that is commonly used is the **interest formula**:

$$A = Pe^{rt}$$

In this formula, interest is compounded continuously. A is the value of the investment after the time, t, in years. P is the initial amount of the investment, r is the interest rate, and e is the constant equal to approximately 2.718. Given an initial amount of $200 and a time of 3 years, if interest is compounded continuously at a rate of 6%, the total investment value can be found by plugging each value into the formula. The invested value at the end is $239.44. In more complex problems, the final investment may be given, and the rate may be the unknown. In this case, the formula becomes:

$$239.44 = 200e^{r3}$$

Solving for r requires isolating the exponential expression on one side by dividing by 200, yielding the equation:

$$1.20 = e^{r3}$$

Taking the natural log of both sides results in:

$$\ln(1.2) = r3$$

Using a calculator to evaluate the logarithmic expression:

$$r = 0.06 = 6\%$$

176

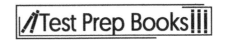

When working with logarithms and exponential expressions, it is important to remember the relationship between the two. In general, the logarithmic form is $y = log_b x$ for an exponential form $b^y = x$. Logarithms and exponential functions are inverses of each other.

Interpreting Variables and Constants in Expressions

Linear functions, also written as linear equations in two variables, can be written to model real-world scenarios. Questions on this material will provide information about a scenario and then request a linear equation to represent the scenario. The algebraic process for writing the equation will depend on the given information. The key to writing linear models is to decipher the information given to determine what it represents in the context of a linear equation (variables, slope, ordered pairs, etc.).

Identifying Variables for Linear Models

The first step to writing a linear model is to identify what the variables represent. A variable represents an unknown quantity, and in the case of a linear equation, a specific relationship exists between the two variables (usually x and y). Within a given scenario, the variables are the two quantities that are changing. The variable x is considered the independent variable and represents the inputs of a function. The variable y is considered the dependent variable and represents the outputs of a function. For example, if a scenario describes distance traveled and time traveled, distance would be represented by y and time represented by x. The distance traveled depends on the time spent traveling (time is independent). If a scenario describes the cost of a cab ride and the distance traveled, the cost would be represented by y and the distance represented by x. The cost of a cab ride depends on the distance traveled.

Identifying the Slope and Y-Intercept for Linear Models

The slope of the graph of a line represents the rate of change between the variables of an equation. In the context of a real-world scenario, the slope will tell the way in which the unknown quantities (variables) change with respect to each other. A scenario involving distance and time might state that someone is traveling at a rate of 45 miles per hour. The slope of the linear model would be 45. A scenario involving the cost of a cab ride and distance traveled might state that the person is charged $3 for each mile. The slope of the linear model would be 3.

The y-intercept of a linear function is the value of y when $x = 0$ (the point where the line intercepts the y-axis on the graph of the equation). It is sometimes helpful to think of this as a "starting point" for a linear function. Suppose for the scenario about the cab ride that the person is told that the cab company charges a flat fee of $5 plus $3 for each mile. Before traveling any distance ($x = 0$), the cost is $5. The y-intercept for the linear model would be 5.

Identifying Ordered Pairs for Linear Models

A linear equation with two variables can be written given a point (ordered pair) and the slope or given two points on a line. An ordered pair gives a set of corresponding values for the two variables (x and y). As an example, for a scenario involving distance and time, it is given that the person traveled 112.5 miles in 2 ½ hours. Knowing that x represents time and y represents distance, this information can be written as the ordered pair $(2.5, 112.5)$.

Practice Quiz

1. Which of the following numbers has the greatest value?
    a. 1.43785
    b. 1.07548
    c. 1.43592
    d. 0.89409

2. The value of 6 × 12 is the same as:
    a. 2 × 4 × 4 × 2
    b. 7 × 4 × 3
    c. 6 × 6 × 3
    d. 3 × 3 × 4 × 2

3. This chart indicates how many sales of CDs, vinyl records, and MP3 downloads occurred over the last year. Approximately what percentage of the total sales was from CDs?

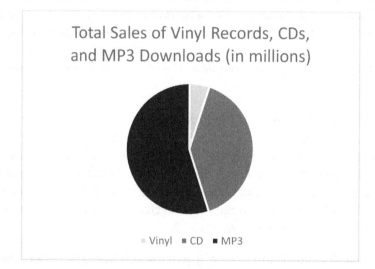

    a. 55%
    b. 25%
    c. 40%
    d. 5%

4. Mo needs to buy enough material to cover the walls around the stage for a theater performance. If he needs 79 feet of wall covering, what is the minimum number of yards of material he should purchase if the material is sold only by whole yards?
    a. 28 yards
    b. 27 yards
    c. 26 yards
    d. 29 yards

5. Which of the following values is the largest?
   a. 0.45
   b. 0.096
   c. 0.3
   d. 0.313

See answers on the next page.

Answer Explanations

1. A: Compare each number after the decimal point to figure out which overall number is greatest. In Choices A (1.43785) and C (1.43592), both have the same tenths place (4) and hundredths place (3). However, the thousandths place is greater in Choice A (7), so A has the greatest value overall.

2. D: By rearranging and grouping the factors in Choice D, we can notice that $3 \times 3 \times 4 \times 2 = (3 \times 2) \times (4 \times 3) = 6 \times 12$, which is what we were looking for.

3. C: The total percentage of a pie chart equals 100%. We can see that CD sales make up less than half of the chart (50%) but more than a quarter (25%), and the only answer choice that meets these criteria is Choice C, 40%.

4. B: A yard is 3 feet. The equation to calculate the minimum number of yards is:

$$79 \div 3 = 26\frac{1}{3}$$

If the material is sold only by whole yards, then Mo would need to round up to the next whole yard in order to cover the extra $\frac{1}{3}$ yard. Therefore, the answer is 27 yards.

5. A: To figure out which value is the largest, look at the first nonzero digits. Choice B's first nonzero digit is in the hundredths place. The other three all have nonzero digits in the tenths place, so it must be Choice A, C, or D. Of these, Choice A's first nonzero digit is the largest.

Practice Test #1

Reading

Questions 1–6 are based on the following passage:

1   In recent years, some modern approaches to public transportation have made significant additions to conventional modes, such as city buses, subways, and taxis. Private transportation has become convenient and affordable to anyone with access to the Internet.

2   One of the most well-known modern transportation companies is Uber. Uber employs individuals to pick up and drop off riders with the touch of a button. When a rider needs to be picked up, they simply log into the Uber app and request a car. Once the app verifies the rider's location, a driver arrives for pick-up within minutes. Payment for the ride is done through the app, so riders don't need to worry about carrying cash in order to catch a ride.

3   Uber is a great resource; it is commonly used by adult commuters. Smaller cities have launched their own versions of Uber. For example, Deer Park, Texas, created DeerHaul. DeerHaul operates under the same idea as Uber, only it caters to kids. Many working parents find it difficult to transport their children themselves during work hours, and DeerHaul is a viable alternative. If a child needs to be picked up from school and dropped off at Little League baseball practice, but his or her parents can't leave work, a ride with DeerHaul can be arranged. All DeerHaul drivers are previous or current teachers who have passed a **battery** of fingerprint background checks. Like Uber, DeerHaul rides are arranged through an Internet app, and all payments are handled electronically, so no cash is exchanged between the child and the driver.

1. The main purpose of this passage is to
    a. Advertise for private transportation companies such as Uber and DeerHaul
    b. Inform readers about new modes of private transportation
    c. Persuade readers to schedule a ride with DeerHaul for their children
    d. Convince readers to consider conventional methods of transportation

2. Which statement about DeerHaul is best supported by the passage?
    a. DeerHaul is a convenient way for parents to transport their kids.
    b. DeerHaul takes no special safety measures to ensure safe rides for kids.
    c. DeerHaul is a better transportation option than Uber.
    d. Anyone can apply to be a driver for DeerHaul.

3. According to the passage, how are payments handled for private transportation?
    a. Bus or subway tickets are purchased.
    b. Riders pay the driver at the end of each ride.
    c. Tipping drivers with cash is always appreciated.
    d. Rides are paid for electronically when the ride is requested.

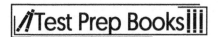

4. The bolded word **battery** most nearly means
   a. Cell
   b. Artillery
   c. Series
   d. Violence

5. Which sentence contains the main idea of this passage?
   a. "In recent years, some modern approaches to public transportation have made significant additions to conventional modes, such as city buses, subways, and taxis."
   b. "Private transportation has become convenient and affordable to anyone with access to the Internet."
   c. "One of the most well-known modern transportation companies is Uber."
   d. "Uber is a great resource; it is commonly used by adult commuters."

6. Which of the following best describes the subject matter of the passage?
   a. Two modes of private transportation are explained.
   b. The best method of private transportation is discussed.
   c. The analysis of one transportation company is refuted by the analysis of a second company.
   d. Conventional transportation methods are compared to more modern transportation.

Questions 7–12 are based on the following passage:

1   Rudolph the Red-Nosed Reindeer hasn't always been an iconic staple in the tradition of Christmas. In 1939, Montgomery Ward department stores gave Robert L. May an assignment that would change the tradition of Christmas around the world. May, a copywriter for Montgomery Ward, was asked to create a promotional Christmas coloring book. The coloring book was to be a gift for children from the store Santa. Montgomery Ward hoped the gift would increase store traffic.

2   The poem, "A Visit from St. Nicholas," published in 1823, originally depicted eight flying reindeer as members of Santa's team. In 1939, May added Rudolph. May's story depicts Rudolph as a **misfit** among the other reindeer because of his red nose. Rudolph has the opportunity to prove his worth as he leads Santa's team through a blizzard on Christmas Eve. For this, Rudolph becomes known as "the most famous reindeer of all". At the time, Montgomery Ward officials were unsure of Rudolph's red nose because this was also known as a symptom of drunkenness. However, after May and coworker Denver Gillan created a sketch of the red-nosed reindeer, officials approved the story.

3   Montgomery Ward's promotion was a great success during the Christmas season, with 2.4 million copies of "Rudolph the Red-Nosed Reindeer" gifted from Santas in their stores. In 1947, "Rudolph the Red-Nosed Reindeer" was commercially printed as a children's literature book available for purchase in bookstores.

7. Which of the following best describes the subject matter in the passage?
   a. A Montgomery Ward advertising project made Rudolph a famous Christmas tradition.
   b. Denver Gillan first created the character of Rudolph for Montgomery Ward.
   c. Robert L. May's work helped him climb the ranks at Montgomery Ward.
   d. Without Montgomery Ward's Rudolph, Christmas would have been canceled in many countries.

8. Which statement is best supported by the passage?
   a. When first presented to the public, the character of Rudolph was associated with drunkenness.
   b. Rudolph became *the most famous reindeer of all* because he saved Christmas.
   c. Gillan is responsible for turning Way's story into a poem.
   d. The Rudolph Christmas promotional saved Montgomery Ward from having to close many stores.

9. According to the passage, *Rudolph the Red-Nosed Reindeer* was
   a. Commercially printed in 1949
   b. Originally a promotional coloring book
   c. Part of an earlier poem called "A Visit from St. Nicholas"
   d. Written by Denver Gillan

10. The bolded word **misfit** most nearly means
    a. Member
    b. Conformist
    c. Insider
    d. Oddball

11. Which of the following best describes the author's tone in this passage?
    a. Humorous
    b. Apologetic
    c. Informative
    d. Sad

12. The phrase *Rudolph the Red-Nosed Reindeer* is what type of figurative language?
    a. Simile
    b. Metaphor
    c. Alliteration
    d. Onomatopoeia

Questions 13–18 are based on the following passage:

1   Water is the only substance on Earth that can occur in three states: liquid, gas, and solid. The liquid state of water is the type of water you drink, cook with, or find in streams and rivers. The gas form is called *water vapor,* or *steam,* and the solid, or frozen, form of water is known as *ice.*

2   Water, also known as H_2O, is made up of hydrogen and oxygen atoms. These atoms join together to form water **molecules.**

3   Water molecules move at various rates of speed and distances from each other depending on the state of water. When the temperature of water reaches its boiling point at 212°F, water molecules move more rapidly and spread farther apart, allowing some of them to escape into the air. This turns liquid water into water vapor, or steam.

4   On the other hand, when the temperature of liquid water becomes cooler, the water molecules begin to slow down and move closer together. Eventually, the water molecules stop moving and stick together to form a solid called ice. **Conversely,** when the temperature of ice becomes warmer, water molecules begin to spread apart, causing the ice to melt and return to a liquid state.

183

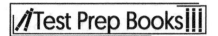
13. According to the passage, the water molecules of boiling water
   a. Move rapidly and spread farther apart
   b. Move more slowly and spread farther apart
   c. Move closer together and slow down
   d. Move rapidly and get closer together

14. If water vapor is formed when the temperature of water reaches 212°F, what happens to water vapor when it rises into the air and cools?
   a. As the water vapor cools, the molecules will return to a liquid state.
   b. The water molecules will move closer together to form a solid.
   c. The water molecules will disappear into the atmosphere.
   d. Once water becomes a gas, it always remains a gas.

15. Which sentence best represents the main idea of this passage?
   a. Water is the only substance on Earth that can occur in three states: liquid, gas, and solid.
   b. Water, also known as H_2O, is made up of hydrogen and oxygen atoms.
   c. Water molecules move at various rates of speed and distances from each other depending on the state of water.
   d. On the other hand, when the temperature of liquid water becomes cooler, the water molecules begin to slow down and move closer together.

16. The bolded word **molecules** most nearly means
   a. Masses
   b. Bundles
   c. Vast amounts
   d. Particles

17. According to this passage, what state of water is steam?
   a. Liquid
   b. Gas
   c. Solid
   d. Molecule

18. The bolded term **conversely** most nearly means
   a. Identically
   b. Comparably
   c. Similarly
   d. The other way around

Questions 19–24 are based on the following passage:

1   My friend Alyssa and I had spent most of the day getting ready. Our moms had treated us to manicures and pedicures, followed by a fancy lunch at Burgdorf's Tea Room and then a trip to the hair salon for some curls and up-dos. Alyssa and I had smiled and giggled all day in disbelief that the big day had finally arrived.

2   At seven o'clock sharp, Ricky and Bobby came to pick us up. There was an exchange of corsages and boutonnieres as our moms took an abundance of pictures to remember

184

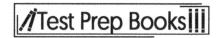

the night. The four of us giggled and laughed as the limo driver whisked us off to the eighth-grade dance.

3   We blared the radio and sang our favorite songs as the limo hustled into town. It was all fun and games until the car suddenly swerved and we tumbled over each other in the back seat like rag dolls. The tires *screeched like an alley cat* just before everything went black.

4   It's been three months since everything went dark that night, although it feels like a lifetime. The driver swerved to avoid a deer in the road. He might have seen it sooner if he hadn't been texting while he was driving. We never made it to the eighth-grade dance. The only dancing lights I got to see that night were those of ambulances and police cars. Ricky, Bobby, and Alyssa never even got to see those.

19. What is the main purpose of this passage?
    a. To persuade readers to attend their eighth-grade dance
    b. To inform readers about the availability of limo rides
    c. To illustrate the impact of texting and driving
    d. To explain how girls get ready for a dance

20. The phrase *screeched like an alley cat* is an example of a(an)
    a. Metaphor
    b. Simile
    c. Alliteration
    d. Cliché

21. This story is told in which point of view?
    a. First person
    b. Second person
    c. Third person
    d. Fourth person

22. According to the last sentence in the passage, readers can conclude that
    a. Ricky, Bobby, and Alyssa did not survive the accident.
    b. Ricky, Bobby, and Alyssa did not have to ride in an ambulance.
    c. Ricky, Bobby, and Alyssa had never planned to attend the dance.
    d. Ricky, Bobby, and Alyssa were blinded in the accident.

23. What is the overall message of this passage?
    a. Limo drivers are not required to take driving safety courses.
    b. Don't text and drive.
    c. Car accidents are common occurrences on special nights.
    d. Friends should not travel together in a limo.

24. Which statement can best be supported by this passage?
    a. The girls had been best friends since kindergarten.
    b. Ricky and Bobby came to pick up the girls in a limo.
    c. The girls' mothers were very supportive of their decision to go to the dance.
    d. The town has a great emergency response team.

185

Questions 25–30 are based on the following passage:

1   Princess Diana, born Diana Spencer on July 1, 1961 in Sandringham, England, left this world on August 31, 1997, at the age of thirty-six.

2   Princess Diana was a graduate of Riddlesworth Hall School and West Heath School. After completing further schooling at Institut Alpin Videmanette in Switzerland, she worked as a teacher's assistant so she could pursue her passion for working with children.

3   Princess Diana was known for her big heart and support of various charities. Some of her most influential work included helping the homeless and children in need. She also worked to provide support to people living with HIV and AIDS. Princess Diana also partnered with her sons, working diligently to raise awareness in Angola about the dangers of landmines left behind after war.

4   Princess Diana is survived by son, Prince William Arthur Philip Louis; son, Prince Henry Charles Albert David; and ex-husband, Prince Charles of Wales.

5   Funeral services will be held September 6 at Westminster Abbey. A family-only graveside ceremony will be held at the Spencer family estate, Althorp.

6   *In lieu of* flowers, the family requests donations be made to the Diana, Princess of Wales Memorial Fund in an effort to continue the valuable charity work Princess Diana cherished.

25. What type of article is this passage?
    a. News article
    b. Preface
    c. Obituary
    d. Short story

26. The phrase *in lieu of* most nearly means
    a. Because of
    b. Instead of
    c. Preferably
    d. Do not send

27. With the information in this passage, readers can conclude Princess Diana was passionate about
    a. Having children
    b. Doing charity work
    c. Getting an education
    d. Funding charities

28. After Princess Diana completed school, she
    a. Moved to Sandringham, England
    b. Had children
    c. Became a teacher's assistant
    d. Did charity work

29. With the information in the passage, readers can infer donations to the Diana, Princess of Wales Memorial Fund will
    a. Pay for her funeral at the family estate
    b. Buy clothes and school supplies for less fortunate children
    c. Be transferred to the family trust
    d. Send her sons to college

30. How is this passage organized?
    a. Biographical information is followed by current events.
    b. An opinion is offered about an individual.
    c. Evidence is presented to refute an individual's popularity.
    d. A thesis statement is followed by supporting paragraphs.

Questions 31–36 are based on the following passage:

1   Mr. Walter lived here in Vinson, Oklahoma, for his entire life. He owned the little green house in town where he and his wife, Hilda, raised four boys. Mr. Walter worked at the paper mill as a welder for forty-eight years.

2   When he retired, he became the school crossing guard. Every day, Mr. Walter stood on that corner and helped kids safely cross the street. He knew the name of every kid who stopped at his corner, and he was always happy to see each one. In the wintertime, he handed out hats and gloves to kids who'd left theirs at home. Mr. Walter was always smiling as he waved to every driver that passed his corner.

3   After he got too old to be the crossing guard, Mr. Walter bought himself a bicycle. It was a three-wheeled bike, metallic red with a basket on the front. At eighty years old, Mr. Walter put on his helmet and started running the roads.

4   Mr. Walter rode that red bike around town picking up cans and trash. He said it was his job to look out for his city. It wasn't uncommon to see his bike parked at the McDonald's on Main. He'd be standing out near the street waving at every car that passed.

5   The whole town showed up at Mr. Walter's funeral. In eighty-four years, there wasn't a day that had gone by where Mr. Walter hadn't touched one of our lives. Mr. Walter had been a hero to us. He'd never saved anyone from a burning house or leapt tall buildings in a single bound, but he had loved our town and each of us in it, wholeheartedly. That is what made him our hero.

31. The phrase *running the roads* is an example of a(an)
    a. Simile
    b. Personification
    c. Idiom
    d. Metaphor

187

32. What can readers conclude from this passage?
    a. Mr. Walter retired from the paper mill and started riding his bike around town.
    b. Mr. Walter could never remember the names of the children he crossed at his corner.
    c. Mr. Walter picked up cans and trash when he worked at the paper mill.
    d. Mr. Walter touched the lives of everyone in the town of Vinson.

33. This passage can be categorized as a(n)
    a. Informational text
    b. Short story
    c. News article
    d. Persuasive letter

34. According to the passage, it was common for Mr. Walter to
    a. Give kids hats and gloves in the winter
    b. Forget to wear his safety helmet
    c. Encourage kids to pick up their trash
    d. Take his cans to the McDonald's

35. What is the overall message of this passage?
    a. Heroes should save people from burning buildings.
    b. Sometimes it's the little things that make you a hero.
    c. Kids think all adults like Mr. Walter are heroes.
    d. All school crossing guards are special people.

36. The phrase *leapt tall buildings in a single bound* is an example of a(n)
    a. Hyperbole
    b. Simile
    c. Onomatopoeia
    d. Allusion

Questions 37–42 are based on the following passage:

1   When researchers and engineers undertake a large-scale scientific project, they may end up making discoveries and developing technologies that have far wider uses than originally intended. This is especially true at NASA, one of the most influential and innovative scientific organizations in America. NASA spinoff technology refers to innovations originally developed for NASA space projects that are now used in a wide range of different commercial fields. Many consumers are unaware that products they are buying are based on NASA research! Spinoff technology proves that it is worthwhile to invest in scientific research because it could enrich people's lives in unexpected ways.

2   The first spinoff technology worth mentioning is baby food. In space, where astronauts have limited access to fresh food and fewer options with their daily meals, malnutrition is a serious concern. Consequently, NASA researchers were looking for ways to enhance the nutritional value of astronauts' food. Scientists found that a certain type of algae could be added to food to improve the food's neurological benefits. When experts in the commercial food industry learned of this algae's potential to boost brain health, they were quick to begin their own research. The nutritional substance from algae then

188

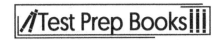

developed into a product called life's DHA, which can be found in over 90 percent of infant food sold in America.

3   Another intriguing example of a spinoff technology can be found in fashion. People who are always dropping their sunglasses may have invested in a pair of sunglasses with scratch-resistant lenses. This innovation is incredibly advantageous for people who are clumsy, but most shoppers don't know that this technology was originally developed by NASA. Scientists first created scratch-resistant glass to help protect costly and crucial equipment from getting scratched in space, especially the helmet visors in space suits. However, sunglass companies later realized that this technology could be profitable for their products, and they licensed the technology from NASA.

37. What is the main purpose of this article?
    a. To advise consumers to do more research before making a purchase
    b. To persuade readers to support NASA's research
    c. To tell a narrative about the history of space technology
    d. To define and describe instances of spinoff technology

38. What is the organizational structure of this article?
    a. A general definition followed by more specific examples
    b. A general opinion followed by supporting evidence
    c. An important moment in history followed by chronological details
    d. A popular misconception followed by counterevidence

39. Why did NASA scientists research algae?
    a. They already knew algae was healthy for babies.
    b. They were interested in how to grow food in space.
    c. They were looking for ways to add health benefits to food.
    d. They hoped to use it to protect expensive research equipment.

40. What does the word *neurological* mean in paragraph 2?
    a. Related to the body
    b. Related to the brain
    c. Related to vitamins
    d. Related to technology

41. Why does the author mention space suit helmets?
    a. To give an example of astronaut fashion
    b. To explain where sunglasses got their shape from
    c. To explain how astronauts protect their eyes
    d. To give an example of valuable space equipment

42. Which statement would the author probably NOT agree with?
    a. Consumers don't always know the history of the products they are buying.
    b. Sometimes new innovations have unexpected applications.
    c. It is difficult to make money from scientific research.
    d. Space equipment is often very expensive.

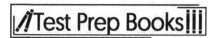

Questions 43–47 are based on the following passage:

1   Koko the gorilla, who passed in 2018 at the age of forty-six, knew more than 2000 words and could sign at least 1000 of those. Although this was a feat unto itself, even more interesting was the belief that Koko, in addition to learning words, was actually communicating with the researchers she worked with. Perhaps even more interesting, in terms of language acquisition and learning, is that Koko created her own word combinations for words she didn't know. For example, she coined "eye hats" to mean a mask and, more famously, "finger watches" to mean rings.

2   Humans are always amazed at an animal's capacity to learn language, although we've long known that most animals communicate in a language all their own. Furthermore, we understand that many mammals have complex languages of their own as well. For example, we've long been obsessed with attempting to translate and decode the languages of both dolphins and whales.

3   Despite their ability to communicate and our ability to teach specific words to mammals, there has long been debate about whether any of this actually constitutes language. More specifically, language, by definition, requires three things: semantics, grammar, and vocabulary acquisition. This is where the debate gets tricky because some evidence, among some animals, seems to demonstrate all of these requirements.

4   Before we delve into these examples, let's clarify what we mean by semantics and grammar. Semantics refers to the fact that there are words or phrases that have meanings that are immutable. Grammar refers to the rules by which sentences are constructed. Finally, vocabulary acquisition refers to the ability for the species to learn and use new words. This means they are not born with language, and ingrained communication, such as a baby's cry, although communication, does not qualify as language. Many scientists argue that for us to truly define animal communication as a language, the communication must demonstrate the noted requirements.

5   The question then becomes, Do we see any of these requirements in animal species, let alone all three? The short answer is yes. In both monkeys and bird species, researchers have recorded and studied calls that denote a threat or predator. The birds' language appears to be more complex, as variations in pitch, repetition, and duration seem to indicate additional information about the predator, including what and where it is. This demonstrates a fixed meaning to the vocalizations.

6   When it comes to grammar, there are more questions than answers. Although some of the avian species appear to have syntax and appear to construct longer strings of sounds together to denote different meanings, grammar is less clear. Research did demonstrate that when the calls were repeated back to the birds, the reaction (to a predator) was the same. However, when researchers played the sounds in reverse, the reaction was not the same. Some researchers assert that this means there is a sentence structure and, therefore, grammar. Others argue that this is a demonstration of syntax, or fixed meaning.

7   Finally, when it comes to language and vocabulary acquisition, researchers are increasingly interested in dolphins and whales. Both whales and dolphins seem to learn

190

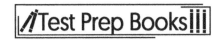

new "words." More specifically, dolphins learn new whistles, and humpback whales learn new songs, which seem to spread across pods, especially as they cross geographical areas. Still, there is much to be learned about the way sea mammals communicate. For that reason, intense focus and effort has been spent in gathering the millions of songs that will be required to make accurate computer algorithms to decipher their language.

43. Birds' failure to respond to a call repeated in reverse is listed as evidence of what part of language?
    a. Vocabulary
    b. Rhetoric
    c. Grammar
    d. Punctuation

44. "... some evidence, among some animals, seems to demonstrate all of these [language] requirements" is an example of which of the following?
    a. Main idea
    b. Supporting detail
    c. Topic sentence
    d. Conclusion

45. Which phrasing is an example of the author's opinion?
    a. "... researchers are increasingly interested in dolphins and whales." (paragraph 7)
    b. "... a baby's cry, although communication, does not qualify as language." (paragraph 4)
    c. "... there is much to be learned about the way sea mammals communicate." (paragraph 7)
    d. "Perhaps even more interesting, in terms of language acquisition and learning ..." (paragraph 1)

46. According to the passage, why is syntax important in language?
    a. It creates sentence structure.
    b. It creates a fixed meaning to vocabulary.
    c. It creates new vocabulary.
    d. It creates complex variations.

47. Which of the following is explained in the passage as support for the idea that communication does not necessarily qualify as language?
    a. The variations in pitch, repetition, and duration in bird calls.
    b. The reactions of birds to bird calls that are played in reverse.
    c. Koko's creation of word combinations.
    d. A baby's cry.

Language

1. Which sentence below does NOT contain an error in comma usage for dates?
    a. My niece arrives from Australia on Monday, February 4, 2016.
    b. My cousin's wedding this Saturday June 9, conflicts with my best friend's birthday party.
    c. The project is due on Tuesday, May, 17, 2016.
    d. I can't get a flight home until Thursday September 21.

2. Which of the following sentences uses correct spelling?
   a. Although he believed himself to be a consciensious judge of character, his judgment in this particular situation was grossly erroneous.
   b. Although he believed himself to be a conscientious judge of character, his judgment in this particular situation was grossly erroneous.
   c. Although he believed himself to be a conscentious judge of character, his judgement in this particular situation was grossly erroneous.
   d. Although he believed himself to be a concientious judge of character, his judgemant in this particular situation was grossly erroneous.

3. The stress of preparing for the exam was starting to take its toll on me.

In the preceding sentence, what part of speech is the word *stress*?
   a. Verb
   b. Noun
   c. Adjective
   d. Adverb

4. Select the example that uses the correct plural form.
   a. Rooves
   b. Octopi
   c. Potatos
   d. Mooses

5. Which of these examples uses correct punctuation?
   a. The presenter said, "The award goes to," and my heart skipped a beat.
   b. The presenter said, "The award goes to" and my heart skipped a beat.
   c. The presenter said "The award goes to" and my heart skipped a beat.
   d. The presenter said, "The award goes to", and my heart skipped a beat.

6. Select the sentence in which the word *counter* functions as an adjective.
   a. The kitchen counter was marred and scratched from years of use.
   b. He countered my offer for the car, but it was still much higher than I was prepared to pay.
   c. Her counter argument was very well presented and logically thought out.
   d. Some of the board's proposals ran counter to the administration's policies.

7. In which of the following sentences does the pronoun correctly agree with its antecedent?
   a. Human beings on the planet have the right to his share of clean water, food, and shelter.
   b. Human beings on the planet have the right to their share of clean water, food, and shelter.
   c. Human beings on the planet have the right to its share of clean water, food, and shelter.
   d. Human beings on the planet have the right to her share of clean water, food, and shelter.

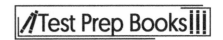

8. Which of the following is the complete subject of the following sentence?

> Every single one of my mother's siblings, their spouses, and their children met in Colorado for a week-long family vacation last summer.

   a. Every single one
   b. Siblings, spouses, children
   c. One
   d. Every single one of my mother's siblings, their spouses, and their children

9. Using the context clues in the following sentence, which of the following is the correct meaning of the word *foliage*?

> Walking through the heavily wooded park by the river in October, I was amazed at the beautiful colors of the foliage, the bright blue sky, and the crystal-clear water.

   a. Leaves of the trees
   b. Feathers of the birds
   c. Tree bark
   d. Rocks on the path

10. Which of the following sentences incorrectly uses italics?
   a. *Old Yeller* is a classic in children's literature, yet very few young people today have read it or even seen the movie.
   b. My favorite musical of all time has to be *The Sound of Music*, followed closely by *Les Miserables.*
   c. Langston Hughes's famous poem *Dreams* is the most anthologized of all his works.
   d. When I went to the Louvre, I was surprised at how small Leonardo de Vinci's *Mona Lisa* is compared to other paintings.

11. Which of the following sentences employs correct usage?
   a. It's always a better idea to ask permission first rather than ask for forgiveness later.
   b. Its always a better idea to ask permission first rather than ask for forgiveness later.
   c. It's always a better idea to ask permission first rather then ask for forgiveness later.
   d. Its always a better idea to ask permission first rather then ask for forgiveness later.

12. Which of the following is an imperative sentence?
   a. The state flower of Texas is the blue bonnet.
   b. Do you know if the team is playing in the finals or not?
   c. Take the first right turn, and then go one block west.
   d. We won in overtime!

13. Identify the compound sentence from the following examples:
   a. John and Adam met for coffee before going to class.
   b. As I was leaving, my dad called and needed to talk.
   c. I ran before work and went to the gym afterward for an hour or so.
   d. Felix plays the guitar in my roommate's band, and Alicia is the lead vocalist.

14. Identify all the words that function as nouns in the following sentence.

Jose had three exams on Monday, so he spent several hours in the library the day before and more time in his dorm room that night studying.
- a. Jose, exams, hours, library, day, time, room, night
- b. Jose, exams, Monday, hours, library, day, time, room, night
- c. Jose, exams, Monday, he, hours, library, day, time, dorm, night
- d. Exams, Monday, hours, library, day, time, room, night

15. Identify the sentence that uses correct subject-verb agreement.
- a. Each of the students have completed the final project and presentation.
- b. Many players on the basketball team was injured in last night's game.
- c. My friends from school has been trying to talk me in to dance classes.
- d. Everyone in my family has broken a bone except for me.

16. Which of the following sentences has an error in capitalization?
- a. My Mom used to live on the East Coast.
- b. I registered for one semester of Famous Women in Film, but there is not enough room in my schedule.
- c. I prefer traveling on Southwest Airlines because they do not charge baggage fees.
- d. I have never been to Martha's Vineyard, or to any other part of New England for that matter.

17. From the answer choices below, select one that is used as an adjective in the following sentence.

The exhilarating morning air, combined with the beautiful mountain scenery, inspired me to want to jump right out of bed every morning for a lengthy run.
- a. Air
- b. Inspired
- c. Exhilarating
- d. Me

18. My favorite teacher gave _____ and _____ extra credit on our project.
- a. me, him
- b. he, I
- c. him, I
- d. him, me

19. Which of these sentences uses correct punctuation?
- a. We traveled through six states on our road trip; Texas, New Mexico, Colorado, Wyoming, Utah, and Montana.
- b. We traveled through six states on our road trip: Texas, New Mexico, Colorado, Wyoming, Utah, and Montana.
- c. We traveled through six states on our road trip Texas, New Mexico, Colorado, Wyoming, Utah, and Montana.
- d. We traveled through six states on our road trip, Texas, New Mexico, Colorado, Wyoming, Utah, and Montana.

20. Which of the following sentences employs correct usage?
    a. You're going to need to go there to get your backpack from their house.
    b. Your going to need to go there to get you're backpack from their house.
    c. You're going to need to go their to get your backpack from there house.
    d. Your going to need to go their to get you're backpack from there house.

21. Which of the following sentences uses passive voice?
    a. My car was terribly dented by hail during the storm the other night.
    b. My car looked great after the car wash and detailing.
    c. The hail damaged not only my car but the roof of my house as well.
    d. The storm rolled through during the night, taking everyone by surprise.

22. Which of the following sentences correctly uses an apostrophe?
    a. The childrens' choir performed at the Music Hall on Tuesday.
    b. The Smith's went to Colorado with us last summer.
    c. The Joneses' house is currently unoccupied while they are out of the country.
    d. Peoples' attitudes about politics are sometimes apathetic.

23. Which of the following sentences does NOT use correct parallel structure?
    a. We worked out every day by swimming, biking, and a run.
    b. The list of craft supplies included scissors, glue, tissue paper, and glitter.
    c. Before I can come over, I need to run to the bank, go to the grocery store, and stop by the dry cleaners.
    d. I love to eat good food, take long walks, and read great books.

24. Which of the following words is spelled incorrectly?
    a. Caffiene
    b. Counterfeit
    c. Sleigh
    d. Receipt

25. The following sentence contains what kind of error?

    Forgetting that he was supposed to meet his girlfriend for dinner, Anita was mad when Fred showed up late.

    a. Parallelism
    b. Run-on sentence
    c. Misplaced modifier
    d. Subject-verb agreement

26. The following sentence contains what kind of error?

    Some workers use all their sick leave, other workers cash out their leave.

    a. Parallelism
    b. Comma splice
    c. Sentence fragment
    d. Subject-verb agreement

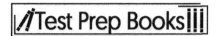
27. A student writes the following in an essay:

Protestors filled the streets of the city. Because they were dissatisfied with the government's leadership.

Which of the following is an appropriately punctuated correction for this sentence?
a.   Protestors filled the streets of the city, because they were dissatisfied with the government's leadership.
b.   Protesters, filled the streets of the city, because they were dissatisfied with the government's leadership.
c.   Because they were dissatisfied with the government's leadership protestors filled the streets of the city.
d.   Protestors filled the streets of the city because they were dissatisfied with the government's leadership.

28. Which word choices will correctly complete the sentence?

Increasing the price of bus fares has had a greater _____ on ridership _____ expected.

a.   affect; then
b.   affect; than
c.   effect; then
d.   effect; than

29. Compared to other students, twelve-year-old Dave is somewhat of an oddity at six feet, two inches (tallness runs in his family).

The parentheses in the preceding sentence indicate what?
a.   The information within is essential to the paragraph.
b.   The information, though relevant, carries less emphasis.
c.   The information is redundant and should be eliminated.
d.   The information belongs elsewhere.

30. The high school student, after witnessing some wrongdoing against others, spoke to teachers and _____ in accordance with his _____.
a.   principals; principles
b.   principles; principals
c.   princapals; princaples
d.   princaples; princapals

31. Each patient, having gone through rehabilitative therapy, needed ____ file returned to the nursing station.
a.   they're
b.   there
c.   his or her
d.   the people's

32. A man decided not to take his family to the zoo after hearing about a bomb threat on the news. The man believed the threat to be real and _____.
    a. eminent
    b. imminent
    c. emanate
    d. amanita

33. Which of the following is punctuated correctly?
    a. Martha read and analyzed *The Taming of the Shrew*: she presented her findings to the class.
    b. Martha read and analyzed *The Taming of the Shrew*, she presented her findings to the class.
    c. Martha read and analyzed *The Taming of the Shrew*; she presented her findings to the class.
    d. Martha read and analyzed *The Taming of the Shrew* she presented her findings to the class.

34. Which of the following exemplifies a compound sentence?
    a. Tod and Elissa went to the movies, got some dessert, and slept.
    b. Though Tod and Elissa decided to go to the movies, Marge stayed home.
    c. Tod and Elissa decided to go to the movies, and Marge read a book.
    d. Tod and Elissa went to the movies while Marge slept.

35. The professor's engaging lecture, though not his best, ran over thirty minutes late.

Which of the following words in this preceding sentence functions as a verb?
    a. Engaging
    b. Though
    c. Ran
    d. Over

36. Dave arrived at work almost thirty minutes late. His boss, who was irritated, lectured him. Dave was inconsolable the rest of the shift.

Which of the following words in this preceding passage functions as an adverb?
    a. Arrived
    b. Almost
    c. Irritated
    d. Rest

37. Which of the following is capitalized correctly?
    a. History 220 is taught by one of my favorite professors. He used to teach an entry-level sociology class but decided he likes teaching Advanced History better.
    b. History 220, taught by Mr. Hart, the Professor, focuses on the conflicts that transformed America: The Revolution, The Civil War, The Korean War, World War I, World War II, and Vietnam.
    c. In particular, he likes to discuss how yankee ingenuity helped overcome the British army and navy, the world's most formidable world power at the time.
    d. Mr. Hart is scheduled to retire in the summer of 2018. President Williams already said he'll be in charge of retirement party planning.

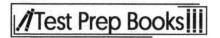
38. Which of the following passages best displays clarity, fluency, and parallelism?
   a. Ernest Hemingway is probably the most noteworthy of expatriate authors. Hemingway's concise writing style, void of emotion and stream of consciousness, had a lasting impact, one which resonates to this very day. In Hemingway's novels, much like in American cinema, the hero acts without thinking, is living in the moment, and is repressing physical and emotional pain.
   b. Ernest Hemingway is probably the most noteworthy of expatriate authors since his concise writing style is void of emotion and stream of consciousness and has had a lasting impact on Americans which has resonated to this very day, and Hemingway's novels are much like in American cinema. The hero acts. He doesn't think. He lives in the moment. He represses physical and emotional pain.
   c. Ernest Hemingway is probably the most noteworthy of authors. His concise writing style, void of emotion and consciousness, had a lasting impact, one which resonates to this very day. In Hemingway's novels, much like in American cinema, the hero acts without thinking, lives in the moment, and represses physical and emotional pain.
   d. Ernest Hemingway is probably the most noteworthy of expatriate authors. His concise writing style, void of emotion and stream of consciousness, had a lasting impact, one which resonates to this very day. In Hemingway's novels, much like in American cinema, the hero acts without thinking, lives in the moment, and represses physical and emotional pain.

39. Which of the following is punctuated correctly?
   a. After reading *Frankenstein*, Daisy turned to her sister and said, "You told me this book wasn't 'all that bad.' You scare me as much as the book!"
   b. After reading "Frankenstein," Daisy turned to her sister and said, "You told me this book wasn't 'all that bad.' You scare me as much as the book!"
   c. After reading *Frankenstein*, Daisy turned to her sister and said, 'You told me this book wasn't "all that bad." You scare me as much as the book!'
   d. After reading *Frankenstein*, Daisy turned to her sister, and said "You told me this book wasn't 'all that bad'. You scare me as much as the book!"

40. Which sentence uses proper subject-verb agreement?
   a. Each of the members of the chess club, who have been successful before on their own, struggled to unite as a team.
   b. Everyone who has ever owned a pet and hasn't had help knows it's difficult.
   c. Neither of the boys, after a long day of slumber, have cleaned their bedrooms.
   d. One of the very applauded and commended lecturers are coming to our campus!

Math

1. What is the sum of $\frac{1}{3}$ and $\frac{2}{5}$?
   a. $\frac{3}{8}$

   b. $\frac{11}{15}$

   c. $\frac{11}{30}$

   d. $\frac{4}{5}$

198

2. What is the value of the expression: $7^2 - 3 \times (4 + 2) + 15 \div 5$?
   a. 12.2
   b. 40.2
   c. 34
   d. 58.2

3. How would $\frac{4}{5}$ be written as a percent?
   a. 40%
   b. 125%
   c. 90%
   d. 80%

4. If $-3(x + 4) \geq x + 8$, what is the value of x?
   a. $x = 4$
   b. $x \geq 2$
   c. $x \geq -5$
   d. $x \leq -5$

5. What is the 42nd item in the pattern: ▲○○□ ▲○○□ ▲...?
   a. ○
   b. ▲
   c. □
   d. None of the above

6. A closet is filled with red, blue, and green shirts. If $\frac{1}{3}$ of the shirts are green and $\frac{2}{5}$ are red, what fraction of the shirts are blue?
   a. $\frac{4}{15}$
   b. $\frac{1}{5}$
   c. $\frac{7}{15}$
   d. $\frac{1}{2}$

7. Shawna buys $2\frac{1}{2}$ gallons of paint. If she uses $\frac{1}{3}$ of it on the first day, how much does she have left?
   a. $1\frac{5}{6}$ gallons
   b. $1\frac{1}{2}$ gallons
   c. $1\frac{2}{3}$ gallons
   d. 2 gallons

8. What value of x would solve the following equation?
$$6x + x - 5 = 20 + 3x$$

   a. $x = -5$

   b. $x = 2$

   c. $x = \dfrac{11}{4}$

   d. $x = \dfrac{25}{4}$

9. Arrange the following numbers from least to greatest value:

$$0.85, \frac{4}{5}, \frac{2}{3}, \frac{91}{100}$$

   a. $0.85, \dfrac{4}{5}, \dfrac{2}{3}, \dfrac{91}{100}$

   b. $\dfrac{4}{5}, 0.85, \dfrac{91}{100}, \dfrac{2}{3}$

   c. $\dfrac{2}{3}, \dfrac{4}{5}, 0.85, \dfrac{91}{100}$

   d. $0.85, \dfrac{91}{100}, \dfrac{4}{5}, \dfrac{2}{3}$

10. Which graph will be a line parallel to the graph of $y = 3x - 2$?
   a. $6x - 2y = -2$
   b. $4x - y = -4$
   c. $3y = x - 2$
   d. $2x - 2y = 2$

11. What is the equation for the line passing through the origin and the point $(2, 1)$?
   a. $y = 2x$

   b. $y = \dfrac{1}{2}x$

   c. $y = x - 2$

   d. $2y = x + 1$

12. A line goes through the point $(-4, 0)$ and the point $(0, 2)$. What is the slope of the line?
   a. 2

   b. 4

   c. $\dfrac{3}{2}$

   d. $\dfrac{1}{2}$

13. Write the expression for three times the sum of twice a number and one, minus six.
   a. $2x + 1 - 6$
   b. $3x + 1 - 6$
   c. $3(x + 1) - 6$
   d. $3(2x + 1) - 6$

14. What would be the coordinates if the point plotted on the grid was reflected over the x-axis?

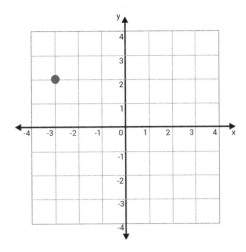

   a. $(-3, 2)$
   b. $(2, -3)$
   c. $(-3, -2)$
   d. $(2, 3)$

15. Jessica buys 10 cans of paint. Red paint costs $1 per can, and blue paint costs $2 per can. In total, she spends $16. How many red cans did she buy?
   a. 2
   b. 3
   c. 4
   d. 5

16. The variable y is directly proportional to x. If $y = 3$ when $x = 5$, then what is y when $x = 20$?
   a. 10
   b. 12
   c. 14
   d. 16

17. Apples cost $2 each, while bananas cost $3 each. Maria purchased a total of 10 pieces of fruit and spent $22. How many apples did she buy?
   a. 5
   b. 6
   c. 7
   d. 8

201

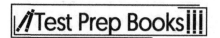

18. If $-3(x + 4) \geq x + 8$, what is the value of x?
    a. $x = 4$
    b. $x \geq 2$
    c. $x \geq -5$
    d. $x \leq -5$

19. Steve has received the following scores on his math tests: 70, 54, 65, 85. What score must Steve get on his next math test to have an overall average of at least 70?
    a. 76
    b. 80
    c. 70
    d. 95

20. What is the overall median of Dwayne's current scores: 78, 92, 83, 97?
    a. 80.5
    b. 85
    c. 90
    d. 87.5

21. Simplify the following fraction:

$$\frac{\frac{5}{7}}{\frac{9}{11}}$$

    a. $\frac{55}{63}$

    b. $\frac{7}{1,000}$

    c. $\frac{13}{15}$

    d. $\frac{5}{11}$

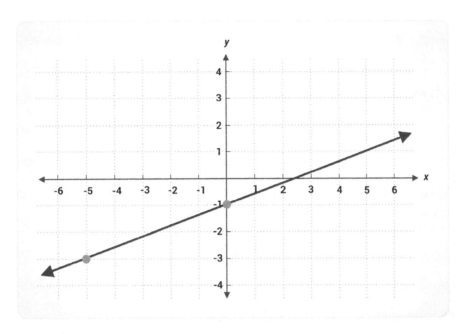

22. What is the slope of this line?

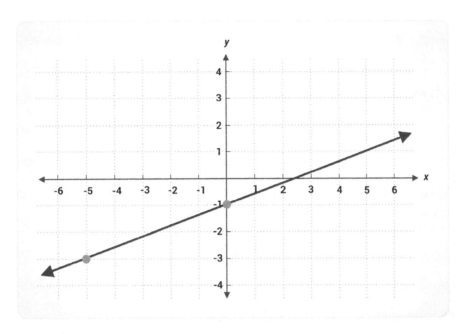

a. 2

b. $\frac{5}{2}$

c. $\frac{1}{2}$

d. $\frac{2}{5}$

23. What is the perimeter of the figure below? Note that the solid outer line is the perimeter.

a. 48.565 in
b. 36.565 in
c. 39.78 in
d. 39.565 in

24. Which four-sided shape is always a rectangle?
   a. Rhombus
   b. Square
   c. Parallelogram
   d. Quadrilateral

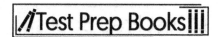

25. Of the numbers -1, 17, -13, or -6, which is farthest from 5 on the number line?
    a. -1
    b. 17
    c. -13
    d. -6

26. If $\sqrt{1 + x} = 4$, what is x?
    a. 10
    b. 15
    c. 20
    d. 25

27. Five students take a test. The scores of the first four students are 80, 85, 75, and 60. If the median score is 80, which of the following could NOT be the score of the fifth student?
    a. 60
    b. 80
    c. 85
    d. 100

28. Which of the following statements is true about the two lines below?

    a. The two lines are parallel but not perpendicular.
    b. The two lines are perpendicular but not parallel.
    c. The two lines are both parallel and perpendicular.
    d. The two lines are neither parallel nor perpendicular.

29. What is the volume of a rectangular prism with a height of 2 inches, a width of 4 inches, and a depth of 6 inches?
    a. 12 in^3
    b. 24 in^3
    c. 48 in^3
    d. 96 in^3

30. What is the volume of a cylinder, in terms of π, with a radius of 5 inches and a height of 10 inches?
    a. $250\pi \text{ in}^3$
    b. $50\pi \text{ in}^3$
    c. $100\pi \text{ in}^3$
    d. $200\pi \text{ in}^3$

31. Ten students take a test. Five students get a 50. Four students get a 70. If the average score is 55, what was the last student's score?
   a. 20
   b. 40
   c. 50
   d. 60

32. An equilateral triangle has a perimeter of 18 feet. The sides of a square have the same length as the triangle's sides. What is the area of the square?
   a. 6 square feet
   b. 36 square feet
   c. 256 square feet
   d. 1,000 square feet

33. Which of the following numbers has the greatest value?
   a. 1.43785
   b. 1.07548
   c. 1.43592
   d. 0.89409

34. What is $(2 \times 20) \div (7 + 1) + (6 \times 0.01) + (4 \times 0.001)$?
   a. 5.064
   b. 5.64
   c. 5.0064
   d. 48.064

35. Last year, the New York City area received approximately $27\frac{3}{4}$ inches of snow. The Denver area received approximately three times as much snow as New York City. How much snow fell in Denver?
   a. 60 inches
   b. $27\frac{1}{4}$ inches
   c. $9\frac{1}{4}$ inches
   d. $83\frac{1}{4}$ inches

36. Solve for x: $\frac{2x}{5} - 1 = 59$.
   a. 60
   b. 145
   c. 150
   d. 115

37. A National Hockey League store in the state of Michigan advertises 50% off all items. Sales tax in Michigan is 6%. How much would a hat originally priced at $32.99 and a jersey originally priced at $64.99 cost during this sale? Round to the nearest penny.
   a. $97.98
   b. $103.86
   c. $51.93
   d. $48.99

205

38. Store-brand coffee beans cost $1.23 per pound. A local coffee bean roaster charges $1.98 per $1\frac{1}{2}$ pounds. How much more would 5 pounds from the local roaster cost than 5 pounds of the store-brand?
   a. $0.55
   b. $1.55
   c. $1.45
   d. $0.45

39. Paint Inc. charges $2,000 for painting the first 1,800 feet of trim on a house and an additional $1.00 per foot for each foot beyond that. How much would it cost to paint a house with 3,125 feet of trim?
   a. $3,125
   b. $2,000
   c. $5,125
   d. $3,325

40. A train traveling 50 miles per hour takes a trip lasting 3 hours. If a map has a scale of 1 inch per 10 miles, how many inches apart are the train's starting point and ending point on the map?
   a. 14 inches
   b. 12 inches
   c. 13 inches
   d. 15 inches

Answer Explanations #1

Reading

1. B: This item asks you to determine the purpose of this passage. Choice *B* is the correct answer because the passage is written to inform readers about companies that offer more modern means of transportation. Choice *A* is incorrect because the author does not promote either company in the passage. Choice *C* is incorrect because the author does not try to persuade readers to schedule a ride for their children, and Choice *D* is incorrect because the author only makes a brief statement about conventional methods of transportation in the first sentence.

2. A: This item asks you to determine which statement can be supported based on information that is given in the passage. Choice A is the correct answer because the text explains how parents can use DeerHaul to help transport their children when they are unavailable. Choices *B* and *D* are incorrect because the third paragraph explains who can drive for DeerHaul and what safety precautions are taken by the company. Choice *C* is incorrect because the author offers no opinion on which company is the better option.

3. D: Your task here is to use information from the text to determine which detail is correct. The passage explains how payments are made electronically through the app. Choice *A* is incorrect since buses and subways are considered public transportation. Choices *B* and *C* are incorrect because when payments are made and tipping are not discussed in the article.

4. C: In this context, battery is synonymous with series, so the correct answer is *C*. Although a battery can be a cell used to provide power to something, an artillery of guns, or an act of violence, none of these are the meaning that best fits this sentence. Thus, Choices *A*, *B*, and *D* are incorrect.

5. B: Choice *B* is correct because the most prevalent idea in the passage is the accessibility of transportation. Choice *A* is incorrect because it is a supporting detail. Choices *C* and *D* are introductory sentences for their paragraphs. They do not represent the entire text.

6. A: Choice *A* is correct because both the second and third paragraphs explain a means of private transportation. Choices *B*, *C*, and *D* are incorrect because the author does not offer an opinion on the best method of transportation or the best company to use.

7. A: Choice *A* is correct because the passage discusses how a department store's advertising project made Rudolph a famous Christmas tradition. Choice *B* is mentioned in the passage as a supporting detail. Choices *C* and *D* are not mentioned in the passage.

8. B: The passage explains that Rudolph leads Santa's team through a blizzard, making him "the most famous reindeer of all", so Choice *B* is the correct answer. The passage does not support the claims made in answers *A, C, or D*.

9. B: Originally, May was asked to create a promotional coloring book, so Choice *B* is correct. The passage does not support the claims made in choices *A, C, or D*.

10. D: Your task here is to identify the meaning of the word *misfit*. The word *misfit* means "oddball," so Choice *D* is correct. The words *member, conformist,* and *insider* are all antonyms, or opposites, for the word *misfit,* so Choices *A*, *B*, and *C* are incorrect.

207

11. C: This item asks you to identify the author's tone in this passage. The author's tone is informative, so Choice *C* is correct. The author is not humorous, apologetic, or sad in this passage, so Choices *A, B,* and *D* are incorrect.

12. C: Your task here is to determine which type of figurative language the phrase *Rudolph the Red-Nosed Reindeer* represents. Choice *C,* alliteration, is correct. Alliteration is the repetition of a consonant at the beginning of multiple consecutive words. Because no comparison is made in this phrase (simile or metaphor) and the phrase is not an onomatopoeia (a word that is formed by its sound), Choices *A, B,* and *D* are incorrect.

13. A: This item asks you to identify information in the passage. The third paragraph indicates that as the temperature of water increases, water molecules move rapidly and spread farther apart, so Choice *A* is correct.

14. A: This item asks you to draw a conclusion based on information learned in the text. Choice *A* is correct because as water vapor cools, the water molecules move closer together and move more slowly to form a liquid.

15. A: The question asks which sentence best represents the main idea in the passage. The passage discusses water having the ability to occupy three states of matter, so Choice *A* is the correct answer. Choices *B, C,* and *D* are main ideas for support paragraphs in the passage, so they are incorrect.

16. D: Your task here is to determine the meaning of the word *molecules.* Molecules are tiny units, or particles, of something, so Choice *D* is correct. Choices *A, B,* and *C* are antonyms for the word *molecule,* so they are incorrect.

17. B: This item asks you to identify specific details in the passage. Because steam, also known as *water vapor,* is water in the form of gas, Choice *B* is correct.

18. D: *Conversely* is a word used to mean "the other way around." The words for choices *A, B,* and *C* say the opposite thing and are incorrect.

19. C: This item asks you to determine the main purpose of this passage. The author tells this sad story to illustrate the impact texting while driving can have, not just on the driver, but also on the passengers, so Choice *C* is correct.

20. B: Your task here is to identify the type of figurative language in the passage. Choice *B* is correct because the phrase *screeched like an alley cat* is a simile. A simile is a comparison of two similar things (the sound of the tires and the screech of an alley cat) using the words *like* or *as.* Choice *A* is incorrect because a metaphor does not contain the words *like* or *as.* An alliteration is the repetition of a consonant sound at the beginning of several consecutive words.

21. A: This item asks you to identify the story's point of view. Choice *A* is correct because the story is told from a first-person point of view. In first-person narratives, the author is a character in the story and uses words such as *I, me,* and *we.* Second person, Choice *B,* which is uncommon, includes words such as *you, your,* and *yours.* In third person, Choice *C,* narratives, the narrator is not a character in the story and uses words such as *he, she,* and *they.* Choice *D,* fourth person, is a made-up choice.

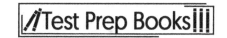

22. A: This task asks you to draw a conclusion based on information provided in the last sentence of the passage. The author says that Ricky, Bobby, and Alyssa never got to see the dancing lights of the ambulances and police cars. Thus, readers can conclude that they didn't survive the accident.

23. B: This task asks you to determine the overall message of this passage. This story serves to highlight the potential consequences of texting and driving to dissuade readers from doing it. This means Choice *B* is the answer.

24. C: This item asks you to examine details from the story. The first paragraph explains in detail how the girls' mothers wanted the day to be fun. Readers can conclude Choice *C* is the correct answer. The story includes no information to indicate *A* or *D* are correct. Choice *B* might be correct, but the text does not provide enough information for that conclusion.

25. C: This item asks you to determine the type of passage. Choice *C*, an obituary, is the correct answer. Obituaries are biographies written to honor someone who has passed away.

26. B: This question asks the meaning of the phrase *in lieu of* in the last paragraph. *In lieu of* means "instead of"; thus, the family is requesting that instead of sending flowers, people donate money to Princess Diana's memorial fund.

27. B: This item asks you to use details in the story to determine what Princess Diana was passionate about. Paragraph three explains her dedication to charity work, so Choice *B* is the correct answer.

28. C: This item asks you to use details in the story to determine a sequence of events. Sentence 3 explains that after school, Princess Diana became a teacher's assistant, so Choice *C* is the correct answer.

29. B: This item asks you to make an inference based on information from the passage. The passage explains that Diana did a great deal of charity work for children in need. The passage also states that the family is asking mourners to donate to the Diana, Princess of Wales Memorial Fund instead of purchasing flowers for the funeral. Readers can safely assume at least some of the donation money will help needy children, so Choice *B* is correct.

30. A: This item asks you to analyze the organization of the passage. Choice *A* is correct because basic information given about Princess Diana's life is followed by current events, such as details about the funeral and where to send donations.

31. C: This item asks you to determine the meaning of a specific phrase in the passage. Idioms are phrases that take on a meaning different from the inherent meaning of the words, like *running the roads*. This means the correct answer is *C*.

32. D: The task here is to draw a conclusion based on information from the text. Throughout the passage, the author speaks of ways Mr. Walter touched the lives of everyone in the town of Vinson, so Choice *D* is correct.

33. B: This item asks you to decide how this passage is categorized. This passage is considered a short story because it has a message, a sequence of events, and characters. Thus, Choice *B* is correct.

34. A: This item asks you to identify details in the passage. Choice *A* is correct because the second paragraph tells readers Mr. Walter gave out gloves and hats during the winter to children who needed them.

35. B: This item asks you to identify the overall message in this passage. Choice *B* is correct because the author is trying to point out that heroes can be everyday people who consistently do little things in their communities to impact the lives of others.

36. A: This item asks you to identify the type of figurative language used in the phrase *leapt tall buildings in a single bound.* A hyperbole is an exaggeration not meant to be taken literally, so Choice *A* is correct.

37. D: This is an example of a purpose question—why did the author write this? The article contains facts, definitions, and other objective information without telling a story or arguing an opinion. In this case, the purpose of the article is to inform the reader. Choices *A* and *B* are incorrect because they argue for an opinion or present a position. Choice *C* is incorrect because the focus of the article is spinoff technology, not the history of space technology.

38. B: This organization question asks readers to analyze the structure of the essay. The topic of the essay is about spinoff technology, and the thesis statement at the end of the first paragraph offers the opinion, "Spinoff technology proves that it is worthwhile to invest in scientific research because it could enrich people's lives in unexpected ways." The next two paragraphs provide evidence to support this opinion, making Choice *B* the best option. Choice *A* is the second-best option because the first paragraph gives a general definition of spinoff technology, while the following two paragraphs offer more detailed examples to help illustrate this idea. However, it is not the best answer because the main idea of the essay is that spinoff technology enriches people's lives in unexpected ways. Choice *C* is incorrect because the essay does not provide details of any specific moment in history. Choice *D* is incorrect because the essay does not discuss a popular misconception.

39. C: This reading comprehension question can be answered based on the second paragraph, which describes how scientists were concerned about astronauts' nutrition and began researching useful nutritional supplements. Choice *A* incorrectly says the algae was identified for baby food use first.

40. B: Even for readers who have never encountered the word *neurological* before, the passage does provide context clues. The sentence following the statement about neurological benefits says algae has "potential to boost brain health." From this context, readers should be able to infer that "neurological" is related to the brain.

41. D: This purpose question requires readers to understand the relevance of the given detail. In this case, the author mentions "*costly and crucial equipment*" before mentioning space suit visors, which are given as an example of something that is very valuable. Choice *A* is not correct because fashion is only related to sunglasses, not to NASA equipment. Choice *B* can be eliminated because it is simply not mentioned in the passage. While Choice *C* seems like it could be a true statement, it is also not relevant to what is being explained by the author.

42. C: The article gives several examples of how businesses have been able to capitalize on NASA research, so it is unlikely that the author would agree with this statement. Evidence for the other answer choices can be found in the article. In Choice *A*, the author mentions that "many consumers are unaware that products they are buying are based on NASA research." Choice *B* is a general definition of spinoff technology. Choice *D* is mentioned in the final paragraph.

This material is provided for exam preparation purposes only and does not indicate an endorsement of any specific scientific, political, or religious point of view. © TPB Publishing. You have been licensed one copy of this document for personal use only. Any other reproduction or redistribution is strictly prohibited. All rights reserved.

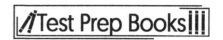

43. C: Some researchers assert that because the call only has meaning in one direction (meaning the reverse does not mean the same), it indicates that there is a sentence structure and, therefore, grammar. Choice *A* is incorrect. There is no debate about the fact that there is a clear meaning to the call or that different calls mean different things and might equate vocabulary. Choice *B* is incorrect. Language debates don't hinge on sentences but rather the structure of those sentences, such as syntax. Choice *D* is incorrect. Punctuation is not included in the passage as a way to define language.

44. A: The fact that some animals demonstrate the building blocks of language is the main idea of the passage. Main ideas address what an author wants readers to know about a topic. Choice *B* and Choice *C* are incorrect. Supporting details and topic sentences support the main idea and present subtopics or ideas. Choice *D* is incorrect. Conclusions are based on evidence and make judgments. This relies on facts but does not make a judgment. Instead, it analyzes the significance of the evidence.

45. D: The word *interesting* is a judgment and therefore demonstrates the author's opinion. Choice *A* and Choice *B* are incorrect because they are both facts and don't include judgment. Choice *C* is incorrect because it is also a statement that reflects the actions of researchers who believe researching sea mammal communication is valuable. This is not the opinion of the author.

46. B: Paragraph 4 establishes the meaning of syntax as providing a fixed meaning to vocabulary. Choice *A* is incorrect. According to the passage, grammar creates sentence structure. Choice *C* is incorrect. Vocabulary has to do with words and their meanings. Choice *D* is incorrect. Complex variations are referenced in relation to birds, which create complex variations to add meaning to sentences. In other words, complex variations may change fixed meanings.

47. D: Choice *D* is correct. The author states that "ingrained communication, such as a baby's cry, although communication, does not qualify as language." Choice *A* is the example used to demonstrate that there is a fixed meaning, or syntax, to the vocalizations made by birds, which is part of the grammar requirement for language. Choice *B* is part of the explanation that indicates that birds use grammar, which is another requirement for language. Choice *C* demonstrates proof of another language requirement, vocabulary acquisition.

Language

1. A: It is necessary to put a comma between the date and the year and between the day of the week and the month. Choice *B* is incorrect because it is missing the comma between the day of the week and the month. Choice *C* is incorrect because it adds an unnecessary comma between the month and date. Choice *D* is missing the necessary comma between day of the week and month.

2. B: *Conscientious* and *judgment* are both spelled correctly in this sentence. These are both considered commonly misspelled words. One or both words are spelled incorrectly in all the other examples.

3. B: In this sentence, the word *stress* is a noun. While the word *stress* can also act as a verb, in this particular case, it is a noun functioning as the subject of the sentence. The word *stress* cannot be used as an adjective or adverb, so these answers are also incorrect.

4. B: The correct answer is *octopi*, the plural form of the word *octopus* (*octupuses* is also correct). Choice *A* is the incorrect spelling of the plural of *roof,* which should be *roofs*. Choice *C* is the incorrect spelling of the plural form of the word *potato*, which should be *potatoes*. Choice *D* is the incorrect plural form of the word *moose*, which remains the same in the singular and the plural, *moose*.

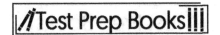

5. A: Quotation marks are used to indicate something someone has said. This is a direct quotation that interrupts, or breaks, the sentence in half. A comma is necessary before the quotation and after it, inside the quotation marks, to set off the quote from the rest of the sentence. Choice *B* is incorrect because there is no comma at the end of the quotation. Choice *C* is incorrect because there is no comma before or after the quotation. Choice *D* is incorrect because the comma at the end of the quotation is placed outside the quotation marks.

6. C: In this sentence, the word *counter* functions as an adjective that modifies the word *argument*. Choice *A* is incorrect because the word *counter* functions as a noun. Choice *B* is incorrect because the word *counter* functions as a verb. Choice *D* is incorrect because the word *counter* functions as an adverb.

7. B: This sentence correctly uses the plural pronoun *their,* which agrees in number with its antecedent, *human beings*. Choice *A* is incorrect because *his* is a singular pronoun and does not agree in number with the antecedent. Choice *C* is incorrect because *its* is a singular pronoun and usually refers to an object. Choice *D* is incorrect because *her* is a singular pronoun and does not agree with the antecedent.

8. D: *Every single one of my mother's siblings, their spouses, and their children* is the complete subject because it includes who or what is doing the action in the sentence as well as the modifiers that go with it. The other answer choices are incorrect because they only include part of the complete subject.

9. A: The word *foliage* is defined as leaves on plants or trees. In this sentence, the meaning can be drawn from the fact that a heavily wooded area in October would be characterized by the beautiful changing colors of the leaves. The other answer choices do not accurately define the word *foliage*, so they are incorrect.

10. C: Choice *C* is the one that incorrectly uses italics; quotation marks should be used for the title of a short work such as a poem, not italics. Choice *A* correctly italicizes the title of a novel. Choice *B* correctly italicizes the title of both musicals, and Choice *D* correctly italicizes the name of a work of art.

11. A: In this sentence, the commonly misused words *it's* and *than* are used correctly. *It's* is a contraction for the pronoun *it* and the verb *is*. The word *than* accurately shows comparison between two things. The other examples all contain some combination of the commonly misused words *then* and *its*. *Then* is an adverb that conveys time, and *its* is a possessive pronoun. Both are incorrectly used in the other examples.

12. C: This example is an imperative sentence because it gives a command and ends with a period (though imperative sentences can also end with an exclamation point). Choice *A* is a declarative sentence that states a fact and ends with a period. Choice *B* is an interrogative sentence that asks a question and ends with a question mark. Choice *D* is an exclamatory sentence that shows strong emotion and ends with an exclamation point.

13. D: This is a compound sentence because it joins two independent clauses, *Felix plays the guitar in my roommate's band* and *Alicia is the lead vocalist*, with a comma and the coordinating conjunction *and*. Choices *A* and *C* are simple sentences, each containing one independent clause with a complete subject and predicate. Choice *A* does contain a compound subject, *John and Adam,* and Choice *C* contains a compound predicate, *ran and went*, but they are still simple sentences that only contain one independent clause. Choice *B* is a complex sentence because it contains one dependent clause, *As I was*

212

leaving, and one independent clause, *my dad called and needed to talk.* This sentence also contains a compound predicate, *called and needed.*

14. B: This answer includes all the words functioning as nouns in the sentence. Choice *A* is incorrect because it does not include the proper noun *Monday.* The word *he* makes Choice *C* incorrect because it is a pronoun. This example also includes the word *dorm,* which can function as a noun, but in this sentence, it functions as an adjective modifying the word *room.* Choice *D* is incorrect because it leaves out the proper noun *Jose.*

15. D: The simple subject of this sentence, *Everyone,* although it names a group, is a singular noun and therefore agrees with the singular verb form *has.* Choice *A* is incorrect because the simple subject *each* does not agree with the plural verb form *have.* In Choice *B,* the plural subject *players* does not agree with the singular verb form *was.* In Choice *C,* the plural subject *friends* does not agree with the singular verb form *has.*

16. A: In this sentence, the word *Mom* should not be capitalized because it is not functioning as a proper noun. If the possessive pronoun *My* was not there, then it would be considered a proper noun and would be capitalized. *East Coast* is correctly capitalized. Choice *B* correctly capitalizes the name of a specific college course, which is considered a proper noun. Choice *C* correctly capitalizes the name of a specific airline, which is a proper noun, and Choice *D* correctly capitalizes the proper nouns *Martha's Vineyard* and *New England.*

17. C: In this sentence, *exhilarating* functions as an adjective that modifies the phrase *morning air. Air* is a noun, *inspired* is a verb, and *me* is a pronoun. Other words functioning as adjectives in the sentence include *beautiful, mountain, every,* and *lengthy.*

18. D: This is the correct answer because the pronouns *him* and *me* are in the objective case. *Him* and *me* are the indirect objects of the verb *gave.* Choice *A* is incorrect because the first-person pronoun (in this example, *me*) should always go last. Choices *B* and *C* are incorrect because they each contain at least one pronoun in nominative case: *he* and *I.*

19. B: In this sentence, a colon is correctly used to introduce a series of items. Choice *A* incorrectly uses a semicolon to introduce the series of states. Choice *C* incorrectly uses a dash to introduce the series. Choice *D* is incorrect because it incorrectly uses a comma to introduce the series.

20. A: This sentence uses the correct form of the contraction *you are* as the subject of the sentence, and it uses the correct form of the possessive pronoun *your* to indicate ownership of the backpack. It also uses the correct form of the adverb *there,* indicating place, and the possessive pronoun *their,* indicating ownership. Choice *B* is incorrect because it reverses the possessive pronoun *your* and the contraction *you are.* Choice *C* is incorrect because it reverses the adverb *there* and the possessive pronoun *their.* Choice *D* is incorrect because it reverses the contraction *you are* and the possessive pronoun *your* and the possessive pronoun *their* and the adverb *there.*

21. A: In Choice *A,* the subject *car* is acted upon, rather than performing the action of the sentence. To put this sentence into active voice, we should make *the hail* be the subject. Example: *The hail during the storm the other night terribly dented my car.* All the other sentences use active voice because the subject is completing the action of the sentence.

22. C: This sentence correctly places an apostrophe after the plural proper noun *Joneses* to show possession. When a proper name ends in s, add es to make it plural, then an apostrophe to make the plural form possessive. In Choice *A*, to make the word children possessive, add an apostrophe and then *s* since the word children is already plural. Choice *B* does not need an apostrophe because *Smiths* is plural, not possessive. Choice *D* incorrectly places an apostrophe after the *s*. In this case, to make *people* possessive, add an apostrophe and then an *s* since the word *people* is already plural.

23. A: When parallel structure is used, all parts of the sentence are grammatically consistent. Choice *A* uses incorrect parallel structure because *swimming* and *biking* are participles, whereas a *run* is a noun phrase, so the structure is grammatically inconsistent.

24. A: The correct spelling of this word is *caffeine*. This answer, along with Choices *B* and *C*, are exceptions to the rule "i before e, except after c". Choice *D* follows this rule because the letters *ie* follow the letter *c*, so the correct order would be *ei*.

25. C: In this sentence, the modifier is the phrase "Forgetting that he was supposed to meet his girlfriend for dinner." This phrase offers information about Fred's actions, but the noun that immediately follows it is Anita, creating some confusion about the "do-er" of the phrase. A more appropriate sentence arrangement would be "Forgetting that he was supposed to meet his girlfriend for dinner, Fred made Anita mad when he showed up late." Choice *A* is incorrect, as parallelism refers to the consistent use of sentence structure and verb tense, and this sentence is appropriately consistent. Choice *B* is incorrect as this sentence contains appropriate punctuation for the number of independent clauses presented; it is not a run-on sentence. Choice *D* is incorrect because subject-verb agreement refers to the appropriate conjugation of a verb relative to the subject, and all verbs have been properly conjugated.

26. B: A comma splice occurs when a comma is used to join two independent clauses together without the additional use of an appropriate conjunction. One way to remedy this problem is to replace the comma with a semicolon. Another solution is to add a conjunction: "Some workers use all their sick leave, but other workers cash out their leave." Choice *A* is incorrect, as parallelism refers to the consistent use of sentence structure and verb tense; all tenses and structures in this sentence are consistent. Choice *C* is incorrect because a sentence fragment is a phrase or clause that cannot stand alone—this sentence contains two independent clauses. Choice *D* is incorrect because subject-verb agreement refers to the proper conjugation of a verb relative to the subject, and all verbs have been properly conjugated.

27. D: The problem in the original passage is that the second sentence is a dependent clause that cannot stand alone as a sentence; it must be attached to the main clause found in the first sentence. Because the main clause comes first, it does not need to be separated by a comma. However, if the dependent clause came first, then a comma would be necessary, which is why Choice *C* is incorrect. Choices *A* and *B* also insert unnecessary commas into the sentence.

28. D: In this sentence, the first answer choice requires a noun meaning *impact* or *influence*, so *effect* is the correct answer. For the second answer choice, the sentence is drawing a comparison. *Than* shows a comparative relationship whereas *then* shows sequence or consequence. Choices *A* and *C* can be eliminated because they contain the choice *then*. Choice *B* is incorrect because *affect* is a verb while this sentence requires a noun.

29. B: Parentheses indicate that the information contained within carries less weight or importance than the surrounding text. The word *essential* makes Choice *A* false. The information, though relevant, is not essential, and the paragraph could survive without it. For Choice *C*, the information is not repeated at any point, and, therefore, is not redundant. For Choice *D*, the information is placed next to his height, which is relevant. Placing it anywhere else would make it out of place.

30. A: Leaders of schools are often called *principals. Principles* are values, morals, or ideology. In Choice *B*, the words are reversed. In Choices *C* and *D*, both answers are misspelled, regardless of position.

31. C: *His* or *her* is correct. Each indicates the need for a singular pronoun, and because the files belong to the patients, the pronoun must be possessive as well. *They're* and *there* do not fit grammatically or make sense in the sentence; *the people's* suggests a single file belonging to all of them, rather than a separate file for each person.

32. B: *Imminent* means impending or happening soon. The man fears going to the zoo because a bomb might soon be detonated. In Choice *A*, *eminent* describes someone of a high rank or status. In Choice *C*, *emanate* means to originate from. In Choice *D*, *amanita* is a type of fungus.

33. C: Semicolons can function as conjunctions. When used thus, they take the place of *and*, joining two independent clauses together. Choice *A* is incorrect because an italicized title should not have quotation marks as well. Choice *B* is an example of a run-on sentence. Commas may not be used to join two independent clauses. Choice *D* is also a run-on sentence. There's no punctuation of any type to indicate two separate clauses that can stand on their own.

34. C: This answer includes two independent clauses that could stand on their own. To test this, try separating the clauses and putting a period at the end. Choice *A*, consists of one independent clause. Choices *B* and *D* consist of an independent clause and a dependent clause.

35. C: For Choice *A*, *engaging* acts as an adjective, describing *lecture.* For Choice *B*, *though* can act as a conjunction or adverb, but not a verb. For Choice *D*, *over* is an adverb that describes *ran*.

36. B: Adverbs describe verbs or adjectives. In this instance, *almost* describes *arrived*, the verb. Adverbs answer questions like how or where, and here *almost* describes how *he arrived*. For Choice *A*, *arrived* is a past-tense verb. For Choice *C*, *irritated* functions as an adjective, describing Dave's boss. *Rest*, Choice *D*, is a noun.

37. D: *Summer* is generic, so it doesn't require capitalization. A title, like *President*, is capitalized when it's specific and precedes the person's name. It's similar to saying *Mr.* or *Mrs.*, followed by a person's name. Choice *A* is incorrect because *advanced history* should not be capitalized. *History 220* is the official name of the class, and *advanced history* is the subject of the class. Choice *B* is incorrect because *professor* should only be capitalized when it precedes the name of the individual. Choice *C* is incorrect because *Yankee* is a proper noun.

38. D: This passage displays clarity (the author states precisely what he or she intended), fluency (the sentences run smoothly together), and parallelism (words are used in a similar fashion to help provide rhythm). Choice *A* lacks parallelism. When the author states, "the hero acts without thinking, is living in the moment, and is repressing physical and emotional pain," the words *acts*, *is living* and *is repressing* are in different tenses, and, consequently, jarring to one's ears. Choice *B* runs on endlessly in the first half ("Ernest Hemingway is probably the most noteworthy of expatriate authors since his concise writing style is void of emotion and stream of consciousness and has had a lasting impact on Americans which

215

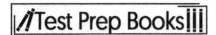

has resonated to this very day, and Hemingway's novels are much like in American cinema."). It demands some type of pause and strains the readers' eyes. The second half of the passage is choppy: "The hero acts. He doesn't think. He lives in the moment. He represses physical and emotional pain." For Choice C, leaving out *expatriate* is, first, vague, and second, alters the meaning. The correct version claims that Hemingway was the most notable of the expatriate authors while the second version claims he's the most notable of any author *ever*, a very bold claim indeed. Also, leaving out *stream of* in "stream of consciousness" no longer references the non-sequential manner in which most people think. Instead, this version sounds like all the characters in the novel are in a coma!

39. A: Books are italicized, like *Frankenstein*, and smaller works are put in quotation marks. A direct quotation takes a single set of quotation marks (" ") and a quote within a quote takes a single set (' '). Choice B is incorrect because *Frankenstein* should be italicized, not put in quotation marks. In Choice C, the double and single-set quotation marks should be reversed. In Choice D, the comma is missing before the first quotation mark, and the period for the quote within a quote is on the outside of the quotation mark, not the inside. Punctuation belongs inside the quotation marks, regardless of whether it a single or double set.

40. B: Indefinite pronouns such as *everyone* always take the singular. The key is to delete unnecessary language mentally ("who has ever owned a pet and hasn't had help"), which allows one to better test the conjugation between noun and verb. In this case, *everyone* and *knows* are joined. Choice A is incorrect because *each* (another indefinite pronoun) is singular while the verb *have* is plural. In Choice C, *neither* is indefinite, so *is* should be *has*, not *have*. In Choice D, *One*, which is indefinite, is the noun. The prepositional phrase "of the very applauded and commended lecturers" can be removed from the sentence. Therefore, the singular *is* is needed, not *are*.

Math

1. B: Fractions must have like denominators to be added. The common denominator is the least common multiple (LCM) of the two original denominators. In this case, the LCM is 15, so both fractions should be changed to equivalent fractions with a denominator of 15. Multiply the bottom of each fraction by whatever number is needed to produce 15, and multiply the top of each fraction by that same number:

$$\frac{1 \times 5}{3 \times 5} = \frac{5}{15} \text{ and } \frac{2 \times 3}{5 \times 3} = \frac{6}{15}$$

Now, add the numerators and keep the denominator the same:

$$\frac{5}{15} + \frac{6}{15} = \frac{11}{15}$$

2. C: When performing calculations consisting of more than one operation, the order of operations should be followed: parentheses, exponents, multiplication & division, addition & subtraction.

Parentheses:

$$7^2 - 3 \times (4 + 2) + 15 \div 5$$

$$7^2 - 3 \times (6) + 15 \div 5$$

216

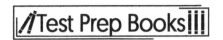

Exponents:

$$49 - 3 \times 6 + 15 \div 5$$

Multiplication & division (from left to right):

$$49 - 18 + 3$$

Addition & subtraction (from left to right):

$$49 - 18 + 3 = 34$$

3. D: To convert a fraction to a percent, we can first convert the fraction to a decimal. To do so, divide the numerator by the denominator: $4 \div 5 = 0.8$. To convert a decimal to a percent, multiply by 100:

$$0.8 \times 100 = 80\%$$

4. D: Solve a linear inequality in a similar way to solving a linear equation. First, start by distributing the −3 on the left side of the inequality.

$$-3x - 12 \geq x + 8$$

Then, add 12 to both sides.

$$-3x \geq x + 20$$

Next, subtract x from both sides.

$$-4x \geq 20$$

Finally, divide both sides of the inequality by −4. Don't forget to flip the inequality sign because you are dividing by a negative number.

$$x \leq -5$$

5. A: The core of the pattern consists of 4 items: ▲○○□. Therefore, the core repeats in multiples of 4, with the pattern starting over on the next step. The highest multiple of 4 that's below 42 is 40. Step 40 is the end of the core (□), so step 41 will start the core over (▲) and step 42 is ○.

6. A: The total fraction taken up by green and red shirts will be:

$$\frac{1}{3} + \frac{2}{5} = \frac{5}{15} + \frac{6}{15} = \frac{11}{15}$$

The remaining fraction is:

$$1 - \frac{11}{15} = \frac{15}{15} - \frac{11}{15} = \frac{4}{15}$$

7. C: If Shawna has used $\frac{1}{3}$ of the paint, she has $\frac{2}{3}$ remaining. The mixed fraction can be converted because $2\frac{1}{2}$ gallons is the same as $\frac{5}{2}$ gallons. The calculation is:

$$\frac{2}{3} \times \frac{5}{2} = \frac{10}{6} = \frac{5}{3} = 1\frac{2}{3} \text{ gallons}$$

8. D:

$$6x + x - 5 = 20 + 3x$$

Combine 6x and x.

$$7x - 5 = 20 + 3x$$

Add 5 to both sides to remove (-5).

$$7x - 5 + 5 = 20 + 3x + 5$$

$$7x = 25 + 3x$$

Subtract 3x from both sides to move it to the other side of the equation.

$$7x - 3x = 25 + 3x - 3x$$

$$4x = 25$$

Divide by 4 to get x by itself.

$$\frac{4x}{4} = \frac{25}{4}$$

$$x = \frac{25}{4}$$

9. C: For each fraction, we can divide the numerator by the denominator to find a decimal value. $\frac{4}{5} = 0.8$, $\frac{2}{3} \approx 0.67$, and $\frac{91}{100} = 0.91$. Ordering these from least to greatest gives us 0.67, 0.8, 0.85, and 0.91, which matches Choice *C*.

10. A: Parallel lines have the same slope. The slope of the given equation is 3. The slope of Choice *C* can be seen to be $\frac{1}{3}$ by dividing both sides by 3. The other choices are in standard form $Ax + By = C$, for which the slope is given by $\frac{-A}{B}$. For Choice *A*, the equation can be written as $6x - 2y = -2$. Therefore, the slope is:

$$\frac{-A}{B} = \frac{-6}{-2} = 3$$

This is the same as the given equation. The slope of Choice *B* is:

$$\frac{-A}{B} = \frac{-4}{-1} = 4$$

The slope of Choice *B* is 4. The slope of Choice *D* is:

$$\frac{-A}{B} = \frac{-2}{-2} = 1$$

The slope of Choice D is 1. Therefore, the only equation with a parallel slope of 3 is $6x - 2y = -2$.

11. B: The origin is (0,0). The slope is given by $\frac{(y^2 - y^1)}{(x^2 - x^1)} = \frac{1-0}{2-0} = \frac{1}{2}$.

The y-intercept will be 0 since it passes through the origin, (0,0). Using slope-intercept form, the equation for this line is:

$$y = \frac{1}{2}x$$

12. D: The slope is given by the change in y divided by the change in x. The change in y is $2 - 0 = 2$, and the change in x is $0 - (-4) = 4$. The slope is $\frac{2}{4} = \frac{1}{2}$.

13. D: "Sum" means the result of addition, so "the sum of twice a number and one" can be written as 2x+1. Next, "three times the sum of twice a number and one" would be $3(2x + 1)$. Finally, "six less than three times the sum of twice a number and one" would be $3(2x + 1) - 6$.

14. C: The coordinates of a point are written as an ordered pair (x, y). To determine the x-coordinate, a line is traced directly above or below the point until reaching the x-axis. This step notes the value on the x-axis. In this case, the x-coordinate is -3. To determine the y-coordinate, a line is traced directly to the right or left of the point until reaching the y-axis, which notes the value on the y-axis. In this case, the y-coordinate is 2. Therefore, the current ordered pair is written $(-3, 2)$. To reflect the point over the x-axis, the x-coordinate stays the same, but the y-coordinate becomes -2, since after a refection over the x-axis, the point would be located equivalently far below the x-axis as it is above the x-axis. Since the current y-coordinate is 2, the y-coordinate would become -2.

15. C: Let r be the number of red cans and b be the number of blue cans. One equation is $r + b = 10$. The total price is \$16, and given the prices for each can, the second equation is $1r + 2b = 16$. Multiplying the first equation on both sides by -1 results in $-r - b = -10$. Add this equation to the second equation, leaving $b = 6$. So, she bought 6 *blue* cans. From the first equation, this means $r = 4$; thus, she bought 4 *red* cans.

16. B: The variable y is directly proportional to x, which means that whenever x is multiplied by a number, y is multiplied by that same number. When x changes from 5 to 20, it is multiplied by 4, so the original y value must also be multiplied by 4. That means $y = 3 \times 4 = 12$

17. D: Let a be the number of apples and let b represent the number of bananas. The total number of fruits is $a + b = 10$, and the total cost is $2a + 3b = 22$. To solve this pair of equations, we can multiply the first equation by -3:

$$-3(a + b) = -3(10)$$

$$-3a - 3b = -30$$

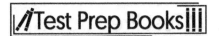

Now we can add this to the other equation, and the b terms cancel out:

$$(-3a - 3b = -30) + (2a + 3b = 22)$$

$$= (-a = -8)$$

This simplifies to $a = 8$.

18. D: When solving a linear inequality, distribution is performed first, if necessary:

$$-3(x + 4) \rightarrow -3x - 12 \geq x + 8$$

The inequality is manipulated to get the variable on one side.

The equation/inequality is manipulated to get the variable on one side. In this case, start by subtracting x from both sides:

$$-4x - 12 \geq 8$$

The variable is isolated using inverse operations to undo subtraction. Adding 12 to both sides produces $-4x \geq 20$.

The variable is isolated using inverse operations to undo multiplication/division. Remember, if dividing by a negative number, the relationship of the inequality reverses, so the sign is flipped. In this case, dividing by -4 on both sides produces $x \leq -5$.

19. C: To find the average of a set of values, add the values together and then divide by the total number of values. In this case, include the unknown value, x, of what Steve needs to score on his next test. The average must equal 70. Set up the equation and solve:

First, combine like terms:

$$\frac{70 + 54 + 65 + 85 + x}{5} = 70$$

$$\frac{274 + x}{5} = 70$$

Next, multiply both sides by 5:

$$(5)(\frac{274 + x}{5}) = (70)(5)$$

$$274 + x = 350$$

Lastly, subtract 274 from both sides:

$$274 + x - 274 = 350 - 275$$

$$x = 76$$

Steve would need to get a minimum score of 76 in order to get an average of at least 70.

220

Test this answer by substituting 76 back into the original formula.

$$\frac{70 + 54 + 65 + 85 + 76}{5} = 70$$

20. D: For an even number of total values, the median is calculated by finding the mean, or average, of the two middle values once all values have been arranged in ascending order from least to greatest. In this case, $\frac{83+92}{2}$ would equal the median 87.5, Choice *D*. Choice *A* is the lowest two values divided by 2, $\frac{78+83}{2} = 80.5$. Choice *B* is the first and third values divided by 2, $\frac{78+92}{2} = 85$. Choice *C* is the second and fourth values divided by 2, $\frac{83+97}{2} = 90$.

21. A: First, simplify the larger fraction by separating it into two fractions. When dividing one fraction by another, remember to invert the second fraction and multiply, like so:

$$\frac{5}{7} \times \frac{11}{9}$$

The resulting fraction $\frac{55}{63}$ cannot be simplified further, so this is the answer to the problem.

22. D: The slope is given by the change in y divided by the change in x. Specifically, it's:

$$slope = \frac{y_2 - y_1}{x_2 - x_1}$$

The first point is $(-5, -3)$, and the second point is $(0, -1)$. Work from left to right when identifying coordinates. Thus, the point on the left is point 1 $(-5, -3)$ and the point on the right is point 2 $(0, -1)$.

Now, we can plug those numbers into the equation:

$$slope = \frac{-1 - (-3)}{0 - (-5)}$$

It can be simplified to:

$$slope = \frac{-1 + 3}{0 + 5}$$

$$slope = \frac{2}{5}$$

23. B: The figure is composed of three sides of a square and a semicircle. The sides of the square are simply added:

$$8 \text{ in} + 8 \text{ in} + 8 \text{ in} = 24 \text{ in}$$

The circumference of a circle is found by the equation $C = 2\pi r$. The radius is 4 in, so the circumference of the circle is approximately 25.13 in. Only half of the circle makes up the outer border of the figure (part of the perimeter), and half of 25.13 in is 12.565 in. Therefore, the total perimeter is:

$$24 \text{ in} + 12.565 \text{ in} = 36.565 \text{ in}$$

The other answer choices use the incorrect formula or fail to include all of the necessary sides.

24. B: A rectangle is a specific type of parallelogram. It has 4 right angles. A square is a rhombus that has 4 right angles. Therefore, a square is always a rectangle because it has two sets of parallel lines and 4 right angles.

25. C: The number line below can be labeled with all 4 given numbers. The number 5 is shown with the open dot. By observing the placement of the dots and their relation to the open dot at 5, the number -1 can be eliminated as an answer because it is the closest. After that, the distance to the other dots can be counted. The distance is shown below with the arcs.

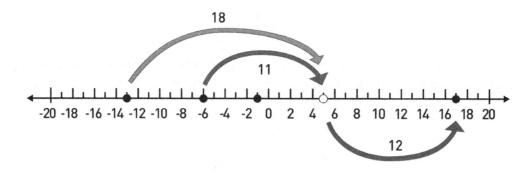

As demonstrated from the arcs showing distance on the number line, the number -13 is furthest from 5 on the number line, at a distance of 18.

26. B: Start by squaring both sides to get $1 + x = 16$. Then, subtract 1 from both sides to get $x = 15$.

27. A: Putting the scores in order from least to greatest, we have 60, 75, 80, and 85, as well as one unknown. The median is 80, so 80 must be the middle data point out of these five. Therefore, the unknown data point must be the fourth or fifth data point, meaning it must be greater than or equal to 80. The only answer that fails to meet this condition is 60.

28. D: Parallel lines will never intersect. Therefore, the lines are not parallel. Perpendicular lines intersect to form a right angle (90°). Although the lines intersect, they do not form a right angle, which is usually indicated with a box at the intersection point. Therefore, the lines are not perpendicular.

29. C: The volume of a rectangular prism is: $volume = length \times width \times height$. Substituting the values given in the problem, we find V $= 2$ in $\times 4$ in $\times 6$ in $= 48$ in^3.

30. A: The volume of a cylinder is $\pi r^2 h$ and $\pi \times 5^2 \times 10$ is 250π in^3.

31. A: Let the unknown score be x. The average will be:

$$\frac{5 \times 50 + 4 \times 70 + x}{10} = \frac{530 + x}{10} = 55$$

Multiply both sides by 10 to get $530 + x = 550$, or $x = 20$.

32. B: An equilateral triangle has 3 sides of equal length, so if the total perimeter is 18 feet, each side must be 6 feet long. A square with sides of 6 feet will have an area of $6^2 = 36$ square feet.

33. A: Compare each numeral after the decimal point to figure out which overall number is greatest. In Choices A (1.43785) and C (1.43592), both have the same value in the tenths (4) and hundredths (3). However, the thousandths is greater in Choice A (7), so A has the greatest value overall.

34. A: Operations within the parentheses must be completed first. Division is completed next, and finally, addition. When adding decimals, digits within each place value are added together. Therefore, the expression is evaluated as:

$$(2 \times 20) \div (7 + 1) + (6 \times 0.01) + (4 \times 0.001)$$

$$40 \div 8 + 0.06 + 0.004$$

$$5 + 0.06 + 0.004 = 5.064$$

35. D: To find Denver's total snowfall, 3 must be multiplied by $27\frac{3}{4}$. In order to easily do this, the mixed number should be converted into an improper fraction.

$$27\frac{3}{4} = \frac{27 \times 4 + 3}{4} = \frac{111}{4}$$

Therefore, Denver had approximately $\frac{3 \times 111}{4} = \frac{333}{4}$ inches of snow. The improper fraction can be converted back into a mixed number through division.

$$\frac{333}{4} = 83\frac{1}{4} \text{ inches}$$

36. C: Set up the initial equation.

$$\frac{2x}{5} - 1 = 59$$

Add 1 to both sides.

$$\frac{2x}{5} - 1 + 1 = 59 + 1$$

Multiply both sides by $\frac{5}{2}$.

$$\frac{2x}{5} \times \frac{5}{2} = 60 \times \frac{5}{2} = 50$$

$$x = 150$$

37. C: We can first find the total cost of the hat and jersey, then multiply by 0.5 to apply the 50% off:

$$(32.99 + 64.99) \times 0.5 = 48.99$$

Finally, we calculate the sales tax of 6% (that is, 0.06) and add it to the total:

$$48.99 + (48.99 \times 0.06) = 51.93$$

38. D: Five pounds of store-brand coffee would cost $\frac{\$1.23}{1\ lbs} \times 5\ lbs = \$6.15$. For five pounds of local coffee, the cost would be $\frac{\$1.98}{1.5\ lbs} \times 5\ lbs = \$6.60$. Calculate the price difference: $\$6.60 - \$6.15 = \$0.45$.

39. D: Find how many feet are left after the first 1,800 ft:

$$3,125\ ft$$

$$\underline{-1,800\ ft}$$

$$1,325\ ft$$

At $1 per foot, this part will cost $1,325. Add this to the $2,000 for the first 1,800 ft to get the total cost:

$$\$2,000 + \$1,325 = \$3,325$$

40. D: First, the train's journey in the real world is:

$$3\ h \times 50\frac{mi}{h} = 150\ mi$$

On the map, 1 inch corresponds to 10 miles, so that is equivalent to:

$$150\ mi \times \frac{1\ in}{10\ mi} = 15\ in$$

Therefore, the start and end points are 15 inches apart on the map.

Practice Test #2

Reading

Questions 1–3 are based on the following passage:

The Global Water Crisis

1   For decades, the world's water supply has been decreasing. At least 10% of the world's population, or over 780 million people, does not have access to potable water. They have to walk for miles, carrying heavy buckets in intense heat, in order to obtain the essential life source that comes freely from our faucets.

2   We are in a global water crisis. Only 2.5% of the water on Earth is suitable for drinking, and over 70% of this water is frozen in the polar ice caps or located deep underground. This leaves a very small percentage available for drinking. And yet, we see millions of gallons of water being wasted on watering huge lawns in deserts like Arizona, running dishwashers that are only half-full, or filling personal pools in Los Angeles. Meanwhile, people in Africa are dying of thirst.

3   In order to reduce water waste, citizens of first world countries should adhere to the following guidelines: only run the dishwasher when it is full, only do full loads of laundry, wash the car with a bucket instead of a hose, only take showers when necessary, and only swim in public pools. Overall, people should be cognizant of how much water they are using in general. Our planet is getting thirstier by the year, and if we do not solve this problem, our species will surely perish.

1. Which of the following best supports the assertion that we need to limit our water usage?
   a. People are wasting water on superfluous things.
   b. There is very little water on Earth suitable for drinking.
   c. At least 10% of the world population does not have access to drinking water.
   d. There is plenty of drinking water in industrialized countries but not anywhere else.

2. Which of the following, if true, would challenge the assertion that we are in a global water crisis?
   a. There are abundant water stores on Earth that scientists are not reporting.
   b. Much of the water we drink comes from rain.
   c. People in Africa only have to walk less than a mile to get water.
   d. Most Americans only run the dishwasher when it is full.

3. Which of the following is implicitly stated within the following sentence?

> This leaves a very small percentage available for drinking. And yet, we see millions of gallons of water being wasted on watering huge lawns in deserts like Arizona, running dishwashers that are only half-full, or filling personal pools in Los Angeles. Meanwhile, people in Africa are dying of thirst.

    a. People run dishwashers that are not full.
    b. People in Africa are dying of thirst.
    c. People take water for granted.
    d. People should stop watering their lawns.

Questions 4–10 are based on the following passage:

1   People who argue that William Shakespeare is not responsible for the plays attributed to his name are known as anti-Stratfordians (from the name of Shakespeare's birthplace, Stratford-upon-Avon). The most common anti-Stratfordian claim is that William Shakespeare simply was not educated enough or from a high enough social class to have written plays overflowing with references to such a wide range of subjects like history, the classics, religion, and international culture. William Shakespeare was the son of a glove-maker, he only had a basic grade-school education, and he never set foot outside of England—so how could he have produced plays of such sophistication and imagination? How could he have written in such detail about historical figures and events, or about different cultures and locations around Europe? According to anti-Stratfordians, the depth of knowledge contained in Shakespeare's plays suggests a well-traveled writer from a wealthy background with a university education, not a countryside writer like Shakespeare. But in fact, there is not much substance to such speculation, and most anti-Stratfordian arguments can be refuted with a little background about Shakespeare's time and upbringing.

2   First of all, those who doubt Shakespeare's authorship often point to his common birth and brief education as stumbling blocks to his writerly genius. Although it is true that Shakespeare did not come from a noble class, his father was a very *successful* glove-maker and his mother was from a very wealthy land-owning family—so while Shakespeare may have had a country upbringing, he was certainly from a well-off family and would have been educated accordingly. Also, even though he did not attend university, grade-school education in Shakespeare's time was actually quite rigorous and exposed students to classic drama through writers like Seneca and Ovid. It is not unreasonable to believe that Shakespeare received a very solid foundation in poetry and literature from his early schooling.

3   Next, anti-Stratfordians tend to question how Shakespeare could write so extensively about countries and cultures he had never visited before. For instance, several of his most famous works like *Romeo and Juliet* and *The Merchant of Venice* were set in Italy, which is located on the opposite side of Europe from England. But again, this criticism does not hold up under scrutiny. For one thing, Shakespeare was living in London, a **bustling** metropolis of international trade, the most populous city in England, and a political and cultural hub of Europe. In the daily crowds of people, Shakespeare would certainly have been able to meet travelers from other countries and hear firsthand

226

accounts of life in their home country. And, in addition to the influx of information from world travelers, this was also the age of the printing press. This jump in technology made it possible to print and circulate books much more easily than in the past. This also facilitated a freer flow of information across different countries, allowing people to read about life and ideas from all over Europe. One needn't travel the continent in order to learn and write about its different cultures.

4. What is the main purpose of this article?
   a. To explain two sides of an argument and allow readers to choose which side they agree with
   b. To encourage readers to be skeptical about the authorship of famous poems and plays
   c. To give historical background on an important literary figure
   d. To criticize a theory by presenting counterevidence

5. Which sentence contains the author's thesis?
   a. People who argue that William Shakespeare is not responsible for the plays attributed to his name are known as anti-Stratfordians.
   b. But in fact, there is not much substance to such speculation, and most anti-Stratfordian arguments can be refuted with a little background about Shakespeare's time and upbringing.
   c. It is not unreasonable to believe that Shakespeare received a very solid foundation in poetry and literature from his early schooling.
   d. Next, anti-Stratfordians tend to question how Shakespeare could write so extensively about countries and cultures he had never visited before.

6. How does the author respond to the claim that Shakespeare was not well-educated because he did not attend university?
   a. By insisting upon Shakespeare's natural genius
   b. By explaining grade-school curriculum in Shakespeare's time
   c. By comparing Shakespeare with other uneducated writers of his time
   d. By pointing out that Shakespeare's wealthy parents probably paid for private tutors

7. The bolded word **bustling** most nearly means
   a. Busy
   b. Foreign
   c. Expensive
   d. Undeveloped

8. What can be inferred from the article?
   a. Shakespeare's peers were jealous of his success and wanted to attack his reputation.
   b. Until recently, classic drama was only taught in universities.
   c. International travel was extremely rare in Shakespeare's time.
   d. In Shakespeare's time, glove-makers were not part of the upper class.

9. Why does the author mention *Romeo and Juliet*?
   a. It is Shakespeare's most famous play.
   b. It was inspired by Shakespeare's trip to Italy.
   c. It is an example of a play set outside of England.
   d. It was unpopular when Shakespeare first wrote it.

10. Which statement would the author probably agree with?
    a. It is possible to learn things from reading rather than from firsthand experience.
    b. If you want to be truly cultured, you need to travel the world.
    c. People never become successful without a university education.
    d. All of the world's great art comes from Italy.

Questions 11–20 are based on the following passage:

1   Three years ago, I think there were not many bird-lovers in the United States who believed it possible to prevent the total extinction of both egrets from our fauna. All the known rookeries accessible to plume-hunters had been totally destroyed. Two years ago, the secret discovery of several small, hidden colonies prompted William Dutcher, President of the National Association of Audubon Societies, and Mr. T. Gilbert Pearson, Secretary, to attempt the protection of those colonies. With a fund contributed for the purpose, wardens were hired and duly **commissioned**. As previously stated, one of those wardens was shot dead in cold blood by a plume hunter. The task of guarding swamp rookeries from the attacks of money-hungry desperadoes, to whom the accursed plumes were worth their weight in gold, is a very chancy proceeding. There is now one warden in Florida who says that "before they get my rookery they will first have to get me."

2   Thus far, the protective work of the Audubon Association has been successful. Now there are 20 colonies, which contain, all told, about 5,000 egrets and about 120,000 herons and ibises which are guarded by the Audubon wardens. One of the most important is on Bird Island, a mile out in Orange Lake, Central Florida, and it is ably defended by Oscar E. Baynard. To-day, the plume hunters who do not dare to raid the guarded **rookeries** are trying to study out the lines of flight of the birds, to and from their feeding-grounds, and shoot them in transit. Their motto is "Anything to beat the law, and get the plumes." It is there that the state of Florida should take part in the war.

3   The success of this campaign is attested by the fact that last year a number of egrets were seen in eastern Massachusetts—for the first time in many years. And so to-day the question is, can the wardens continue to hold the plume-hunters at bay?

11. The author's use of first-person pronouns in the following text does NOT have which of the following effects?

> Three years ago, I think there were not many bird-lovers in the United States who believed it possible to prevent the total extinction of both egrets from our fauna.

    a. The phrase "I think" acts as a sort of hedging, where the author's tone is less direct and absolute.
    b. It allows the reader to more easily connect with the author.
    c. It encourages the reader to empathize with the egrets.
    d. It distances the reader from the text by overemphasizing the story.

228

12. What purpose does the quote serve at the end of the first paragraph?
    a. The quote shows proof of a hunter threatening one of the wardens.
    b. The quote lightens the mood by illustrating the colloquial language of the region.
    c. The quote provides an example of a warden protecting one of the colonies.
    d. The quote provides much needed comic relief in the form of a joke.

13. The bolded word **rookeries** most nearly means
    a. Houses in a slum area
    b. A place where hunters gather to trade tools
    c. A place where wardens go to trade stories
    d. A colony of breeding birds

14. What is on Bird Island?
    a. Hunters selling plumes
    b. An important bird colony
    c. Bird Island Battle between the hunters and the wardens
    d. An important egret with unique plumes

15. What is the main purpose of the passage?
    a. To persuade the audience to act in preservation of the bird colonies
    b. To show the effect hunting egrets has had on the environment
    c. To argue that the preservation of bird colonies has had a negative impact on the environment
    d. To demonstrate the success of the protective work of the Audubon Association

16. According to the passage, why are hunters trying to study the lines of flight of the birds?
    a. To further their studies of ornithology
    b. To help wardens preserve the lives of the birds
    c. To have a better opportunity to hunt the birds
    d. To build their homes under the lines of flight because they believe it brings good luck

17. A year before the passage was written, where were a number of egrets seen?
    a. California
    b. Florida
    c. Eastern Massachusetts
    d. Western Texas

18. The bolded word **commissioned** most nearly means
    a. Appointed
    b. Compelled
    c. Beguiled
    d. Fortified

19. What happened two years before the passage was written?
    a. The plume hunters didn't dare to raid the rookeries, as they are heavily guarded.
    b. Twenty colonies have emerged as thousands of egrets are protected and make their homes in safe havens.
    c. The plume hunters tried to shoot the birds in their line of flight.
    d. Several hidden colonies were found which prompted Dutcher and Pearson to protect them.

20. As it is used in paragraph 2, the phrase *in transit* most nearly means:
    a. On a journey or trip
    b. To give authority to
    c. On the way to the destination
    d. To make angry

Questions 21–30 are based on the following passage:

1   Four hundred years ago, in 1612, the north-west of England was the scene of England's biggest peacetime witch trial: the trial of the Lancashire witches. Twenty people, mostly from the Pendle area of Lancashire, were imprisoned in the castle as witches. Ten were hanged, one died in gaol, one was sentenced to stand in the pillory, and eight were acquitted. The 2012 anniversary saw a small flood of **commemorative** events, including works of fiction by Blake Morrison, Carol Ann Duffy, and Jeanette Winterson. How did this witch trial come about, and what accounts for its **enduring** fame?

2   We know so much about the Lancashire Witches because the trial was recorded in unique detail by the clerk of the court, Thomas Potts, who published his account soon afterwards as *The Wonderful Discovery of Witches in the County of Lancaster*. I have recently published a modern-English edition of this book, together with an essay piecing together what we know of the events of 1612. It has been a fascinating exercise, revealing how Potts carefully edited the evidence, and also how the case against the "witches" was constructed and manipulated to bring about a spectacular show trial. It all began in mid-March when a pedlar from Halifax named John Law had a frightening encounter with a poor young woman, Alizon Device, in a field near Colne. He refused her request for pins and there was a brief argument during which he was seized by a fit that left him with "his head ... drawn awry, his eyes and face deformed, his speech not well to be understood; his thighs and legs stark lame." We can now recognize this as a stroke, perhaps triggered by the stressful encounter. Alizon Device was sent for and surprised all by confessing to the bewitching of John Law and then begging for forgiveness.

3   When Alizon Device was unable to cure the pedlar, the local magistrate, Roger Nowell was called in. Characterized by Thomas Potts as "God's justice," he was alert to instances of witchcraft, which were regarded by the Lancashire's Puritan-inclined authorities as part of the cultural rubble of "popery"—Roman Catholicism—long overdue to be swept away at the end of the country's very slow Protestant Reformation. "With weeping tears," Alizon explained that she had been led astray by her grandmother, "old Demdike," well-known in the district for her knowledge of old Catholic prayers, charms, cures, magic, and curses. Nowell quickly interviewed Alizon's grandmother and mother, as well as Demdike's supposed rival, "old Chattox," and her daughter Anne. Their panicky attempts to explain themselves and shift the blame to others eventually only ended up incriminating them, and the four were sent to Lancaster gaol in early April to await trial at the summer assizes. The initial picture revealed was of a couple of poor, marginal local families in the forest of Pendle with a longstanding reputation for magical powers, which they had occasionally used at the request of their wealthier neighbours. There had been disputes but none of these were

part of ordinary village life. Not until 1612 did any of this come to the attention of the authorities.

4 The net was widened still further at the end of April when Alizon's younger brother James and younger sister Jennet, only nine years old, came up between them with a story about a "great meeting of witches" at their grandmother's house, known as Malkin Tower. This meeting was presumably to discuss the plight of those arrested and the threat of further arrests, but according to the evidence extracted from the children by the magistrates, a plot was hatched to blow up Lancaster castle with gunpowder, kill the gaoler, and rescue the imprisoned witches. It was, in short, a conspiracy against royal authority to rival the gunpowder plot of 1605—something to be expected in a county known for its particularly strong underground Roman Catholic presence.

5 Those present at the meeting were mostly family members and neighbours, but they also included Alice Nutter, described by Potts as "a rich woman [who] had a great estate, and children of good hope: in the common opinion of the world, of good temper, free from envy or malice." Her part in the affair remains mysterious, but she seems to have had Catholic family connections, and may have been one herself, providing an added motive for her to be prosecuted.

21. What's the point of this passage, and why did the author write it?
    a.   The author is documenting a historic witchcraft trial while uncovering/investigating the role of suspicion and anti-Catholicism in the events.
    b.   The author seeks long-overdue reparations for the ancestors of those accused and executed for witchcraft in Lancashire.
    c.   The author is educating the reader about actual occult practices of the 1600s.
    d.   The author argues that the Lancashire witch trials were more brutal than the infamous Salem trials.

22. Which term BEST captures the meaning of the author's use of the bolded word **enduring**?
    a.   Un-original
    b.   Popular
    c.   Wicked
    d.   Circumstantial

23. What textual information is present within the passage that most lends itself to the author's credibility?
    a.   His prose is consistent with the time.
    b.   This is a reflective passage; the author doesn't need to establish credibility.
    c.   The author cites specific quotes.
    d.   The author has published a modern account of the case and has written on the subject before.

24. What might the following excerpt suggest about the trial or, at the very least, Thomas Potts' account of the trial?

> It has been a fascinating exercise, revealing how Potts carefully edited the evidence, and also how the case against the "witches" was constructed and manipulated to bring about a spectacular show trial.

a. The events were so grand that the public was allowed access to such a spectacular set of cases.
b. Sections may have been exaggerated or stretched to create notoriety on an extraordinary case.
c. Evidence was faked, making the trial a total farce.
d. The trial was corrupt from the beginning.

25. Which statement best describes the political atmosphere of the 1600s that influenced the Alizon Device witch trial/case?
a. Fear of witches was prevalent during this period.
b. Magistrates were seeking ways to cement their power during this period of unrest.
c. In a highly superstitious culture, the Protestant church and government were highly motivated to root out any potential sources that could undermine the current regime.
d. Lancashire was originally a prominent area for pagan celebration, making the modern Protestants very weary of whispers of witchcraft and open to witch trials to resolve any potential threats to Christianity.

26. Which best describes the strongest "evidence" used in the case against Alizon and the witches?
a. Knowledge of the occult and witchcraft
b. "Spectral evidence"
c. Popular rumors of witchcraft and Catholic association
d. Self-incriminating speech

27. What type of passage is this?
a. Persuasive
b. Expository
c. Narrative
d. Descriptive

28. According to the passage, how many people were arrested as witches in the Lancashire trials?
a. Ten
b. Twenty
c. Thirty
d. Forty

29. The bolded word **commemorative** most nearly means
a. Associated with being acquitted
b. An act of disloyalty
c. A circumstance to be disliked
d. In honor of something

232

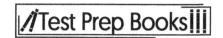

30. According to the passage, what is Malkin tower?
    a. The building where the trial of the Lancashire witches took place.
    b. The grandmother's house of the peddler who sought revenge on Alizon.
    c. Alizon's grandmother's house where a meeting of witches was held.
    d. The residence of a jury member who witnessed the cursing of the peddler.

Questions 31–40 are based upon the following passage:

1   Insects as a whole are **preeminently** creatures of the land and the air. This is shown not only by the possession of wings by a vast majority of the class, but by the mode of breathing to which reference has already been made, a system of branching air-tubes carrying atmospheric air with its combustion-supporting oxygen to all the insect's tissues. The air gains access to these tubes through a number of paired air-holes or spiracles, arranged segmentally in series.

2   It is of great interest to find that, nevertheless, a number of insects spend much of their time under water. This is true of not a few in the perfect winged state, as for example aquatic beetles and water-bugs ('boatmen' and 'scorpions') which have some way of protecting their spiracles when submerged, and, possessing usually the power of flight, can pass on occasion from pond or stream to upper air. But it is advisable in connection with our present subject to dwell especially on some insects that remain continually under water till they are ready to undergo their final **molt** and attain the winged state, which they pass entirely in the air. The preparatory instars of such insects are aquatic; the adult instar is aerial. All may-flies, dragon-flies, and caddis-flies, many beetles and two-winged flies, and a few moths thus divide their life-story between the water and the air. For the present we confine attention to the Stone-flies, the May-flies, and the Dragon-flies, three well-known orders of insects respectively called by systematists the Plecoptera, the Ephemeroptera, and the Odonata.

3   In the case of many insects that have aquatic larvae, the latter are provided with some arrangement for enabling them to reach atmospheric air through the surface-film of the water. But the larva of a stone-fly, a dragon-fly, or a may-fly is adapted more completely than these for aquatic life; it can, by means of gills of some kind, breathe the air dissolved in water.

31. Which statement best details the central idea in this passage?
    a. It introduces certain insects that transition from water to air.
    b. It delves into entomology, especially where gills are concerned.
    c. It defines what constitutes insects' breathing.
    d. It invites readers to have a hand in the preservation of insects.

32. The bolded word **molt** most nearly means
    a. An adventure of sorts, especially underwater
    b. Mating act between two insects
    c. The act of shedding part or all of the outer shell
    d. Death of an organism that ends in a revival of life

33. What is the purpose of paragraph 1 in relation to paragraph 2?
   a. The first paragraph serves as a cause, and the second paragraph serves as an effect.
   b. The first paragraph serves as a contrast to the second.
   c. The first paragraph is a description for the argument in the second paragraph.
   d. The first and second paragraphs are merely presented in a sequence.

34. What does the following sentence most nearly mean?

   The preparatory instars of such insects are aquatic; the adult instar is aerial.

   a. The volume of water is necessary to prep the insect for transition rather than the volume of the air.
   b. The abdomen of the insect is designed like a star in the water as well as the air.
   c. The early stages in between periods of molting are acted out in the water, while the last stage is in the air.
   d. These insects breathe first in the water through gills yet continue to use the same organs to breathe in the air.

35. Which of the statements reflects information that one could reasonably infer based on the author's tone?
   a. The author's tone is persuasive and attempts to call the audience to action.
   b. The author's tone is passionate due to excitement over the subject and personal narrative.
   c. The author's tone is informative and exhibits interest in the subject of the study.
   d. The author's tone is somber, depicting some anger at the state of insect larvae.

36. Which statement best describes stoneflies, mayflies, and dragonflies?
   a. They are creatures of the land and the air.
   b. They have a way of protecting their spiracles when submerged.
   c. Their larvae can breathe the air dissolved in water through gills of some kind.
   d. The preparatory instars of these insects are aerial.

37. According to the passage, what is true of "boatmen" and "scorpions"?
   a. They have no way of protecting their spiracles when submerged.
   b. They have some way of protecting their spiracles when submerged.
   c. They usually do not possess the power of flight.
   d. They remain continually under water till they are ready to undergo their final molt.

38. Paragraph 3 indicates that the author believes
   a. That the stonefly, dragonfly, and mayfly larvae are better prepared to live beneath the water because they have gills that allow them to do so.
   b. That the stonefly is different from the mayfly because the stonefly can breathe underwater and the mayfly can only breathe above water.
   c. That the dragonfly is a unique species in that its larvae lives mostly underwater for most of its young life.
   d. That the stonefly larvae can breathe only by reaching the surface film of the water.

39. According to the passage, why are insects as a whole preeminently creatures of the land and the air?
    a. Because insects are born on land but eventually end up adapting to life underwater for the rest of their adult lives.
    b. Because most insects have legs made for walking on land and tube-like structures on their bellies for skimming the water.
    c. Because a vast majority of insects have wings and also have the ability to breathe underwater.
    d. Because most insects have a propulsion method specifically designed for underwater use, but they can only breathe on land.

40. The bolded word **preeminently** most nearly means
    a. Unknowingly
    b. Above all
    c. Most truthfully
    d. Not importantly

Questions 41–43 are based on the following passage.

1   Christopher Columbus is often credited with discovering America. This is a matter of perspective; America was unknown to fifteenth-century Europe, but bear in mind that the places he "discovered" were already filled with people who had been living there for centuries. What's more, Christopher Columbus was not the first European explorer to reach the present-day Americas! Rather, it was Leif Erikson who first came to the New World and contacted the natives nearly 500 years before Christopher Columbus.

2   Leif Erikson, the son of Erik the Red (a famous Viking outlaw and explorer in his own right), was born in either 970 or 980, depending on which historian you read. His own family, though, did not raise Leif, which was a Viking tradition. Instead, one of Erik's prisoners taught Leif reading and writing, languages, sailing, and weaponry. At age 12, Leif was considered a man and returned to his family. He killed a man during a dispute shortly after his return, and the council banished the Erikson clan to Greenland.

3   In 999, Leif left Greenland and traveled to Norway, where he would serve as a guard to King Olaf Tryggvason. It was there that he became a convert to Christianity. Leif later tried to return home with the intention of taking supplies and spreading Christianity to Greenland, but his ship was blown off course and he arrived in a strange new land: present-day Newfoundland, Canada.

4   When he finally returned to his adopted homeland of Greenland, Leif consulted with a merchant who had also seen the shores of this previously unknown land. The son of the legendary Viking explorer then gathered a crew of 35 men and set sail. Leif became the first European to set foot in the New World as he explored present-day Baffin Island and Labrador, Canada. His crew called the land Vinland since it was plentiful with grapes.

5   During their time in present-day Newfoundland, Leif's expedition made contact with the natives whom they referred to as Skraelings (which translates to "wretched ones" in Norse). There are several secondhand accounts of their meetings. Some contemporaries described trade between the peoples. Other accounts describe clashes where the Skraelings defeated the Viking explorers with long spears, while still others claim the Vikings dominated the natives. Regardless of the circumstances, it seems that the

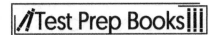

Vikings made contact of some kind. This happened around the year 1000, nearly five hundred years before Columbus famously sailed the ocean blue.

6   Eventually, in 1003, Leif set sail for home and arrived at Greenland with a ship full of timber. In 1020, 17 years later, the legendary Viking died. Many believe that Leif Erikson should receive more credit for his contributions in exploring the New World.

41. Which of the following is an opinion, rather than a historical fact, expressed by the author?
    a.   Leif Erikson was definitely the son of Erik the Red; however, historians debate the year of his birth.
    b.   Leif Erikson's crew called the land Vinland since it was plentiful with grapes.
    c.   Leif Erikson deserves more credit for his contributions in exploring the New World.
    d.   Leif Erikson explored the Americas nearly 500 years before Christopher Columbus.

42. Which of the following most accurately describes the author's main conclusion?
    a.   Leif Erikson is a legendary Viking explorer.
    b.   Leif Erikson deserves more credit for exploring America hundreds of years before Columbus.
    c.   Spreading Christianity motivated Leif Erikson's expeditions more than any other factor.
    d.   Leif Erikson contacted the natives nearly five hundred years before Columbus.

43. Which of the following can be logically inferred from the passage?
    a.   The Vikings disliked exploring the New World.
    b.   Leif Erikson's banishment from Iceland led to his exploration of present-day Canada.
    c.   Leif Erikson never shared his stories of exploration with the King of Norway.
    d.   Historians have difficulty definitively pinpointing events in the Vikings' history

Questions 44–47 are based on the following passage:

Learning how to write a 10-minute play may seem like a monumental task at first, but if you follow a simple creative writing strategy, similar to writing a narrative story, you will be able to write a successful drama. The first step is to open your story as if it is a puzzle to be solved. This will allow the reader a moment to engage with the story and to mentally solve the story with you, the author. You should immediately provide descriptive details that steer the main idea, the tone, and the mood according to the overarching theme you have in mind. For example, if the play is about something ominous, you may open Scene 1 with a thunderclap. Next, use dialogue to reveal the attitudes and personalities of each of the characters who have a key part in the unfolding story. Keep the characters off balance in some way to create interest and dramatic effect. Maybe what the characters say does not match what they do. Show images on stage to speed up the narrative; remember, one picture speaks a thousand words. As the play progresses, the protagonist must cross the point of no return in some way; this is the climax of the story. Then, as in a written story, you create a resolution to the life-changing event of the protagonist. Let the characters experience some kind of self-discovery that can be understood and appreciated by the patient audience. Finally, make sure all things come together in the end so that every detail in the play makes sense right before the curtain falls.

44. Based on the passage above, which of the following statements is NOT true?
   a. Writing a 10-minute play may seem like an insurmountable task.
   b. Providing descriptive details is not necessary until after the climax of the storyline.
   c. Engaging the audience by jumping into the storyline immediately helps them solve the story's developing ideas with you, the writer.
   d. Descriptive details give clues to the play's intended mood and tone.

45. In the passage above, the writer suggests that writing a 10-minute play is accessible for a novice playwright because of which of the following reasons?
   a. It took the author of the passage only one week to write his first play.
   b. The format follows strategies similar to those for writing a narrative story.
   c. There are no particular themes or points to unravel; a playwright can use a stream-of-consciousness style to write a play.
   d. Dialogue that reveals the characters' particularities is uncommonly simple to write.

46. Based on the passage above, which basic feature of narrative writing is NOT mentioned with respect to writing a 10-minute play?
   a. Character development
   b. Descriptive details
   c. Dialogue
   d. Style

47. Based on the passage above, which of the following is true?
   a. Eighth graders usually learn how to write a ten-minute play more easily than adults do.
   b. The playwrights of the 21st century all use the narrative writing basic feature guide to outline their initial scripts.
   c. In order to follow a simple structure, a person can write a ten-minute play based on some narrative writing features.
   d. Women find playwriting easier than men because they are used to communicating in writing.

Language

1. Select the best word for the blank in the following sentence:

   Tom couldn't decide which shirt to ____.

   a. ware
   b. where
   c. wear
   d. were

2. Identify the adjective clause in the following sentence:

   A boy who loves to ride bikes gets plenty of exercise.

   a. a boy who loves
   b. who loves to ride bikes
   c. to ride bikes
   d. gets plenty of exercise

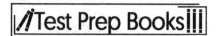

3. Identify the adverbial clause in the following sentence:

I want to work in the garden longer unless you are too tired.

a. I want to work in the garden
b. In the garden
c. Are too tired
d. Unless you are too tired

4. Identify the noun phrase in the following sentence:

The actor and actress rode in the long black limousine.

a. Actor and actress
b. Rode in the
c. The long black limousine
d. Actress rode in

For the next two questions, select the answer choice that best corrects the underlined portion of the sentence:

5. It is necessary for instructors to offer tutoring <u>to any students who need extra help in the class.</u>
a. to any students who need extra help in the class.
b. for any students needs extra help in the class.
c. with any students who need extra help in the class.
d. for any students needed extra help in the class.

6. <u>Because many people</u> feel there are too many distractions to get any work done, I actually enjoy working from home.
a. Because many people
b. While many people
c. Maybe many people
d. With most people

7. Which sentence shows grammatically correct parallelism?
a. He is the clown who inflated balloons and honked his nose.
b. He is the clown who inflated balloons and who honked his nose.
c. He is the clown that inflated balloons and who honked his nose.
d. He is the clown that inflated balloons and that honked his nose.

8. Which sentence shows grammatically correct parallelism?
a. My grandparents have been traveling and have been sightseeing.
b. My grandparents has been traveling and sightseeing.
c. My grandparents were traveling and have been sightseeing.
d. My grandparents have been traveling and they're sightseeing.

9. Which sentence shows grammatically correct subordination?
    a. The building was sturdy and solid; it crumbled during the earthquake.
    b. The building was study and solid although it crumbled during the earthquake.
    c. The building was sturdy and solid, it crumbled during the earthquake.
    d. Despite being sturdy and solid, the building crumbled during the earthquake.

10. Which sentence is grammatically correct?
    a. Every morning we would wake up, ate breakfast, and broke camp.
    b. Every morning we would wake up, eat breakfast, and broke camp.
    c. Every morning we would wake up, eat breakfast, and break camp.
    d. Every morning we would wake up, ate breakfast, and break camp.

11. Which word or words would best link these sentences?

    Polls show that more and more people in the US distrust the government and view it as dysfunctional and corrupt. Every election, the same people are voted back into office.

    a. Not surprisingly,
    b. Understandably,
    c. And yet,
    d. Therefore,

12. A student wants to rewrite the following sentence:

    Entrepreneurs use their ideas to make money.

He wants to use the word *money* as a verb, but he isn't sure which word ending to use. What is the appropriate suffix to add to *money* to complete the following sentence?

    Entrepreneurs _____ their ideas.

    a. –ize
    b. –ical
    c. –en
    d. –ful

13. Based on the following words, what is the correct meaning of the suffix *–fy*?

    Glorify, fortify, gentrify, acidify

    a. Marked by, given to
    b. Doer, believer
    c. Make, cause, cause to have
    d. Process, state, rank

239

14. After a long day at work, Tracy had dinner with her family, and then took a walk to the park.

What are the transitional words in the preceding sentence?
   a. After, then
   b. At, with, to
   c. Had, took
   d. A, the

15. Which words function as nouns in the following sentence?

   Robert needed to find at least four sources for his final project, so he searched several library databases for reliable academic research.

   a. Robert, sources, project, databases, research
   b. Robert, sources, final, project, databases, academic, research
   c. Robert, sources, project, he, library, databases, research
   d. Sources, project, databases, research

16. Which sentence has a misplaced modifier?
   a. The children love their cute and cuddly teddy bears.
   b. Teddy bears are cute and cuddly; the children love them.
   c. Cute and cuddly, the children love their teddy bears.
   d. Cute and cuddly, the teddy bears are loved by many children.

17. Which of the following uses correct spelling?
   a. Jed was disatisfied with the acommodations at his hotel, so he requested another room.
   b. Jed was dissatisfied with the accommodations at his hotel, so he requested another room.
   c. Jed was dissatisfied with the accomodations at his hotel, so he requested another room.
   d. Jed was disatisfied with the accommodations at his hotel, so he requested another room.

18. Which example shows correct comma usage for dates?
   a. The due date for the final paper in the course is Monday, May 16, 2016.
   b. The due date for the final paper in the course is Monday, May 16 2016.
   c. The due date for the final project in the course is Monday, May, 16, 2016.
   d. The due date for the final project in the course is Monday May 16, 2016.

19. Which sentence shows grammatically correct parallelism?
   a. The puppies enjoy chewing and to play tug-o-war.
   b. The puppies enjoy to chew and playing tug-o-war.
   c. The puppies enjoy to chew and to play tug-o-war.
   d. The puppies enjoy chewing and playing tug-o-war.

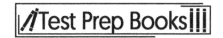

20. In the following sentence, what part of speech is the word *function*?

>   At last night's company function, in honor of Mr. Robertson's retirement, several employees spoke kindly about his career achievements.

   a. Adjective
   b. Adverb
   c. Verb
   d. Noun

21. Which of the examples uses the correct plural form?
   a. Tomatos
   b. Analysis
   c. Cacti
   d. Criterion

22. Which of the following examples uses correct punctuation?
   a. The moderator asked the candidates, "Is each of you prepared to discuss your position on global warming?".
   b. The moderator asked the candidates, "Is each of you prepared to discuss your position on global warming?"
   c. The moderator asked the candidates, 'Is each of you prepared to discuss your position on global warming?'
   d. The moderator asked the candidates, "Is each of you prepared to discuss your position on global warming"?

23. Select the best word for the blank in the following sentence.

>   Garth _____ many pets that he cares for.

   a. has
   b. had
   c. have
   d. haves

24. In which of the following sentences does the word *part* function as an adjective?
   a. The part Brian was asked to play required many hours of research.
   b. She parts ways with the woodsman at the end of the book.
   c. The entire team played a part in the success of the project.
   d. Ronaldo is part Irish on his mother's side of the family.

25. All of Shannon's family and friends helped her to celebrate her 50th birthday at Café Sorrento.

Which of the following is the complete subject of the preceding sentence?
   a. Family and friends
   b. All
   c. All of Shannon's family and friends
   d. Shannon's family and friends

26. Which of the following sentences uses second person point of view?
    a. I don't want to make plans for the weekend before I see my work schedule.
    b. She had to miss the last three yoga classes due to illness.
    c. Pluto is no longer considered a planet because it is not gravitationally dominant.
    d. Be sure to turn off all of the lights before locking up for the night.

27. Based on the context of the following sentence, which of the following words shows the correct meaning of the word *prodigious*?

> As the tour group approached the bottom of Chichen Itza, the prodigious Mayan pyramid, they became nervous about climbing its distant peak.

    a. Very large
    b. Famous
    c. Very old
    d. Fancy

28. Which of the following sentences correctly uses a hyphen?
    a. Last-year, many of the players felt unsure of the coach's methods.
    b. Some of the furniture she selected seemed a bit over - the - top for the space.
    c. Henry is a beagle-mix and is ready for adoption this weekend.
    d. Geena works to maintain a good relationship with her ex-husband to the benefit of their children.

29. Which of the following examples correctly uses quotation marks?
    a. "A Wrinkle in Time" was one of my favorite novels as a child.
    b. Though he is famous for his roles in films like "The Great Gatsby" and "Titanic," Leonardo DiCaprio did not win an Oscar for his role in either film.
    c. Sylvia Plath's poem "Daddy" will be the subject of this week's group discussion.
    d. "The New York Times" reported that many fans are disappointed in some of the trades made by the Yankees this off-season.

30. Which of the following sentences shows correct word usage?
    a. It's often been said that work is better then rest.
    b. Its often been said that work is better then rest.
    c. It's often been said that work is better than rest.
    d. Its often been said that work is better than rest.

31. Which of the following should be evaluated to ensure the credibility of a source?
    a. The publisher, the author, and the references
    b. The subject, the title, and the audience
    c. The organization, stylistic choices, and transition words
    d. The length, the tone, and the contributions of multiple authors

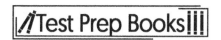

32. Which pronoun makes the following sentence grammatically correct?

    The giraffe nudged _____ baby.

    a. it's
    b. hers
    c. them
    d. its

33. The following sentence contains what kind of error?

    This summer, I'm planning to travel to Italy, take a Mediterranean cruise, going to Pompeii, and eat a lot of Italian food.

    a. Parallelism
    b. Sentence fragment
    c. Misplaced modifier
    d. Subject-verb agreement

34. An English student has been assigned an essay about Oscar Wilde's time in prison. Which of the following sources would be the most relevant for their research?
    a. Oscar Wilde's fictional novels, such as *The Picture of Dorian Gray*
    b. A biography about Wilde
    c. Movie adaptations of Wilde's novels
    d. Internet reviews about Wilde's novels

35. Which of the following sentences uses correct capitalization?
    a. Jeremy learned about the Leaning Tower of Pisa in a college course.
    b. My class went on a trip to Washington, d.c., last week.
    c. I went over to my neighbor's house to meet her cat, daisy.
    d. Brandy was excited to learn the french language.

The next four questions are based on the following passage:

(1) The country of Japan is a chain of islands located along the coast of Asia. (2) Japan is made up of four major islands, with Honshu being the largest. (3) Honshu is also the seventh largest island in the world. (4) Underneath Japan, there are many volcanoes, some active and some dormant, but only about 108 of them are active today.

(5) There are many exciting places to visit in Japan. (6) Osaka is home to Dontobori, the main entertainment district. (7) The popular sport of sumo wrestling is often hosted in the town's arena. (8) People from all over Japan ride the Shinkansen or bullet train to Osaka to watch the events. (9) Hakone is famous for black eggs. (10) The town of Hakone sits on top of a mountain near Mount Fuji, the tallest mountain in Japan. (11) The eggs are boiled in a hot spring on the mountainside. (12) The natural water turns the shell of the egg black; however, it does not change the taste of it. (13) Tokyo is the capital city of Japan. (14) The town of Kyoto is full of shrines and temples, some lined with gold. (15) It is also a well-known place for geisha sightings.

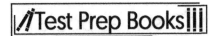

(16) Traditional Japanese food consists mostly of fish and rice. (17) Sushi is raw fish and vegetables rolled in rice and wrapped in seaweed. (18) It is typically dipped in a sauce made of soy sauce and wasabi paste. (19) Tempura is a light, crispy batter used to fry fish, chicken, or vegetables. (20) Soba is another traditional Japanese dish. (21) It is a type of noodle that is oftentimes eaten cold and served in a broth made with soy sauce.

36. Which transition sentence should be added to the beginning of Sentence 16?
   a. Typical Japanese lunch boxes are called *bentos* and usually consist of foods such as dried fruit, rice, and sushi.
   b. Japanese cuisine is very different from American cuisine.
   c. Yakisoba is a traditional Japanese noodle dish served with slices of beef.
   d. Gyoza is a traditional Japanese dish that many Americans refer to as *pot stickers*.

37. Which sentence should be moved to follow Sentence 8 to correct the flow of information in the paragraph?
   a. Sentence 5
   b. Sentence 7
   c. Sentence 10
   d. Sentence 15

38. Which revision of Sentence 4 uses the most precise language?
   a. Japan sits just above 108 active volcanos.
   b. Japan has many volcanos, with only 108 being active.
   c. Active volcanos are common in Japan, especially the biggest 108.
   d. Japan lies on a chain of volcanos, and more than 108 of them are active.

39. Which sentence should be revised to correct an error in sentence structure?
   a. Sentence 4
   b. Sentence 8
   c. Sentence 12
   d. Sentence 14

40. Select the answer that describes the type of error present in the following sentence:

   Benny and Billy went to the mall to buy him a new pair of pants.

   a. Pronoun-antecedent agreement
   b. Sentence fragment
   c. Parallelism
   d. Subject-verb agreement.

Math

1. Frank has been saving up money in order to replace the old appliances in his house. After a 20% sale discount, Frank purchased a new refrigerator for $850. How much did he save compared to the original price?

    a. $170
    b. $212.50
    c. $105.75
    d. $200

2. What is the simplified form of the expression $1.2 \times 10^{12} \div 3.0 \times 10^8$?

    a. 0.4×10^4
    b. 4.0×10^4
    c. 4.0×10^3
    d. 3.6×10^{20}

3. What is the value of x for the right triangle shown below?

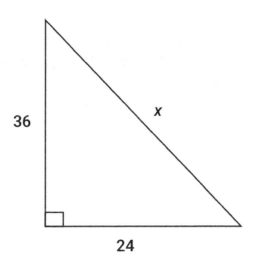

    a. 43.3
    b. 26.8
    c. 42.7
    d. 44.1

4. Express the following in decimal form:

$$\frac{3}{5} \times \frac{7}{10} \div \frac{1}{2}$$

    a. 0.042
    b. 84%
    c. 0.84
    d. 0.42

5. If Sarah reads at an average rate of 21 pages in 4 nights, how long will it take her to read 140 pages?
   a. 6 nights
   b. 26 nights
   c. 8 nights
   d. 27 nights

6. Alan currently weighs 200 pounds, but he wants to lose weight to get down to 175 pounds. What is this difference in kilograms? (1 pound is approximately equal to 0.45 kilograms.)
   a. 9 kg
   b. 11.25 kg
   c. 78.75 kg
   d. 90 kg

7. Johnny earns $2,334.50 from his job each month. He pays $1,437 for monthly expenses and saves the rest. Johnny is planning a vacation in 3 months that he estimates will cost $1,750 total. How much will Johnny have left over from 3 months of saving once he pays for his vacation?
   a. $948.50
   b. $584.50
   c. $852.50
   d. $942.50

8. Sarah has collected 420 miniature figurines from a vendor she passes every day on the way home. There are 98 figurines in a set. Sarah wants to know, approximately, how many full sets she could possibly have. What is $\frac{420}{98}$ rounded to the nearest integer?
   a. 3
   b. 4
   c. 5
   d. 6

9. What value of x makes the following equality true?

$$\sqrt{3x + 5} - 2 = 1$$

   a. $\frac{3}{5}$

   b. $\frac{4}{3}$

   c. 5

   d. $\frac{1}{2}$

10. A house-shaped decoration used as a bookend has a rectangular base. The total perimeter of the base is 36 cm. If the length is 12 cm, what is the width of each side?
   a. 3 cm
   b. 12 cm
   c. 6 cm
   d. 8 cm

11. Dwayne has received the following scores on his math tests: 78, 92, 83, 97. What score must Dwayne get on his next math test to have an overall average of 90?
   a. 89
   b. 98
   c. 95
   d. 100

12. If three squared is subtracted from the product of the square root of thirty-six and the square root of sixteen, what is its value?
   a. 30
   b. 21
   c. 15
   d. 13

13. Before a race of 4 horses, you make a random guess of which horse will get first place and which will get second place. What is the probability that both your guesses will be correct?
   a. $\frac{1}{4}$
   b. $\frac{1}{2}$
   c. $\frac{1}{16}$
   d. $\frac{1}{12}$

14. If the square of the difference between twenty-five and twenty-one is divided by two and added to four times seven, what is the value of that expression?
   a. 512
   b. 36
   c. 60.5
   d. 22

15. Kimberley earns $10 an hour babysitting, and after 10 p.m., she earns $12 an hour. The time she works is rounded to the nearest hour for payment purposes. On her last job, she worked from 5:30 p.m. to 11:00 p.m. In total, how much did Kimberley earn on her last job?
   a. $45
   b. $57
   c. $62
   d. $42

16. What value of x would solve the following equation?

$$9x + x - 7 = 16 + 2x$$

   a. $x = -4$
   b. $x = 3$
   c. $x = \frac{9}{8}$
   d. $x = \frac{23}{8}$

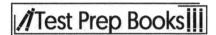

17. Keith's bakery had 252 customers go through its doors last week. This week, that number increased to 378. Express this increase as a percentage.
    a. 26%
    b. 50%
    c. 35%
    d. 12%

18. The following graph compares the various test scores of the top three students in each of these teachers' classes. Based on the graph, which teacher's students had the lowest range of test scores?

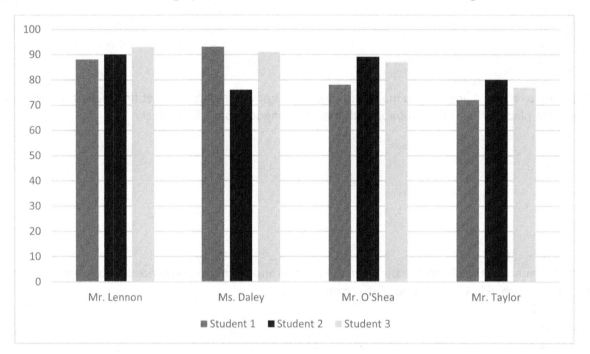

    a. Mr. Lennon
    b. Mr. O'Shea
    c. Mr. Taylor
    d. Ms. Daley

19. What is the solution to the following system of equations?

$$x^2 - 2x + y = 8$$

$$x - y = -2$$

    a. $(-2, 3)$
    b. There is no solution.
    c. $(-2, 0)\ (1, 3)$
    d. $(-2, 0)\ (3, 5)$

20. Using the following diagram, calculate the total circumference, rounding to the nearest tenth place:

5cm

a. 25.0 cm
b. 15.7 cm
c. 78.5 cm
d. 31.4 cm

21. Which measure for the center of a small sample set would be most affected by outliers?
a. Mean
b. Median
c. Mode
d. None of the above

22. A line that travels from the lower left of a graph to the upper right of the graph indicates what kind of relationship between an independent and a dependent variable?
a. Positive
b. Negative
c. Exponential
d. Logarithmic

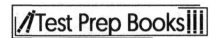
23. Which inequality corresponds to the following graph?

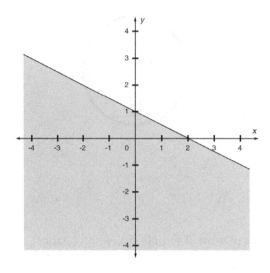

a. $y \leq 1 - \frac{1}{2}x$

b. $y > 1 - \frac{1}{2}x$

c. $y \leq 1 + 2x$

d. $y < 1 + \frac{1}{2}x$

24. Which of the following is the best description of the relationship between x and y?

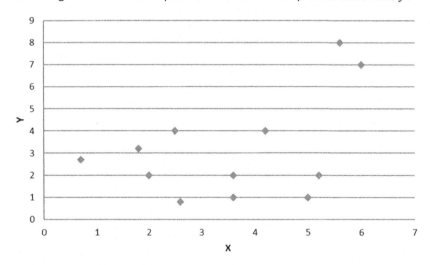

a. The data has normal distribution.

b. x and y have a negative relationship.

c. x and y have no apparent relationship.

d. x and y have a positive relationship.

25. Mike set up a simple experiment to measure the rate at which his dough rose over time. He plotted several points onto a blank coordinate plane to track the distance from the top of his pan when he started five hours ago, and the height now. He graphed the highest and lowest two points at (−5, −3) and (0, −1). What is the slope of the line that this makes?

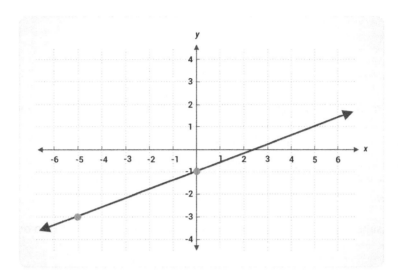

    a. 2

    b. $\frac{5}{2}$

    c. $\frac{1}{2}$

    d. $\frac{2}{5}$

26. Which of the following equations best represents the problem below?

> The width of a rectangle is 2 centimeters less than the length. If the perimeter of the rectangle is 44 centimeters, then what are the dimensions of the rectangle?

    a. $2l + 2(l − 2) = 44$
    b. $(l + 2) + (l + 2) + l = 48$
    c. $l \times (l − 2) = 44$
    d. $(l + 2) + (l + 2) + l = 44$

27. A ball is drawn at random from a ball pit containing 8 red balls, 7 yellow balls, 6 green balls, and 5 purple balls. What's the probability that the ball drawn is yellow?

    a. $\frac{1}{26}$

    b. $\frac{19}{26}$

    c. $\frac{7}{26}$

    d. 1

28. A shuffled deck of 52 cards contains 4 kings. One card is drawn and is not put back in the deck. Then, a second card is drawn. What's the probability that both cards are kings?

   a. $\dfrac{1}{169}$

   b. $\dfrac{1}{221}$

   c. $\dfrac{1}{13}$

   d. $\dfrac{4}{13}$

29. For a group of 20 men, the median weight is 180 pounds, and the range is 30 pounds. If each man gains 10 pounds, which of the following would be true?

   a. The median weight will increase, and the range will remain the same.
   b. The median weight and range will both remain the same.
   c. The median weight will stay the same, and the range will increase.
   d. The median weight and range will both increase.

30. For the following similar triangles, what are the values of x and y (rounded to one decimal place)?

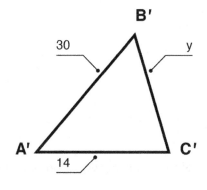

   a. $x = 16.5, y = 25.1$
   b. $x = 19.5, y = 24.1$
   c. $x = 17.1, y = 26.3$
   d. $x = 26.3, y = 17.1$

31. A pizzeria owner regularly creates jumbo pizzas, each with a radius of 9 inches. She is mathematically inclined, and wants to know the area of the pizza to purchase the correct boxes and know how much she is feeding her customers. What is the area of a circle with a radius of 9 inches, in terms of π?

   a. 81π in^2
   b. 18π in^2
   c. 90π in^2
   d. 9π in^2

32. Expand $(2x - 4y)^2$
    a. $4x^2 - 16xy + 16y^2$
    b. $4x^2 - 8xy + 16y^2$
    c. $4x^2 - 16xy - 16y^2$
    d. $2x^2 - 8xy + 8y^2$

33. If $x^2 - x - 3 = 0$, what is the value of $\left(x - \frac{1}{2}\right)^2$?
    a. $\frac{13}{2}$
    b. $\frac{13}{4}$
    c. 13
    d. $\frac{169}{4}$

34. If $x^2 - 2x - 8 = 0$, what value of x makes the equation true?
    a. $2 \pm \frac{\sqrt{30}}{2}$
    b. $2 \pm 4\sqrt{2}$
    c. 1 ± 3
    d. $4 \pm \sqrt{2}$

35. On Monday, Robert mopped the floor in 4 hours. On Tuesday, he did it in 3 hours. If on Monday, his average rate of mopping was p sq. ft. per hour, what was his average rate on Tuesday?
    a. $\frac{4}{3} p$ sq. ft. per hour
    b. $\frac{3}{4} p$ sq. ft. per hour
    c. $\frac{5}{4} p$ sq. ft. per hour
    d. $p + 1$ sq. ft. per hour

36. Which of the following inequalities is equivalent to $3 - \frac{1}{2}x \geq 2$?
    a. $x \geq 2$
    b. $x \leq 2$
    c. $x \geq 1$
    d. $x \leq 1$

37. For which of the following are $x = 4$ and $x = -4$ solutions?
    a. $x^2 + 16 = 0$
    b. $x^2 + 4x - 4 = 0$
    c. $x^2 - 2x - 2 = 0$
    d. $x^2 - 16 = 0$

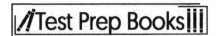

38. What is the probability of selecting an ace or a red card out of a standard pack of cards?

   a. $\frac{1}{2}$

   b. $\frac{1}{13}$

   c. $\frac{7}{13}$

   d. $\frac{15}{26}$

39. In a state's lottery, a player chooses a four-digit number; repetition of those individual digits is allowed. What is the probability that a winning ticket will have all 4 digits the same?

   a. 0.01
   b. 0.999
   c. 0.1
   d. 0.001

40. A box-and-whisker plot of yearly salaries for car salespersons has a Q_1 of \$45,000, Q_2 of \$51,000, and a Q_3 of \$59,000. Which of the following salaries would be considered outliers for the set?

      I. \$21,000
      II. \$28,000
      III. \$65,000
      IV. \$85,000

   a. I only
   b. IV only
   c. I and IV
   d. I, II, III, and IV

Answer Explanations #2

Reading

1. B: Choice *B* is correct because having very little drinking water on Earth is a very good reason for limiting one's water usage. That way, the human population will not run out of drinking water and die out. People wasting water on superfluous things does not support the fact that we need to limit our water usage. It merely states that people are wasteful. Therefore, Choice *A* is incorrect. Answer Choice *C* may be tempting, but it is not the correct one, as this article is not about reducing water usage in order to help those who don't have easy access to water. It is about the fact that the planet is running out of drinking water. Choice *D* is incorrect because nowhere in the article does it state that only industrialized countries have access to drinking water.

2. A: If the assertion is that the Earth does not have enough drinking water, then having abundant water stores that are not being reported would certainly challenge this assertion. Choice *B* is incorrect because even if much of the water we drink does come from rain, that means the human population would be dependent on rain in order to survive, which would support the assertion instead of challenge it. Because the primary purpose of the passage is not to help those who cannot get water, Choice *C* is not the correct answer. Even if Choice *D* were true, it does not dismiss the other ways in which people are wasteful with water and is also not the point.

3. C: Choice *C* is correct because people who waste water on lawns, half-full dishwashers, or personal pools are not taking into account how much water they are using because they get an unlimited supply; therefore, they are taking it for granted. Choices *A* and *B* are incorrect because they are both explicitly stated within the given sentence. While Choice *D* is implicitly stated within the whole article, it is not implicitly stated within the sentence.

4. D: The author mentions anti-Stratfordian arguments in the first paragraph, but then goes on to debunk these theories with more facts about Shakespeare's life in the second and third paragraphs. Choice *A* is not correct because, while the author does present arguments from both sides, the author is far from unbiased; in fact, the author clearly disagrees with anti-Stratfordians. Choice *B* is also not correct because it is more closely aligned to the beliefs of anti-Stratfordians, whom the author disagrees with. Choice *C* can be eliminated because, while it is true that the author gives historical background, the main purpose of the article is using that information to disprove a theory.

5. B: The thesis is a statement that contains the author's topic and main idea. As seen in question 4, the main purpose of this article is to use historical evidence to provide counterarguments to anti-Stratfordians. Choice *A* is simply a definition; Choice *C* is a supporting detail, not a main idea; and Choice *D* represents an idea of anti-Stratfordians, not the author's opinion.

6. B: This question asks readers to refer to the organizational structure of the article and demonstrate understanding of how the author provides details to support their argument. This particular detail can be found in the second paragraph where the author says, "even though he did not attend university, grade-school education in Shakespeare's time was actually quite rigorous."

7. A: This is a vocabulary question that can be answered using context clues. Other sentences in the paragraph describe London as "the most populous city in England" filled with "crowds of people," giving an image of a busy city full of people. Choice *B* is not correct because London was in Shakespeare's

255

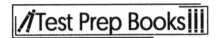

home country, not a foreign one. Choice *C* is not mentioned in the passage. Choice *D* is not a good answer choice because the passage describes how London was a popular and important city, probably not an underdeveloped one.

8. D: Anti-Stratfordians doubt Shakespeare's ability because he was not from the upper class. His father was a glove-maker. Therefore, in at least this instance, glove-makers were not included in the upper class (this is an example of inductive reasoning, or using two specific pieces of information to draw a more general conclusion).

9. C: This detail comes from the third paragraph, where the author responds to skeptics who claim that Shakespeare wrote too much about places he never visited, so *Romeo and Juliet* is mentioned as a famous example of a play with a foreign setting. In order to answer this question, readers need to understand the author's main purpose in the third paragraph and how the author uses details to support this purpose. Choices *A* and *D* are not mentioned in the passage, and Choice *B* is clearly not true because the passage mentions more than once that Shakespeare never left England.

10. A: This inference can be made from the final paragraph, where the author refutes anti-Stratfordian skepticism by pointing out that books about life in Europe could easily circulate throughout London. From this statement, readers can conclude that the author believes it is possible that Shakespeare learned about European culture from books, rather than visiting the continent on his own. Choice *B* is not true because the author believes that Shakespeare contributed to English literature without traveling extensively. Similarly, Choice *C* is not a good answer because the author explains how Shakespeare got his education without university. Choice *D* can also be eliminated because the author describes Shakespeare's genius and clearly Shakespeare is not from Italy.

11. D: The use of "I" could serve to have a "hedging" effect, allow the reader to connect with the author in a more personal way and cause the reader to empathize more with the egrets. However, it doesn't distance the reader from the text, making Choice *D* the answer to this question.

12. C: The quote gives the warden's direct statement regarding his dedication to the rookery. Choice *A* is incorrect because the speaker of the quote is a warden, not a hunter. Choice *B* is incorrect because the quote does not lighten the mood but shows the danger of the situation between the wardens and the hunters. Choice *D* is incorrect because there is no humor found in the quote.

13. D: A *rookery* is a colony of breeding birds. Although *rookery* could mean Choice *A,* houses in a slum area, it does not make sense in this context. Choices *B* and *C* are both incorrect, as this is not a place for hunters to trade tools or for wardens to trade stories.

14. B: The previous sentence is describing "20 colonies" of birds, so what follows should be a bird colony. Choice *A* may be true, but we have no evidence of this in the text. Choice *C* does touch on the tension between the hunters and wardens, but there is no official "Bird Island Battle" mentioned in the text. Choice *D* does not exist in the text.

15. D: The text mentions several different times how and why the association has been successful and gives examples to back this fact. Choice *A* is incorrect because the passage doesn't mention the need for people to take action. Likewise, Choices *B* and *C* are not mentioned in the text.

16. C: Choice *A* might be true in a general sense, but it is not relevant to the context of the text. Choice *B* is incorrect because the hunters are not studying lines of flight to help wardens, but to hunt birds.

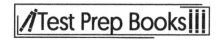

Choice *D* is incorrect because nothing in the text mentions that hunters are trying to build homes underneath lines of flight of birds for good luck.

17. C: The passage states in the third paragraph that a year before, "a number of egrets were seen in eastern Massachusetts." Florida is mentioned in the passage as a place where bird colonies reside. The other two locations are not mentioned in the passage.

18. A: The word *commissioned* most nearly means *appointed*. Choice *B, compelled,* means forced. Choice *C, beguiled,* means entertained. Choice *D, fortified,* means defended.

19. D: Several hidden colonies were found which prompted Dutcher and Pearson to protect them. This information is presented in the first paragraph starting with the sentence "Two years ago." The other answer choices are current to the passage.

20. C: *In transit* means on the way to the destination. Choice *A* is the definition of *travelling*. Choice *B* is the definition of *delegate*. Choice *D* is the definition of *provoke*.

21. A: Choice *D* can be eliminated because the Salem witch trials aren't mentioned. While sympathetic to the plight of the accused, the author doesn't demand or urge the reader to demand reparations to the descendants; therefore, Choice *B* can also be ruled out. It's clear that the author's main goal is to educate the reader and shed light on the facts and hidden details behind the case. However, his focus isn't on the occult, but the specific Lancashire case itself. He goes into detail about suspects' histories and ties to Catholicism, revealing how the fears of the English people at the time sealed the fate of the accused witches. Choice *A* is correct.

22. B: It's important to note that these terms may not be an exact analog for *enduring*. However, through knowledge of the definition of *enduring*, as well as the context in which it's used, an appropriate synonym can be found. Plugging "circumstantial" into the passage in place of "enduring" doesn't make sense. Nor does "un-original" work, since this particular case of witchcraft stands out in history. "Wicked" is very descriptive, but this is an attribute applied to people, not events; therefore, this is an inappropriate choice as well. *Enduring* literally means long lasting, referring to the continued interest in this particular case of witchcraft. Therefore, it's a popular topic of 1600s witch trials, making "popular," Choice *B,* the best choice.

23. D: Choices *A* and *B* are irrelevant and incorrect. The use of quotes lends credibility to the author. However, the presence of quotes alone doesn't necessarily mean that the author has a qualified perspective. What establishes the writer as a reliable voice is that the author's previous writing on the subject has been published before. This qualification greatly establishes the author's credentials as a historical writer, making Choice *D* the correct answer.

24. B: Choice *B* is the best answer because it ultimately encompasses the potentiality of Choices *C* and *D*. Choice *A* is incorrect because it takes the statement literally. For Choice *C,* it's possible that evidence was tampered with or even falsified, but this statement doesn't refer to this. While the author alludes that there may have been evidence tampering and potentially corruption, Choice *D,* what the writer is directly saying is that the documentation of the court indicates an elaborate trial.

25. C: Several of these answers could have contributed to the fear and political motivations around the Lancashire witch trials. What this answer is looking for is very specific: political motivations and issues that played a major role in the case. Choice *C* clearly outlines the public fears of the time. It also describes how the government can use this fear to weed out and eliminate traces of Catholicism (and

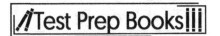

witchcraft too). Catholicism and witchcraft were seen as dangerous and undermining to English Protestantism and governance. Choice *D* can be eliminated; while this information may have some truth and is certainly consistent with the general fear of witchcraft, the details about Lancashire's ancient history aren't mentioned in the text. Choice *A* is true but not necessarily political in nature. Choice *B* is very promising, though not outright mentioned.

26. D: The best evidence comes from Alizon herself. The text mentions that she confessed to bewitching John Law, thinking that she did him harm. From here she names her grandmother, who she believes corrupted her. Choice *B* can be ruled out; spectral evidence isn't mentioned. The case draws on knowledge of superstition of witchcraft, but this in itself can't be considered evidence, so Choice *A* is incorrect. Choice *C* isn't evidence in a modern sense; rumors have no weight in court and therefore are not evidence. While this is used as evidence to some degree, this still isn't the *best* evidence against Alizon and the witches.

27. B: This type of passage would be considered expository, which is an informative passage. Choice *A,* persuasive, means to take a side of an argument, and this essay is merely divulging information. Choice *C,* narrative, means to tell a story. Although a story is being told indirectly, the essay doesn't follow a traditional narrative. Choice *D,* descriptive, means a detailed description of a person or place.

28. B: According to the passage, 20 people were arrested as witches in the Lancashire trials. The essay tells us that "ten were hanged, one died in gaol (jail), one was sentenced to death in the pillory, and eight were acquitted."

29. D: The word *commemorative* means in honor of something. The context clue here includes the "works of fiction" by the authors Blake Morrison, Ann Duffy, and Jeanette Winterson, no doubt to celebrate the preserved history of the famous trial.

30. C: Malkin tower is the house of Alizon's grandmother. It is also a place where a meeting of witches was said to be held in the passage. The passage says, "The net was widened still further at the end of April when Alizon's younger brother James and younger sister Jennet, only nine years old, came up between them with a story about a "great meeting of witches" at their grandmother's house, known as Malkin Tower."

31. A: The central idea of this passage is to introduce certain insects that transition from water to air. Choice *B* is incorrect because although the passage talks about gills, it is not the central idea of the passage. Choices *C* and *D* are incorrect because the passage does not define insect breathing or invite readers to participate in insect preservation. Rather, the passage serves as an introduction to stoneflies, dragonflies, and mayflies and their transition from water to air.

32. C: To molt is to shed part or all of the outer shell, as noted in Choice *C.* Choices *A, B,* and *D* are incorrect. The word in the passage is mentioned here: "But it is advisable in connection with our present subject to dwell especially on some insects that remain continually under water till they are ready to undergo their final molt and attain the winged state, which they pass entirely in the air."

33. B: Notice how the first paragraph goes into detail describing how insects are able to breathe air. The second paragraph acts as a contrast to the first by stating, "[i]t is of great interest to find that, nevertheless, a number of insects spend much of their time under water." Watch for transition words such as *nevertheless* to help find what type of passage you're dealing with.

34. C: *Instars* are the phases between two periods of molting, and the text explains when these transitions occur. The preparatory stages are acted out in the water, while the last stage is in the air. Choices *A*, *B*, and *D* are all incorrect.

35. C: Overall, the author presents us with information on the subject. One moment where personal interest is depicted is when the author states, "It is of great interest to find that, nevertheless, a number of insects spend much of their time under water."

36. C: Their larvae can breathe the air dissolved in water through gills of some kind. This is stated in the last paragraph. Choice *A* is incorrect because the text mentions this in a general way at the beginning of the passage concerning "insects as a whole." Choice *B* is incorrect because this is stated of beetles and water-bugs, and not the insects in question. Choice *D* is incorrect because this is the opposite of what the text says of instars.

37. B: According to the passage, boatmen and scorpions have some way of protecting their spiracles when submerged. We see this in the second paragraph, which says "(boatmen and scorpions) which have some way of protecting their spiracles when submerged."

38. A: The best answer Choice is *A*: the author believes that the stonefly, dragonfly, and mayfly larvae are better prepared to live beneath the water because they have gills that allow them to do so. We see this when the author says "But the larva of a stone-fly, a dragon-fly, or a may-fly is adapted more completely than these for aquatic life; it can, by means of gills of some kind, breathe the air dissolved in water."

39. C: Because a vast majority of insects have wings and also have the ability to breathe underwater. The entire first paragraph talks of how insects have wings, and how insects also have "a system of branching air-tubes" that carries oxygen to the insect's tissues.

40. B: The word *preeminently* most nearly means *above all* or *in particular*. The author is saying that above all, insects are creatures of both land and water.

41. C: Choice *A* is incorrect because it describes facts: Leif Erikson was the son of Erik the Red and historians debate Leif's date of birth. These are not opinions. Choice *B* is incorrect; Erikson calling the land Vinland is a verifiable fact, as is Choice *D*, because he did contact the natives almost 500 years before Columbus. Choice *C* is the correct answer because it is the author's opinion that Erikson deserves more credit. Choice *C* is the correct answer because it is the author's opinion that Erikson deserves more credit. Another person could argue that Columbus or another explorer deserves more credit, which makes it an opinion rather than a historical fact.

42. B: Choice *A* is incorrect because the author aims to go beyond describing Erikson as merely a legendary Viking. Choice *C* is incorrect because the author does not focus on Erikson's motivations, let alone name the spreading of Christianity as his primary objective. Choice *D* is incorrect because it is a premise that Erikson contacted the natives 500 years before Columbus, which is simply a part of supporting the author's conclusion. Choice *B* is correct because it accurately identifies the author's statement that Erikson deserves more credit than he has received for being the first European to explore the New World.

43. D: Choice *A* is incorrect because the author never addresses the Vikings' state of mind or emotions. Choice *B* is incorrect because the author does not elaborate on Erikson's exile and whether he would have become an explorer if not for his banishment. Choice *C* is incorrect because there is not enough information to support this premise. It is unclear whether Erikson informed the King of Norway of his findings. Although it is true that the king did not send a follow-up expedition, he could have simply chosen not to expend the resources after receiving Erikson's news. It is not possible to logically infer whether Erikson told him. Choice *D* is correct because the uncertainty about Leif Erikson's birth year is an example of how historians have trouble pinning down important details in Viking history.

44. B: Readers should carefully focus their attention on the beginning of the passage to answer this question. Even though the sentences may be worded a bit differently, all but one statement is true. It presents a false idea that descriptive details are not necessary until the climax of the story. Even someone who does not read the passage might know that good writing includes descriptive details throughout the narrative, not only around the climax.

45. B: To suggest that a 10-minute play is accessible does not imply any timeline, nor does the passage mention how long a playwright spends with revisions and rewrites. So, Choice *A* is incorrect. Choice *B* is correct because of the opening statement that reads, "Learning how to write a 10-minute play may seem like a monumental task at first; but, if you follow a simple creative writing strategy, similar to the ones used for writing narrative stories, you will be able to write a successful drama." None of the remaining choices are supported by points in the passage.

46. D: The only element of a narrative writer's tool kit not mentioned in the passage is style. This is not to say that ten-minute plays do not have style, but the element of style was not illustrated in this particular passage.

47. C: Choice *C* allows room for the fact that not all people who attempt to write a play will find it easy. If the writer follows the basic principles of narrative writing described in the passage, however, writing a play does not have to be an excruciating experience. None of the other options can be supported by points from the passage.

Language

1. C: While all of these words are spelled similarly and sound the same or similar, the correct answer is Choice *C*, *wear*, which means to cover or equip. We wear clothes. Choice *A*, *ware*, refers to an item that is created or manufactured. Choice *B* is incorrect because *where* asks for a specific location. Choice *D*, *were*, is the second person plural version of *to be*, so it is completely irrelevant to the sentence.

2. B: The clause *who loves to ride bikes* is a restrictive adjective clause modifying the noun *boy*. Choice *A* is incorrect because *a boy who loves* is a phrase, not a clause. Choice *C* is incorrect because *to ride bikes* is an infinitive phrase and does not have a subject. Choice *D* is incorrect because *gets plenty of exercise* is not a clause; it has no subject.

3. D: The adverbial clause *unless you are too tired* modifies the verb *want*. Choice *A* is incorrect because *I want to work in the garden* is an independent clause. Choice *B* is incorrect because *in the garden* has no subject and is a prepositional phrase. Choice *C* is incorrect because *are too tired* is not a clause because it has no subject.

4. C: A noun phrase is a noun and all of its modifiers; in this case, *long* and *black* are adjectives modifying the noun *limousine* and *the* is an article modifying *limousine*. Choice *A* is incorrect because it identifies the compound subject of the sentence. Choice *B* is incorrect because it includes the verb *rode*. Choice *D* is incorrect because it includes a subject and a verb, and phrases do not have both.

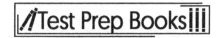

5. A: Choice *B* and *D* drop the word *who* and use the wrong tense of the verb *need*. Choice *C* incorrectly uses the preposition *with*.

6. B: Choice *B* uses the best choice of words to create a subordinate and independent clause. In Choice *A*, *because* makes it seem like this is the reason the person enjoys working from home, which is incorrect. In Choice *C*, the word *maybe* creates two independent clauses, which would need to be joined by a semicolon, not a comma. Choice *D* uses *with*, which does not make grammatical sense.

7. A: Choice *B* is not grammatically incorrect, but the repetition of the word *who* is unnecessary and awkward in this sentence. Choice *C* uses *that* before one verb and *who* before the other to refer to the same subject. Like Choice *B*, Choice *D* unnecessarily repeats the pronoun, creating an awkward sentence.

8. A: Choice *B* is incorrect because the singular verb *has* doesn't match the plural noun *grandparents*. Choice *C* is incorrect because *were traveling* does not match with *have been sightseeing*. Choice *D* is incorrect because the tenses of the verbs do not match and because it's missing a comma before *and*.

9. D: Choice *A* is grammatically correct, but it doesn't convey the connection between the two statements. Choice *B* implies that the building was still sturdy and solid after crumbling in the earthquake because the word *although* is misplaced. Choice *C* is incorrect because it uses a comma to join two independent clauses.

10. C: This sentence uses verbs in a parallel series, so each verb must follow the same pattern. In order to fit with the helping verb would, each verb must be in the present tense. In Choices *A*, *B*, and *D*, one or more of the verbs switches to past tense. Only Choice *C* remains in the same tense, maintaining the pattern.

11. C: The second sentence tells of an unexpected outcome of the first sentence. Choice *A*, Choice *B*, and Choice *D* indicate a logical progression, which does not match this surprise. Only Choice *C* indicates this unexpected twist.

12. A: Only two of these suffixes, *–ize* and *–en*, can be used to form verbs, so *B* and *D* are incorrect. Those choices create adjectives. The suffix *–ize* can mean "to convert or turn into." Because this sentence is about converting ideas into money, *monetize* is the appropriate word to use.

13. C: The suffix *-fy* means to make, cause, or cause to have. Choices *A*, *B*, and *D* are incorrect because they show meanings of other suffixes. Choice *A* shows the meaning of the suffix *-ous*. Choice *B* shows the meaning of the suffix *–ist*, and Choice *D* shows the meaning of the suffix *-age*.

14. A: *After* and *then* are transitional words that indicate time or position. Choice *B* is incorrect because the words *at, with,* and *to* are used as prepositions in this sentence, not transitions. Choice *C* is incorrect because the words *had* and *took* are used as verbs in this sentence. In Choice *D*, *a* and *the* are used as articles in the sentence.

15. A: Choice *A* includes all of the words functioning as nouns in the sentence. Choice *B* is incorrect because it includes the words *final* and *academic,* which are functioning as adjectives in this sentence. The word *he* makes Choice *C* incorrect because it is a pronoun. This answer choice also includes the word *library*, which can function as a noun, but is functioning as an adjective modifying the word *databases* in this sentence. Choice *D* is incorrect because it leaves out the proper noun *Robert*.

261

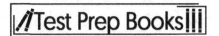

16. C: The dependent adjective clause *cute and cuddly* does not modify *the children*, it modifies *teddy bears*. The modifier is misplaced. Choice *A* does not contain a misplaced modifier. It is a grammatically correct independent clause. Choice *B* does not have a misplaced modifier. It is a grammatically correct compound sentence with two independent clauses joined with a semicolon. Choice *D* does not have a misplaced modifier. The modifier *cute and cuddly* correctly modifies *teddy bears*. The sentence is grammatically correct.

17. B: *Dissatisfied* and *accommodations* are both spelled correctly in Choice *B*. These are both considered commonly misspelled words. One or both words are spelled incorrectly in Choices *A*, *C*, and *D*.

18. A: It is necessary to put a comma between the date and the year. It is also required to put a comma between the day of the week and the month. Choice *B* is incorrect because it is missing the comma between the day and year. Choice *C* is incorrect because it adds an unnecessary comma between the month and date. Choice *D* is missing the necessary comma between the day of the week and the month.

19. D: To create parallelism, make both verbal gerunds. Choice *A* is incorrect. Chewing is a gerund and to play is an infinitive. Choice *B* is incorrect. To chew is an infinitive and playing is a gerund. Choice *C* is incorrect. To chew and to play are both infinitives, but they do not match with the verb enjoy.

20. D: In Choice *D*, the word *function* is a noun. While the word *function* can also act as a verb, in this particular sentence it is acting as a noun as the object of the preposition *at*. Choices *A* and *B* are incorrect because the word *function* cannot be used as an adjective or adverb.

21. C: *Cacti* is the correct plural form of the word *cactus*. Choice *A* (*tomatos*) includes an incorrect spelling of the plural of *tomato*. Both Choice *B* (*analysis*) and Choice *D* (*criterion*) are incorrect because they are in singular form. The correct plural form for these choices would be *criteria* and *analyses*.

22. B: Quotation marks are used to indicate something someone said. The example sentences feature a direct quotation that requires the use of double quotation marks. Also, the question mark should be contained within the quotation marks because the quoted text is asking a question. Choice *A* is incorrect because there is an unnecessary period after the quotation mark. Choice *C* is incorrect because it uses single quotation marks, which are used for a quote within a quote. Choice *D* is incorrect because it places the punctuation outside of the quotation marks.

23. A: Choice *A* is correct because *has* is the same tense and number as the subject *Garth*, so the verb and subject agree. Choice *B* is incorrect because *had* is past tense while the sentence is clearly present tense, indicated by *that he cares for*. Choice *C* incorrectly uses *have*, which is plural and doesn't agree with the singular subject. Choice *D* is incorrect because *haves* is a plural noun indicating people with possessions, not a verb as is needed here.

24. D: In Choice *D*, the word *part* functions as an adjective that modifies the word *Irish*. Choices *A* and *C* are incorrect because the word *part* functions as a noun in these sentences. Choice *B* is incorrect because the word *part* functions as a verb.

25. C: *All of Shannon's family and friends* is the complete subject because it includes who or what is doing the action in the sentence as well as the modifiers that go with it. Choice *A* is incorrect because it only includes the simple subject of the sentence. Choices *B* and *D* are incorrect because they only include part of the complete subject.

26. D: Choice *D* directly addresses the reader, so it is in second person point of view. This is an imperative sentence since it issues a command; imperative sentences have an understood *you* as the subject. Choice *A* uses first person pronouns *I* and *my*. Choices *B* and *C* are incorrect because they use third person point of view.

27. A: The word *prodigious* is defined as very impressive, amazing, or large. In this sentence, the meaning can be drawn from the words *they became nervous about climbing its distant peak*, as this would be an appropriate reaction upon seeing a very large peak that's far in the distance. Choices *B*, *C*, and *D* do not accurately define the word *prodigious*, so they are incorrect.

28. D: Choice *D* correctly places a hyphen after the prefix *ex* to join it to the word *husband*. Many words that begin with the prefixes *great, trans, ex, all,* and *self require* a hyphen. Choices *A* and *C* place hyphens in words where they are not needed. *Beagle mix* would only require a hyphen if coming before the word *Henry*, since it would be serving as a compound adjective in that instance. Choice *B* contains hyphens that are in the correct place but are formatted incorrectly since they include spaces between the hyphens and the surrounding words.

29. C: Choice *C* is correct because quotation marks should be used for the title of a short work such as a poem. Choices *A*, *B*, and *D* are incorrect because the titles of novels, films, and newspapers should be placed in italics, not quotation marks.

30. C: This question focuses on the correct usage of the commonly confused word pairs of *it's/its* and *then/than*. *It's* is a contraction for *it is* or *it has*. *Its* is a possessive pronoun. The word *than* shows comparison between two things. *Then* is an adverb that conveys time. Choice *C* correctly uses *it's* and *than*. *It's* is a contraction for *it has* in this sentence, and *than* shows comparison between *work* and *rest*. None of the other answers choices use both of the correct words.

31. A: The publisher, author, and references are elements of a resource that determine credibility. If the publisher has published more than one work, the author has written more than one piece on the subject, or the work references other recognized research, the credibility of a source will be stronger. Choice *B* is incorrect because the subject and title may be used to determine relevancy, not credibility, and the audience does not have much to do with the credibility of a source. Choice *C* is incorrect because the organization, stylistic choices, and transition words are all components of an effectively written piece, but they have less to do with credibility, other than to ensure that the author knows how to write. The length and tone of a piece are a matter of author's preference, and a work does not have to be written by multiple people to be considered a credible source.

32. D: The word *its* in the sentence is the singular possessive form of the pronoun that stands in place for the word *giraffe's*. There is one baby that belongs to one giraffe. Choice *A* is incorrect. It is a contraction of the words *it* and *is*. You would not say, *"The giraffe nudged it is baby."* Choice *B* is incorrect. We do not know the gender of the giraffe; even if it was female, the proper word would be *her* baby, not *hers* baby. Choice *C* is incorrect. The word *them* is a plural objective pronoun and we need a singular possessive pronoun because there is only one giraffe doing the nudging.

33. A: Parallelism refers to consistent use of sentence structure or word form. In this case, the list within the sentence does not utilize parallelism; three of the verbs appear in their base form—*travel, take,* and *eat*—but one appears as a gerund—*going*. A parallel version of this sentence would be "This summer, I'm planning to travel to Italy, take a Mediterranean cruise, go to Pompeii, and eat a lot of Italian food." Choice *B* is incorrect because this description is a complete sentence. Choice *C* is incorrect, as a

263

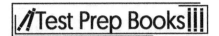
misplaced modifier is a modifier that is not located appropriately in relation to the word or words they modify. Choice *D* is incorrect because subject-verb agreement refers to the appropriate conjugation of a verb in relation to its subject.

34. B: Choice *B* is the correct answer. A biography will be the most helpful resource when writing about Wilde's time in prison. The main purpose of a biography is to detail the life of a specific person. Since imprisonment was a major experience in Wilde's life, a biography would be the best resource to learn about it. Choice *A* might provide insight into Wilde's writing, but fictional works would typically not detail the author's own life. The same goes for movie adaptations. Internet reviews can be written by anyone and do not typically contain helpful or reliable information about the author.

35. A: Choice *A* uses correct capitalization of proper nouns and does not have any errors. Choice *B* fails to properly capitalize the proper noun, Washington, D.C. Choice *C* fails to capitalize the name of the cat, which is a proper noun because it refers to a specific animal's name. Choice *D* fails to capitalize *French* which is a language and should always be capitalized.

36. B: Choice *B* is the correct answer because it states a general fact about Japanese food and serves as a main idea for the paragraph. Although Choices *A, C,* and *D* are true facts about Japanese cuisine, they are details that would further support a main idea about Japanese food.

37. C: Choice *C* is the correct answer. Sentence 10 should follow Sentence 8. It introduces the town of Hakone and provides the framework for the specific information about the town presented in Sentences 9 through 12.

38. D: Choice *D* is the correct answer. This sentence is more concise and still incorporates all of the information trying to be conveyed in the original sentence. Choices *A, B,* and *C* either mix up the information in the original sentence or give incorrect facts.

39. B: Choice *B* is the correct answer. In this sentence, the words *or bullet train* serve as an appositive, or extra information provided in the sentence. These words are added to the sentence to define *Shinkansen*. However, the sentence would be correct even if these words hadn't been added, so this phrase should be set apart with commas. A correct version of the sentence would look like this: [8]*People from all over Japan ride the Shinkansen, or bullet train, to Osaka to watch the events.*

40. A: Choice *A* accurately describes the error in this sentence. It is unclear who the antecedent (*him*) is referring to. It could refer to Benny or Billy. The sentence should be edited so that the pronoun and antecedent match in a clear way. Choices *A, C,* and *D* are errors that are not present in the original sentence.

Math

1. B: Since $850 is the price after a 20% discount, $850 represents 80% (or 0.8) of the original price. In other words, $850 = 0.8x$ (where x is the original price). Solving this, we find $x = \frac{850}{0.8} = 1,062.5$. Now, to find the savings, calculate the original price minus the sale price: $1,062.50 - $850 = $212.50.

2. C: Division in scientific notation can be solved by grouping the first terms together and grouping the tens together. The first terms can be divided, and the tens terms can be simplified using the rules for exponents. The initial expression becomes 0.4×10^4. This is not in scientific notation because the first

264

number is not between 1 and 10. Shifting the decimal and subtracting one from the exponent, the answer becomes 4.0×10^3.

3. A: The Pythagorean theorem states that for right triangles $c^2 = a^2 + b^2$, with c being the side opposite the 90° angle. Substituting 24 as a and 36 as b, and x as c, the equation becomes:

$$x^2 = 24^2 + 36^2$$

$$x^2 = 24^2 + 36^2 = 576 + 1,296 = 1,872$$

The last step is to take the square root of both sides to remove the exponent:

$$x = \sqrt{1,872} \approx 43.3$$

4. C: The first step in solving this problem is expressing the result in fraction form. Multiplication and division are typically performed in order from left to right, but they can be performed in any order. For this problem, let's start by performing the division operation on the last two fractions. When dividing one fraction by another, invert—or flip—the second fraction and then multiply the numerators and denominators.

$$\frac{7}{10} \times \frac{2}{1} = \frac{14}{10}$$

Next, multiply the first fraction by this value:

$$\frac{3}{5} \times \frac{14}{10} = \frac{42}{50}$$

Decimals are expressions of 1, or 100%, so Multiply both the numerator and denominator by 2 to get the fraction into the form 100.

$$\frac{42}{50} \times \frac{2}{2} = \frac{84}{100}$$

In decimal form, this would be expressed as 0.84.

5. D: This problem can be solved by setting up a proportion involving the given information and the unknown value. The proportion is:

$$\frac{21 \text{ pages}}{4 \text{ nights}} = \frac{140 \text{ pages}}{x \text{ nights}}$$

Solving the proportion by cross-multiplying, the equation becomes $21x = 4 \times 140$, where $x = 26.67$. Since it is not an exact number of nights, the answer is rounded up to 27 nights. Twenty-six nights would not give Sarah enough time.

6. B: Using the conversion rate, multiply the projected weight loss of 25 lb by $0.45 \frac{\text{kg}}{\text{lb}}$ to get the amount in kilograms (11.25 kg).

7. D: First, subtract $1,437 from $2,334.50 to find Johnny's monthly savings; this equals $897.50. Then, multiply this amount by 3 to find out how much he will have (in 3 months) before he pays for his

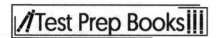

vacation; this equals $2,692.50. Finally, subtract the cost of the vacation ($1,750) from this amount to find how much Johnny will have left: $942.50.

8. B: Dividing by 98 can be approximated by dividing by 100, which would mean shifting the decimal point of the numerator to the left by 2. The result is 4.2, which rounds to 4. Sarah may have about 4 full sets of figurines at the most.

9. B: The value of x within the radical can be solved by first isolating the radical expression:

$$\sqrt{3x + 5} - 2 = 1$$

$$\sqrt{3x + 5} = 3$$

Next, the radical can be cancelled out by squaring both sides of the equation:

$$\left(\sqrt{3x + 5}\right)^2 = 3^2$$

$$3x + 5 = 9$$

Finally, the equation can be solved in terms of x by subtracting 5 from both sides and dividing by 3:

$$3x + 5 - 5 = 9 - 5$$

$$3x = 4$$

$$\frac{3x}{3} = \frac{4}{3}$$

$$x = \frac{4}{3}$$

Thus, the value of x that makes the equality true is $\frac{4}{3}$.

10. C: The formula for the perimeter of a rectangle is $P = 2L + 2W$, where P is the perimeter, L is the length, and W is the width. The first step is to substitute all of the data into the formula:

$$36 = 2(12) + 2W$$

Simplify by multiplying 2×12:

$$36 = 24 + 2W$$

Simplifying this further by subtracting 24 on each side gives:

$$36 - 24 = 24 - 24 + 2W$$

$$12 = 2W$$

Divide by 2:

$$6 = W$$

266

The width is 6 cm. Remember to test this answer by substituting this value into the original formula:

$$36 = 2(12) + 2(6)$$

11. D: To find the average of a set of values, add the values together and then divide by the total number of values. In this case, include the unknown value of what Dwayne needs to score on his next test, in order to solve it.

$$\frac{78 + 92 + 83 + 97 + x}{5} = 90$$

Multiply each side by 5 to simplify the equation, resulting in:

$$78 + 92 + 83 + 97 + x = 450$$

$$350 + x = 450$$

$$x = 100$$

Dwayne would need to get a perfect score of 100 in order to get an average of at least 90.

Test this answer by substituting 100 back into the original formula.

$$\frac{78 + 92 + 83 + 97 + 100}{5} = 90$$

12. C: Three squared subtracted from the product of the square roots of 36 and 16 is the same as:

$$\left(\sqrt{36} \times \sqrt{16}\right) - 3^2$$

Follow the *order of operations* in order to solve this problem. Solve inside the parentheses first, followed by multiplication and then subtraction:

$$(6 \times 4) - 9$$

This is equal to $24 - 9$, or 15, Choice *C*.

13. D: The probability of picking the winner of the race is $\frac{1}{4}$, or $\left(\frac{number\ of\ favorable\ outcomes}{number\ of\ total\ outcomes}\right)$. Assuming the winner was picked on the first selection, three horses remain from which to choose the runner-up (these are dependent events). Therefore, the probability of picking the runner-up is $\frac{1}{3}$. To determine the probability that multiple events all happen, multiply the probabilities of the events:

$$\frac{1}{4} \times \frac{1}{3} = \frac{1}{12}$$

14. B: The square of the difference between 25 and 21 divided by 2 and added to 4 times 7 is equal to:

$$4 \times 7 + (25 - 21)^2 \div 2$$

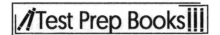

To solve this correctly, keep in mind the order of operations with the mnemonic PEMDAS (Please Excuse My Dear Aunt Sally). This stands for Parentheses, Exponents, Multiplication & Division, Addition & Subtraction. Taking it step by step, solve inside the parentheses first:

$$4 \times 7 + (4)^2 \div 2$$

Then, apply the exponent:

$$4 \times 7 + 16 \div 2$$

Multiplication and division are both performed next:

$$28 + 8$$

Addition and subtraction are done last.

$$28 + 8 = 36$$

The solution is 36.

15. C: Kimberley worked 4.5 hours at the rate of $10 / h and 1 hour at the rate of $12 / h. The problem states that her time is rounded to the nearest hour, so the 4.5 hours would round up to 5 hours at the rate of $10 / h.

$$(5 \text{ hours}) \times (\$10/\text{hour}) + (1 \text{ hour}) \times (\$12/\text{hour}) = \$50 + \$12 = \$62$$

16. D:

$9x + x - 7 = 16 + 2x$	Combine $9x$ and x.
$10x - 7 = 16 + 2x$	
$10x - 7 + 7 = 16 + 2x + 7$	Add 7 to both sides to remove (−7).
$10x = 23 + 2x$	
$10x - 2x = 23 + 2x - 2x$	Subtract $2x$ from both sides to move it to the other side of the equation.
$8x = 23$	
$\dfrac{8x}{8} = \dfrac{23}{8}$	Divide by 8 to get x by itself.
$x = \dfrac{23}{8}$	

17. B: First, calculate the difference between the larger value and the smaller value.

$$378 - 252 = 126$$

To calculate this difference as a percentage of the original value, and thus calculate the percentage *increase*, divide 126 by 252 to get 0.5, then multiply by 100 to reach the percentage 50%, Choice *B*.

18. A: To calculate the range in a set of data, subtract the lowest value from the highest value. In this graph, the range of Mr. Lennon's students is 4, which can be seen physically in the graph as having the smallest difference between the highest value and the lowest value compared with the other teachers.

19. D: This system of equations involves one quadratic equation and one linear equation. One way to solve this is through substitution.

Solving for y in the second equation yields:

$$y = x + 2$$

Plugging this equation in for the y of the quadratic equation yields:

$$x^2 - 2x + x + 2 = 8$$

Simplify the equation:

$$x^2 - x + 2 = 8$$

Set this equal to zero and factor:

$$x^2 - x - 6 = 0 = (x - 3)(x + 2)$$

Solving these two factors for x gives the zeros:

$$x = 3, -2$$

To find the y-value for the point, plug in each number to either original equation. Solving each one for y yields the points $(3, 5)$ and $(-2, 0)$.

20. D: To calculate the circumference of a circle, use the formula $2\pi r$, where r equals the radius (half of the diameter) of the circle, and $\pi \approx 3.14$. Substitute the given information to get:

$$2 \times 3.14 \times 5 = 31.4$$

21. A: Mean. An outlier is a data value that's either far above or below the majority of values in a sample set. The mean is the average of all values in the set. In a small sample, a very high or low number could greatly change the average. The median is the middle value when arranged from lowest to highest. Outliers would have no more of an effect on the median than any other value. Mode is the value that repeats most often in a set. Assuming that the same outlier doesn't repeat, outliers would have no effect on the mode of a sample set.

22. A: This kind of line indicates a positive relationship. A negative relationship would match a line traveling from the upper left of the graph to the lower right. Exponential and logarithmic functions aren't linear—their graphs do not make a straight line.

23. A: The line graphed by the inequality has an x-intercept of 2 and a y-intercept of 1, which gives the equation a slope of $-\frac{1}{2}x$, found by taking the change in y, –1, and dividing it by the change in x, 2. So, the equation of the line is $y = 1 - \frac{1}{2}x$ Because the shaded region lies below the equation, and the line is solid, the inequality must contain all the points on and below the line: $y \le 1 - \frac{1}{2}x$.

24. C: The data points do not appear to form any sort of line, even approximately, as we would expect for a positive or negative relationship. They also do not form the characteristic bell-shaped curve of a normal distribution. No relationship is apparent.

25. D: The slope is given by the change in y divided by the change in x. Specifically, it's:

$$slope = \frac{y_2 - y_1}{x_2 - x_1}$$

The first point is $(-5, -3)$, and the second point is $(0, -1)$. Work from left to right when identifying coordinates. Thus the point on the left is point 1 $(-5, -3)$ and the point on the right is point 2 $(0, -1)$.

Now we just need to plug those numbers into the equation:

$$slope = \frac{-1 - (-3)}{0 - (-5)}$$

It can be simplified to:

$$slope = \frac{-1 + 3}{0 + 5}$$

$$slope = \frac{2}{5}$$

26. A: The perimeter of a rectangle is $P = 2l + 2w$. We are told $P = 44$, so $2l + 2w = 44$. We are also told that the width is 2 cm less than the length: $w = l - 2$. Substituting this for w in the perimeter equation, we get $2l + 2(l - 2) = 44$, which is Choice A. Although it's not necessary to answer the test question, we could solve the equation to find the length and width. The equation simplifies to $4l - 4 = 44$, or $l = 12$, and since $w = l - 2$, we find $w = 10$.

27. C: The sample space is made up of $8 + 7 + 6 + 5 = 26$ balls. The probability of pulling each individual ball is $\frac{1}{26}$. Since there are 7 yellow balls, the probability of pulling a yellow ball is $\frac{7}{26}$.

28. B: For the first card drawn, the probability of a king being pulled is $\frac{4}{52}$. Since this card isn't replaced, if a king is drawn first, the probability of a king being drawn second is $\frac{3}{51}$. The probability of a king being drawn in both the first and second draw is the product of the two probabilities:

$$\frac{4}{52} \times \frac{3}{51} = \frac{12}{2,652}$$

To reduce this fraction, divide the top and bottom by 12 to get $\frac{1}{221}$.

29. A: If each man gains 10 pounds, every original data point will increase by 10 pounds. Therefore, the man with the original median will still have the median value, but that value will increase by 10. The smallest value and largest value will also increase by 10, so the difference between the two (the range) will remain the same.

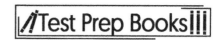

30. C: Because the triangles are similar, the lengths of the corresponding sides are proportional. Therefore:

$$\frac{30 + x}{30} = \frac{22}{14} = \frac{y + 15}{y}$$

This results in the equation:

$$14(30 + x) = 22 \times 30$$

When solved, this gives:

$$x = 17.1$$

The proportion also results in the equation:

$$14(y + 15) = 22y$$

When solved, this gives:

$$y = 26.3$$

31. A: The formula for the area of a circle is $A = \pi r^2$. Here, $r = 9$, so we calculate $A = \pi(9^2) = 81\pi$.

32. A: To expand a squared binomial, it's necessary to use the FOIL (*First, Inner, Outer, Last*) Method. Start with the original equation:

$$\underset{\text{First}}{(2x \times 2x)} + \underset{\text{Outer}}{(2x \times -4y)} + \underset{\text{Inner}}{(2x \times -4y)} + \underset{\text{Last}}{(-4y \times -4y)}$$

$$= 4x^2 - 8xy - 8xy + 16y^2$$

$$= 4x^2 - 16xy + 16y^2$$

33. B: The first step is to use the quadratic formula on the first equation ($x^2 - x - 3 = 0$) to solve for x. In this case, a is 1, b is −1, and c is −3, yielding:

$$x = \frac{-b \pm \sqrt{b^2 - 4ac}}{2a}$$

$$x = \frac{1 \pm \sqrt{1 - 4 \times 1(-3)}}{2}$$

$$x = \frac{1}{2} \pm \frac{\sqrt{13}}{2}$$

Therefore, $x - \frac{1}{2}$, which is in our second equation, equals $\pm \frac{\sqrt{13}}{2}$. We are looking for $\left(x - \frac{1}{2}\right)^2$ though, so we square the $\pm \frac{\sqrt{13}}{2}$. Doing so causes the $\pm$ to cancel and we are left with:

$$\left(x - \frac{1}{2}\right)^2 = \left(\frac{\sqrt{13}}{2}\right)^2 = \frac{13}{4}$$

34. C: The equation is a polynomial, so the first step is to try factoring the equation. The quadratic formula can be used to solve this problem. Given the equation, use the values $a = 1$, $b = -2$, and $c = -8$.

$$x = \frac{-b \pm \sqrt{b^2 - 4ac}}{2a} = \frac{-(-2) \pm \sqrt{(-2)^2 - 4(1)(-8)}}{2(1)}$$

From here, simplify to solve for x.

$$x = \frac{2 \pm \sqrt{4 + 32}}{2} = \frac{2 \pm \sqrt{36}}{2} = \frac{2 \pm 6}{2} = 1 \pm 3$$

35. D: If s is the size of the floor in square feet and r is the rate on Tuesday, then, based on the information given, $p = \frac{s}{4}$ and $r = \frac{s}{3}$. Solve the Monday rate for s, $s = 4p$, and then substitute that in the expression for Tuesday.

36. B: To simplify this inequality, subtract 3 from both sides:

$$3 - 3 - \frac{1}{2}x \geq 2 - 3$$

$$-\frac{1}{2}x \geq -1$$

Then, multiply both sides by –2 (remembering that this flips the direction of the inequality):

$$(-\frac{1}{2}x)(-2) \geq (-1)(-2)$$

$$x \leq 2.$$

37. D: Because we know that $x = 4$ and $x = -4$ are solutions to a quadratic equation, we know that $(x - 4)$ and $(x + 4)$ are factors of the quadratic equation. To find the quadratic equation, use the FOIL method to multiply these two factors by one another.

$$(x - 4)(x + 4) = 0$$

$$x^2 + 4x - 4x - 16 = 0$$

$$x^2 - 16 = 0$$

38. C: A standard pack of cards has 52 cards and 4 of those are aces. There are also 26 red cards in a deck. However, there is an overlap of the 2 red aces. The probability of getting one of these cards is

$$\frac{4}{52} + \frac{26}{52} - \frac{2}{52} = \frac{28}{52} = \frac{7}{13}$$

39. D: Because repetition of digits is allowed and each digit can be one out of 10 options (the digits 0 to 9), there are $10 \times 10 \times 10 \times 10 = 10,000$ ways that a player can select a number to play. If all the digits are the same in the 4 options, the possibilities are 0000, 1111, 2222, . . . , 9999. Therefore, there are 10 options if all 4 digits are the same. The probability of a winning ticket having the same digit four times is $\frac{10}{10,000} = 0.001$.

40. C: I and IV. Outliers in a box-and-whisker plot are data points that fall below the lower extreme or above the upper extreme. The lower extreme is calculated by subtracting 1.5 times the interquartile range from Q_1. And the upper extreme is calculated by adding 1.5 times the interquartile range to Q_3. In this case, the interquartile range (Q_3-Q_1) is 14,000. Therefore, the lower extreme is \$24,000 and the upper extreme is \$80,000.

Practice Test #3

To keep the size of this book manageable, save paper, and provide a digital test-taking experience, the 3rd practice test can be found online. Scan the QR code or go to this link to access it:

testprepbooks.com/bonus/tabe

The first time you access the test, you will need to register as a "new user" and verify your email address.

If you have any issues, please email support@testprepbooks.com

Index

275

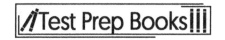

Dear TABE Test Taker,

We would like to start by thanking you for purchasing this study guide for your TABE exam. We hope that we exceeded your expectations.

Our goal in creating this study guide was to cover all of the topics that you will see on the test. We also strove to make our practice questions as similar as possible to what you will encounter on test day. With that being said, if you found something that you feel was not up to your standards, please send us an email and let us know.

We have study guides in a wide variety of fields. If you're interested in one, try searching for it on Amazon or send us an email.

Thanks Again and Happy Testing!
Product Development Team
info@studyguideteam.com

FREE Test Taking Tips Video/DVD Offer

To better serve you, we created videos covering test taking tips that we want to give you for FREE. **These videos cover world-class tips that will help you succeed on your test.**

We just ask that you send us feedback about this product. Please let us know what you thought about it—whether good, bad, or indifferent.

To get your **FREE videos**, you can use the QR code below or email freevideos@studyguideteam.com with "Free Videos" in the subject line and the following information in the body of the email:

      a. The title of your product
      b. Your product rating on a scale of 1-5, with 5 being the highest
      c. Your feedback about the product

If you have any questions or concerns, please don't hesitate to contact us at info@studyguideteam.com.

Thank you!